The Hebrew Bible:
New Insights and Scholarship

JEWISH STUDIES IN THE 21ST CENTURY

The Hebrew Bible

New Insights and Scholarship

EDITED BY

Frederick E. Greenspahn

New York University Press

NEW YORK AND LONDON

NEW YORK UNIVERSITY PRESS
New York and London
www.nyupress.org

Library of Congress Cataloging-in-Publication Data
The Hebrew Bible : new insights and scholarship / edited by
Frederick E. Greenspahn.
    p.   cm. — (Jewish studies in the 21st century)
Includes bibliographical references and index.
ISBN-13: 978-0-8147-3187-1 (cloth : alk. paper)
    ISBN-10: 0-8147-3187-2 (cloth : alk. paper)
ISBN-13: 978-0-8147-3188-8 (pbk. : alk. paper)
    ISBN-10: 0-8147-3188-0 (pbk. : alk. paper)
1. Bible. O.T.—Criticism, interpretation, etc. 2. Bible. O.T.—
Criticism, interpretation, etc., Jewish.   I. Greenspahn,
Frederick E., 1946–
    BS1171.3.H43 2007
    221.6—dc22   2007023840

New York University Press books are printed on acid-free paper,
and their binding materials are chosen for strength and durability.

Manufactured in the United States of America
c 10 9 8 7 6 5 4 3 2 1
p 10 9 8 7 6 5 4 3 2 1

In memory of
Nahum M. Sarna

Contents

Abbreviations

ABD	*Anchor Bible Dictionary,* ed. David Noel Freedman (New York: Doubleday, 1992)
B.	Babylonian Talmud
BA	*Biblical Archaeologist*
BASOR	*Bulletin of the American Schools of Oriental Research*
BDB	*A Hebrew and English Lexicon of the Old Testament,* ed. Francis Brown, S. R. Driver, and Charles A. Briggs (Oxford: Clarendon Press, 1907)
BRLJ	Brill Reference Library of Judaism
BZAW	Beihefte zur *Zeitschrift für die alttestamentliche Wissenschaft*
CAT	*The Cuneiform Alphabetic Texts from Ugarit, Ras Ibn Hani and Other Places* (Münster: Ugarit-Verlag, 1995)
CBQ	*Catholic Biblical Quarterly*
CE	Codex Eshnunna
CH	Codex Hammurabi
CL	Codex Lipit-Ishtar
COS	*Context of Scripture,* ed. William W. Hallo and K. Lawson Younger Jr. (Leiden: E. J. Brill, 2003)
CT	Cuneiform Texts from Babylonian Tablets in the British Museum
CU	Codex Urnamma
HL	Hittite Laws
HTR	*Harvard Theological Review*
HTS	Harvard Theological Studies
HUCA	*Hebrew Union College Annual*
IEJ	*Israel Exploration Journal*
JBL	*Journal of Biblical Literature*
JBR	*Journal of Bible and Religion*
JESHO	*Journal of the Economic and Social History of the Orient*
JNES	*Journal of Near Eastern Studies*

JNSL	*Journal of Northwest Semitic Languages*
JQR	*Jewish Quarterly Review*
JSOT	*Journal for the Study of the Old Testament*
JSOTS	*Journal for the Study of the Old Testament,* Supplement Series
KBo	Keilschrifttexte aus Boghazköi
KTU	*Die Keilalphabetische Texte aus Ugarit einschliesslich der Keilalphabetische Texte außerhalb Ugarits,* ed. M. Dietrich, O. Loretz, and J. Sanmartin (Kevelaer: Butzon & Bercker; Neukirchen-Vluyn: Neukirchener Verlag, 1976, 1995)
KUB	*Keilschrifturkunden aus Boghazköi* (Berlin: Akademie Verlag, 1921–)
M.	Mishna
MAL	Middle Assyrian Laws
NBL	Neo-Babylonian Laws
NEA	*Near Eastern Archaeology*
OBT	Overtures to Biblical Theology
OTL	Old Testament Library
PRU	*Le Palais royal d'Ugarit* (Paris: Imprimerie Nationale, 1955–70)
RIH	field numbers of tablets excavated at Ras Ibn-Hani
RS	field numbers of tablets excavated at Ras Shamra
SAA	State Archives of Assyria
SBL	Society of Biblical Literature
SCS	Septuagint and Cognate Studies
T.	Tosefta
TBR	*Textes syriens de l'âge du Bronze recent,* Daniel Arnaud (Barcelona: Editorial AUSA, 1991)
Ugaritica V	ed. C. F. A. Schaeffer (Paris: Imprimerie Nationale)
VT	*Vetus Testamentum*
VTSup	Supplements to *Vetus Testamentum*
ZAW	Zeitschrift für die alttestamentliche Wissenschaft

Preface

On April 13, 2001, the headline in the *Los Angeles Times* read, "Doubting the Story of the Exodus." The accompanying article described a sermon that had been delivered by the rabbi of a prominent local congregation over the holiday of Passover. In it the rabbi had said, "The truth is that virtually every modern archaeologist who has investigated the story of the exodus, with very few exceptions, agrees that the way the Bible describes the exodus is not the way it happened, if it happened at all." It must have been a dramatic moment in the life of that congregation; however, as Rabbi David Wolpe himself acknowledged, his sermon contained nothing new. The theories he described in that sermon had been common knowledge among biblical scholars for more than thirty years. It is even possible that he had learned about them decades earlier as a student at the Jewish Theological Seminary of America. Yet it was his sermon in early 2001 that captured worldwide attention. What the philosopher Franz Rosenzweig observed in the 1920s—that "What the sparrows chirp from the rooftops of intellectual Germany, still seems terrible heresy to us" (*On Jewish Learning* [New York: Schocken Books, 1955], 60)—remains true today, an ocean and nearly a century away.

Most of the archaeological discoveries that relate to the Bible took place in the last part of the nineteenth century and the early part of the twentieth, yet few people outside the profession know their relevance. The names Hammurabi and Gilgamesh may ring a bell, but not many have any idea of their relevance to the Bible other than some vague sense that they prove or disprove what it says. The facts are actually more complicated than that. Moreover, there has been a veritable revolution, and possibly more than one, in biblical studies over the past generation. Scholarly debate is no longer limited to the reliability and authenticity of the Bible, but extends to the very existence and nature of Israel itself: Was there actually a nation of Israel in any meaningful sense during what is somewhat peculiarly called "the biblical period," and if so, what experiences did it undergo? Those kinds of questions have led to a dramatic reexamination of the very nature of the biblical account, including both its literary quality and the ideas expressed in it.

These challenges did not emerge in a vacuum. The concerns they raise reflect issues that plague our society as a whole. During the past generation, all kinds of accepted social norms have come under question: Should races be treated the way they have been? Can the government be trusted to tell the truth? Are the sexes different in the way we thought? In such an environment, it is no wonder that the Bible has come in for extraordinary scrutiny, nor that the views of its authors on topics such as women and minorities are now being reexamined.

Over the past century, the center for such study has moved into secular settings. As universities have taken a more central role in examining various aspects of religion, the way that religion is studied and understood has been dramatically affected. In such an environment, the Bible is not likely to receive the privileged treatment it enjoyed in religious settings. Instead, university professors are likely to raise the same kinds of questions that are directed at other cultural phenomena. Meanwhile, the fact that the Bible plays a significant role in several quite different communities forces those studying it (at least to the extent that they interact) to think about how it is treated in each tradition. And so the Bible's role *within* religious communities has itself become a topic of inquiry as much for those within such communities as for those outside them.

The goal of this book is to share these conversations, which have been going on in academic circles for decades, with a larger audience. The authors are all experts in the areas of biblical studies they describe. They have national and even international reputations. Here they report recent developments in the areas of their expertise and assess the current state of scholarship on these issues. None of them would claim that their accounts are the last word; they are all too familiar with the constantly changing state of the field. But they have tried to lift the curtain on contemporary scholarship so that the public can hear the discussion and debates that are currently taking place, while offering guidance for those who would like further insight.

The results are not conclusive; that is not how scholarship works. And so there are no pat answers, although the authors have certainly presented their own views as to how this material should be understood, based on years of study and firsthand access to the material they discuss. Instead, the purpose of this book is to make it possible for those who wish to engage topics of great import to reach their own conclusions.

This book would not have been possible without the support and assistance of a great many people. Herbert and Elaine Gimelstob provided the resources that made it possible to assemble this group of experts in the first place; we are all the beneficiaries of their vision and generosity. From the moment that the idea for this project crystallized through every step of its implementation, Jennifer Hammer has been generous with her guidance and assistance, contributing to the cohesion of the final product and generously offering her thoughts on how it could come closer to achieving its stated goals. The general outline was generated by a group of scholars that included Henry Abramson, Alan Berger, Arlene Fradkin, Myriam Ruthenberg, Marianne Sanua, and Michael Zager. In addition, the office of the dean of the College of Arts and Letters at Florida Atlantic University, including William Covino, Lynn Appleton, Kathleen Brunscheen, Kathy DiMaggio, Mary Falconer, Aldett Francis, Nicole Jacobsen, Charles Lingen, Stacia Smith, and Anthony Tamburri, provided the support that made it possible to turn this plan into a reality. Implementation of that plan benefited from the guidance of Victor Castellani and Fay Coulouris. Teresa Maybee's hard work and helpful suggestions also made it possible to turn the idea into reality. And at every stage—from dream to execution—Barbara Pearl provided the support, the assistance, and the enthusiasm that one yearns for but rarely receives; her encouragement and participation made it possible to appreciate as well as conceive this project and so much more.

This book is dedicated to the memory of Nahum M. Sarna. Not only was he instrumental in creating the Jewish Studies program at Florida Atlantic University, where this material was assembled, but through a lifetime devoted to imparting the very best of contemporary biblical scholarship to a larger public, he provided the model for this endeavor. Through works like *Understanding Genesis* and the later JPS commentary series, he managed to bridge the gap this book tries to address, demonstrating that scholarship should be not feared, but confronted so that its findings can be absorbed and made part of our faith. This book attempts to contribute to that venture at which he was such a master.

Part I

The Bible and History

Chapter 1

Israel Without the Bible

Gary A. Rendsburg

The Bible does not exist. That is correct: The Bible does not exist. Permit me to explain what I mean by that statement with the following background material. For most of the twentieth century there was a general consensus among scholars that the Bible is a reliable guide to the history of ancient Israel. The towering figures in the field, people such as W. F. Albright and Cyrus Gordon in the United States and Benjamin Mazar and Yigael Yadin in Israel, led the way in believing that the Bible reflected true history. In their view, everything from the Patriarchs to Ezra was real.

Cuneiform tablets from Nuzi in Mesopotamia described social and legal practices that paralleled the customs reflected in the book of Genesis, including, for example, the duty of a barren wife to present her husband with a maidservant through whom the man would father children, exactly as Sarah presents Hagar to Abraham, leading to the birth of Ishmael.

Egyptian material demonstrated that the customs reflected in the Joseph story fit perfectly in the environment of the Nile Valley, including the presence of certain key Egyptian words in the story, such as *'abrēk* (אברך), which is derived from Egyptian *ib r-k* (literally "heart to you," the equivalent of our English phrase "hail to you"), proclaimed by the Egyptian people as the new viceroy Joseph was paraded through the streets (Genesis 41:43).

The story of the Exodus was real. The cities of Pithom and Rameses (Exodus 1:11) were constructed by Rameses II using foreign slaves; and the Merneptah Stele attests to the existence of the people of Israel in the year 1210 B.C.E.

The Conquest was real. Archaeological work at Bethel, Hazor, Lachish, and Tell Beit Mirsim, among others, revealed the destruction of a series of

Canaanite cities in the latter half of the thirteenth century B.C.E., clearly
the work of the Israelites.

And if these earlier periods of biblical history were real, then the later
material must have reflected true history as well. David and Solomon
ruled over a large empire; the kings of Israel and Judah during the divided
monarchy did exactly what the book of Kings says they did; the Assyrians
destroyed the northern kingdom in 721 B.C.E., the Babylonians destroyed
the southern kingdom in 586 B.C.E., and both Mesopotamian powers exiled the population to the Tigris and Euphrates Valley and beyond; Cyrus
the Great, the forward-looking Persian king, allowed the Jews to return in
538 B.C.E., the Second Temple was built, and Ezra and Nehemiah worked
to restore Jewish life in Jerusalem at the end of the biblical period. To re-
peat: everything from Abraham to Ezra was real.[1]

This was the consensus concerning the history of ancient Israel. It was
"canonized," as it were, in the standard history of the biblical period authored by John Bright, himself a student of Albright. Entitled *A History of
Israel*, Bright's work went through three editions between 1959 and 1981,[2]
was widely used on college campuses and in seminaries, and is still in
print.[3]

Today, however, the picture is very different. Why? What happened?
Obviously, the pendulum of intellectual trends swings continually. The
positive historicism of Albright and his contemporaries gave way, not only
in biblical studies, but in the humanities in general, to the relativism, skepticism, and indeed nihilism that now dominates. Chinks in the Albrightian
armor were already visible thirty years ago, but the chinks soon became
cracks and the cracks developed into full-scale eruptions.

The Conquest affords us the best opportunity to see this process at
work. Already in the 1920s, the great German scholar Albrecht Alt had
challenged the idea of an Israelite military conquest of the land of Canaan.[4] According to Alt, there simply was no archaeological evidence to
confirm the scenario depicted in the book of Joshua. For every site such as
Bethel and Hazor, which clearly were destroyed at the end of the thirteenth century, there were other sites such as Ai and most famously Jericho, which not only show no destruction at this time period, but in fact
little or no settlement at all. These findings led Alt to propose an alternative explanation for the emergence of the Israelites in the land of Canaan
—what scholars came to call the peaceful infiltration or peaceful settlement model. According to this theory, the main tradition of the Bible is
accurate, the Israelites entered the land from the outside, from the desert

fringe region, but there was no military conquest. Instead, one must speak of Israelites entering and peacefully settling open territory. Alt's reconstruction of events, as I said, was but a chink in the Albrightian armor, but it set the stage for more drastic departures.

A third model developed in the 1950s and 1960s, much more radical in its approach. The archaeological evidence now was interpreted to demonstrate that the Israelites did not originate from outside the land, but were in origin Canaanites who had shifted gears. According to this view, Israelite pottery was indistinguishable from Canaanite pottery; Israelite architecture was indistinguishable from Canaanite architecture; Israelite water systems were indistinguishable from Canaanite water systems; and so on. All of this meant that the Israelites *were* Canaanites, most likely former Canaanite rural peasants who had thrown off the yoke of their Canaanite urban overlords. According to this view, class struggle, not religious revolution, is what gave rise to Israel. The arm of Marxism had spread to biblical studies.[5]

As such, so the theory goes, the Israelites had never been to Egypt. The Bible's foundational story about the Israelites as slaves in Egypt is not a reflection of any historical reality, but rather a reflection of the fact that Israel had been slaves in the land of Canaan, slaves to Canaanite urban centers, whose rulers in turn were puppets of the Egyptian empire during the New Kingdom eighteenth and nineteenth dynasties. That is to say, the Israelites were slaves not *in* Egypt, but *to* Egypt.[6]

This theory that the Israelites originated as Canaanites explains why there is so much polytheism present in the Bible's description of the people of Israel. Israel was not a monotheistic or a monolatrous people fighting polytheistic inroads under the influence of their Canaanite neighbors, but rather just another group of Canaanite polytheists, albeit one with a small but vocal and (in the end) successful group of radical thinkers who conceived of the idea of one god.

Stretching further back in the Bible, if there was no Conquest and there was no Exodus and there was no Slavery, then clearly there was no Patriarchal Period either. Indeed, further investigation into the Genesis narratives claimed that there are closer parallels to the customs reflected in the Abraham and Jacob stories in first-millennium B.C.E. Babylonian legal texts than in the second-millennium documents.[7] Accordingly, the Genesis tales are the inventions of Jews during the Babylonian exile when such customs were the way of life. And why have patriarchal stories at all? Why have Abraham originating in Mesopotamia and emigrating to Canaan? Because this was part of early Zionist propaganda to get Jews to leave their homes in comfortable Babylon and to make the long journey to begin a new and arduous life in the land of their forefathers. It is clear from Second Isaiah and Ezra and Nehemiah, and from Babylonian textual remains—I refer here to a set of cuneiform texts known as the Murashu documents, which describe affluent Jewish businessmen in Mesopotamia during this period[8]—that not all Jews wanted to return to Israel. Thus was Abraham invented. He had left his home in Ur for the brave new world of Canaan, and so should you.

I am not done. This approach is only mildly radical. For the approach that I have just outlined at least recognizes that the Israelites, even if they originated as Canaanites, at least existed before 586 B.C.E. First they were organized as tribes, but eventually changed their polity to that of a monarchy. Under David and Solomon they achieved some success, then receded in power to the minor kingdoms of Israel and Judah. The extreme radicals go so far as to deny the existence of Israel and/or Judah before 586. Certainly there never was a David or a Solomon. If after two hundred years of archaeological research, from Napoleon's men discovering the Rosetta Stone in 1799 to the present day, there is not a single shred of evidence that David or Solomon ever existed, then they too must be fictional inventions. The Jews of the sixth and fifth centuries B.C.E. lived in world empires, under Babylonian and Persian domination, with the former Assyrian empire still a recent memory. The idea of the United Kingdom of David and Solomon ruling over conquered peoples, then, represented an inventive effort to show that the Jews too once had power.

And the most radical reconstruction of all goes even further. According to this extreme view, the Jews originated as a group of Semites in Mesopotamia during the sixth and fifth centuries B.C.E., and were transplanted by the Persians to the land of Canaan to serve them as political stooges, as it were. Once there in the land, Jewish writers created an entire history that had never existed, to create for themselves not only a glorious past but also a connection to the land they lacked. Yes, there actually are scholars who believe this.[9]

To put this in the simplest terms: the paradigm has shifted from a maximalist stance to a minimalist one. A few definitions of these terms: The maximalists hold that since so much of the biblical record has been confirmed by archaeological work and by other sources from the ancient Near East (for example, the aforementioned Merneptah Stele), we can therefore assume even in the absence of any corroborating evidence that the Bible reflects true history, unless it can be proved otherwise. The minimalist approach is exactly the opposite: Because so much of the biblical record is contradicted by archaeological work and by other sources from the ancient Near East—for example, the lack of any conquest at Jericho and Ai —we must assume that the Bible is literary fiction, unless it can be proved otherwise.

I do not want to give you the impression that there are no maximalists left standing today. Indeed there are, and as you probably have gathered, I situate myself firmly in their camp. I need to add here that representatives of the two schools often do not speak to each other; there is much vitriol and namecalling involved; and yes, modern politics spills over into this debate as well, the denials of scholars notwithstanding. I am not sure that I can quantify the schools, that is, tell you that the majority of biblical scholars today are maximalist or minimalist—I suppose the divide is probably about 50-50—but I can tell you this: there is no doubt that the minimalists are the more vocal, and they are the ones who set the agenda, publish books at a very rapid pace, organize conferences to present their views (especially in Europe), and take advantage of the popular press. The maximalists, in turn, frequently are left to respond to these diatribes, often needing to take time away from their own research to counter the views expressed in the many publications emanating from the pens of minimalist scholars.[10]

Given this lack of consensus and avoidance of dialogue, how are we to proceed? I propose to do something new, something which to the best of my knowledge has not been attempted yet. For the purposes of this chapter, let us return to my opening statement: pretend that the Bible does not exist. Let us reconstruct the history of ancient Israel based solely on the information provided by archaeology. This is, after all, the way archaeologists have reconstructed many ancient Near Eastern societies, such as the Sumerians, the Hittites, the Hurrians, the Urartians, the Elamites, and others, about all of whom nothing was known before the twentieth century. If we can do this for all these people, why not for Israel as well? Let us attempt to do so, using both epigraphic remains and material remains. The former refers to inscriptions found in archaeological excavations;[11] the latter refers to all other finds, including pottery, artwork, architecture, and animal bones. Only when we are done with this exercise will we bring the Bible back into the picture, to see to what extent the two overlap: the archaeological picture on the one hand, and the history as outlined in the Bible on the other.

We begin with a look at inscriptions from the land of Israel, especially from the central hill country of Canaan, the mountainous area that stretches from the Galilee in the north through Samaria in the center, further south to Jerusalem, and then furthest south to places like Hebron and Arad in southern Judah. I begin with inscriptions because, if a picture is worth a thousand words, an ancient Hebrew inscription is worth a thousand pieces of pottery. With apologies to my archaeologist friends, it is true that we can learn more about ancient history from a single inscription, and even more from a group of inscriptions, than we can from analyzing material remains. So let us start there.

We have hundreds of very tiny inscriptions from the central hill country in Canaan, most of them seals and bullae—the former are little stone or metal items; the latter are the clay imprints of the seals—giving us hundreds of personal names of people who lived in those hills. Jeffrey Tigay of the University of Pennsylvania wrote a handy little book twenty years ago, in which he collected all these names and classified them by their theophoric elements (that is, the divine names that are included as an element of many ancient personal names).[12] For example, the Egyptian pharaoh Rameses includes the name of the sun-god Ra, the Babylonian king Nebuchadnezzar includes the name of the deity Nabu, and the Carthaginian general Hannibal includes the name of the Canaanite storm-god Baal. When we look at the inscriptions from the central hill country of Canaan, from places such as Samaria, Gibeon, Jerusalem, Lachish, and Arad, we note that by far the commonest element in the personal names is Yah or Yahu, placed at either the beginning or the end of these names. Tigay finds 263 names that have a theophoric element: of these, 213 are Yahwistic, that is, they contain Yah or Yahu at either the beginning or the end of the name; 30 of them are Elohistic, that is, they contain El at either the beginning or the end of the name, and 20 of them contain an element that might suggest a pagan deity, such as the Canaanite god Baal or the Egyptian god Horus. There are, of course, plenty of names that do not include any theophoric element, such as Ḥanan and Natan; these names are of interest, but they do not disclose anything about the deity worshipped by the bearers of these names or by the parents who gave their children these names. (Incidentally, the numbers I am using here reflect only those names found on inscriptions excavated by archaeologists. I do not include names found on materials purchased on the antiquities market, especially in light of recent discussions about the prevalence of forgeries.) To illustrate these data, note such Yahwistic names as Aḥiyahu, Amaryahu, Gedalyahu,

Hoshiʿyahu, Ḥananyahu, Yeho'ab, Yehoʿaz, Yonatan, and so on. Among the names with El, note, for example, Eli'ur, Elyaqim, Elishamaʿ, Yishmaʿʿel, and so on.[13] At first we might conclude that these people, whom we have not identified yet, worshipped two gods, one called El and one called Yah or Yahu. But since we know that El is a common Semitic element for "god, deity," we have reason to believe that the people who lived in these mountains considered El and Yah/Yahu to be one and the same.

When we look at inscriptions that provide more information than merely personal names, something interesting happens. Here we see that a fuller form of the name Yah or Yahu appears, in the form YHWH. No vowels are provided, of course, but we posit Yahweh as an educated guess or reconstruction, based on our knowledge of comparative Semitic grammar. What inscriptions am I referring to? First, two silver amulets found in Jerusalem that invoke the god YHWH to bless the bearers of these amulets.[14] Second, references to YHWH in a collection of letters from Lachish, letters mainly of a military nature, describing various preparations and stratagems for war.[15] Third, references to YHWH in a group of texts from Arad, documents mainly of an administrative nature, but with one reference to BYT YHWH as well, referring to a temple, either in Arad itself or in some other location.[16] Moreover, archaeological excavations at Arad revealed a sanctuary site, so that most likely the expression BYT YHWH refers to the local temple.

We also find something quite interesting in several other inscriptions. Blessings from two sites, Khirbet el-Qom in southern Judah and Kuntillet ʿAjrud in the Sinai, refer to YHWH and his Asherah.[17] The latter we recognize as a goddess attested in texts from Ugarit, among the Philistines, and even in Arabia. We register this point in our minds for the moment, as something to ponder in our reconstruction of ancient Israel. For as noted above, until this point we have assumed that the people whose history we are reconstructing worshipped only one God. We also note that YHWH gains two epithets in the Kuntillet Ajrud inscriptions: YHWH TYMN and YHWH ŠMRN. The former clearly means "Yahweh of the Southland," and we propose that in some fashion Yahweh is connected with the desert land, perhaps even the very spot of Kuntillet Ajrud deep in the Sinai desert. The latter is subject to two different interpretations. Like TYMN it could be a place name, identifying Yahweh with a particular locale; or the term could derive from the Semitic root *shin-mem-resh* meaning "to guard," which would, of course, be a most appropriate epithet for a deity.

We still would like to know the identity of these people, and various clues from different sources point to the answer. The Mesha Stele, a well-known inscription from Moab, across the Jordan River, provides us with the best answer.[18] The king of Moab, named Mesha, claims to have conquered the people of Israel, who were led by their king Omri and his unnamed son, and to have captured cultic objects dedicated to the god YHWH. This text, which makes the explicit connection between the god YHWH and the people Israel, affords us our smoking gun. The people who worship this deity are called Israel.

Other sources, especially Assyrian inscriptions, provide the names of additional kings of Israel. The Kurkh Monolith of Shalmaneser III refers to a king named Ahab the Israelite, who was able to muster 10,000 soldiers and 2,000 chariots in the battle of Qarqar on the Orontes River in northern Syria.[19] We can even date this event to exactly 853 B.C.E. From slightly later in the reign of Shalmaneser III comes the Black Obelisk, which refers to a king named Jehu, son of Omri, paying tribute to Assyria. This too is datable, to the year 841 B.C.E., and the obelisk even gives us a picture of king Jehu and his emissaries.[20] We are not able to work out the Israelite dynasty with absolute precision, since we are led to believe that Jehu is the son of Omri and yet we know that Ahab must have preceded Jehu, but for the moment we do not worry about such details.

From about a half-century later, c. 800 B.C.E., we have reference in another Assyrian text to a king named Ia-'a-su the Samarian. The name looks Yahwistic, so we assume that he is an Israelite. His label "the Samarian" immediately brings to mind the term attested at Kuntillet ʿAjrud, YHWH ŠMRN (see above), and we connect the two. We conclude, therefore, that of the two choices indicated earlier, the former was the correct choice—that like TYMN, the word ŠMRN is also a place name. Apparently YHWH, the god of the Israelites, could be called "YHWH of Samaria" by the Israelites themselves; and the king of Israel could be called by the epithet "the Samarian" by the conquering Assyrians. We do not yet know where this place is located, but at least we have made the connection.

The annals of Assyrian kings from another half-century later inform us that Assyria conquered the land of Omri and deported its people to Assyria. More than a century after Omri ruled, the Assyrians still referred to the country as the land of Omri, so we assume that he must have been quite a powerful king and/or the founder of the Israelite dynasty. Moreover, these texts that describe the deportation of the Israelites to Assyria provide us with the names of still two other kings, Peqaḥ and Hoshea, whom we assume were the last two kings of the kingdom.

Another source provides additional information, though it is very fragmentary. The Aramaic inscription from Tel Dan, found in 1993–94, refers to an individual whose name ends in *-ram* as MLK YSR'L "king of Israel."[21] We know nothing more about this individual, but at least we have another small puzzle piece with which to contend. We will return to this very important inscription below.

We now bring an additional source into the picture: the Merneptah Stele.[22] Merneptah was an important pharaoh of the nineteenth dynasty in Egypt, the son of Rameses II, the most powerful pharaoh in all of Egyptian history. In about 1210 B.C.E., Merneptah claims to have conquered the land of Canaan, with specific reference to three cities and to one people. The three cities are Ashkelon, Gezer, and Yenoam; the one people referred to is Israel. The reference to the *people* of Israel is actually rather unique within the corpus of Egyptian texts, and we are not quite sure what to make of this reference. The best guess is that the Israelites were a people within the general region of Canaan, but without a specific chunk of land unto themselves. Regardless of the exact meaning of the passage in the Merneptah Stele, we are able to conclude that in some fashion the people of Israel existed as a recognized entity as early as the late thirteenth century B.C.E., sufficiently organized into a group that the powerful Egyptians took some notice of them. This is in fact the earliest reference to Israel in the historical record.

There is still more evidence from Egypt that is relevant to our quest to reconstruct Israel in the archaeological record. One of the Pharaohs of the New Kingdom—we are not certain which one—left us two long lists of the places his army visited during its various campaigns. These lists were found at Soleb and Amara, both in far Upper Egypt south of Aswan. Among the places and peoples appearing in these lists are the Shasu of Se'ir and the Shasu of YHWH. "Shasu" is the term the Egyptians used for the bedouin or the pastoralists on the desert fringe, essentially anyone who did not live in the Nile Valley or in urban centers in foreign countries. We have nothing more to say about the word Se'ir, because (remember?) the Bible does not exist, and the term Se'ir, which is to be associated with the land of Edom to the south of Israel, is known only from the Bible. So we have to put that knowledge aside for our present enterprise. The latter term, however, the Shasu of YHWH, piques our interest, for the second term looks like an Egyptian rendering of the name of the god of Israel. We are not quite sure how to correlate the two, for Yahweh is the name of a divinity, and the Shasu of YHWH would suggest a place by that name. That problem notwithstanding, we incorporate this valuable piece of evidence into our general picture. Given that the Shasu are bedouin or desert-fringe types and given that earlier we saw Yahweh referred to as YHWH TYMN "Yahweh of the Southland," we reach the general conclusion that the people who worshipped Yahweh had some traditional connection to the desert region.

There is still more Egyptian evidence that aids us in our quest. On the walls of the great temple to the god Amun, the famous Karnak temple in Luxor, we find four panels depicting battle scenes. Most of them are very worn, but there is enough there to reach the following conclusions. In the first three panels we see the Egyptian army besieging enemy cities, one of which is clearly identified as Ashkelon.[23] In the fourth panel, we see the Egyptian army attacking a group in the open terrain. Moreover, the portrayal of the subdued people in this scene matches the portrayal of the Shasu well known from other Egyptian artwork. Now earlier we saw in the Merneptah Stele reference to three conquered cities, including Ashkelon, and one conquered people, Israel. And since we have just suggested some connection between Israel and the Shasu, a clearer picture begins to emerge. In its early stages, in the thirteenth century B.C.E., Israel was a pastoralist or bedouin people, identified by the Egyptians as part of the larger Shasu group, resident in the general southland, that is, the vast desert that stretches across Sinai, the Negev, Edom, and northern Arabia. The Merneptah Stele refers to the people of Israel, whom we know from later times worshipped the god Yahweh, identified at times as Yahweh of the Southland; the artwork depicting the battle scenes shows the people of Israel to be Shasu in some general sense, and two Egyptian lists of place names include a reference to the Shasu of YHWH.

We are not quite sure how all of this correlates with the evidence we surveyed earlier, which places Israel in the central hill country of Canaan, but hopefully that missing link will emerge as our project unfolds. For now, though, we have to contend with another problem. At times, it appears that the worship of Yahweh is associated with another political entity, called Judah. What is the evidence for this group? And who are they?

The best evidence comes once more from Assyria. Royal inscriptions from Assyria refer not only to Israel, but to Judah as well. In fact, of the four kings of Judah mentioned in Assyrian annals, three of them have Yahwistic names. The earliest are Azriyau and Yehoaḥaz from the middle of the eighth century B.C.E., both of whom paid tribute to Assyria; next comes Hezekiah, whose realm was laid waste by the army of Sennacherib; and finally comes Manasseh in the seventh century B.C.E., the only one of these individuals without a Yahwistic name. The most famous of these Assyrian texts is the Sennacherib prism, which goes on at length about the Assyrian attack on Judah, with specific mention of King Hezekiah.[24]

At this stage in our investigation, we are not quite sure where this Judah entity is to be located, but somehow it must relate to the better established Israel entity. Fortunately, we find several clues that help us resolve this question. First is a single mention of Judah in one of the Arad ostraca (inscribed potsherds)—in fact the text reads MLK YHD(H), "king of Judah" —and thus we have reason to believe that Judah is found in the southern part of the country.[25] Second is the mention of Judah in a burial inscription from a place called Khirbet Bet Lei, about twenty miles southwest of Jerusalem, at least according to one opinion—the text is poorly preserved and very difficult to read—again pointing to Judah in the southern part of the country.[26] Finally, we confirm our conclusion from later references to the name Judah, dated to the Persian period: we possess about twenty attestations of the term in a series of jar stamps and coins from places like Ramat Rahel and elsewhere, in either the Hebrew form YHDH or the Aramaic form YHD.

Having now located Judah geographically, we also can learn more about this entity historically. We know from Mesopotamian records that eventually the Assyrian empire declined and was defeated by the new power in that region, the Babylonians. Specific to our quest, the annals of the great Babylonian king Nebuchadnezzar inform us that in the seventh year of his reign, corresponding to 598–597 B.C.E., he captured "the city of Judah," seized its king, and placed a new king on the throne, no doubt one more to his liking who would serve him as a puppet.[27] Clearly, "the city of Judah" must refer to the capital of the country, though we are not quite sure where it is located.

We will return to that question in a moment, but first let us discuss in greater detail the Tel Dan inscription, to which we referred earlier. Alongside the reference to the person whose name ends in *-ram* identified as the king of Israel, there is reference to another person whose name ends in *-yahu* identified as the king of the house of David, BYTDWD in the original Aramaic.[28] This one presents a real puzzle for a moment, but upon further investigation we recall that Aramaic inscriptions frequently refer to national entities as BYT-something, or BYT-X, one might say. In such cases, the X element may be a place name or it may refer to the founder of the royal dynasty, at least according to some scholars. Either of these options is possible here—we simply cannot be sure. One scholar, by the way, Andre Lemaire of Paris, believes that he can read the same words BT.DWD "house of David" at the end of the Mesha Stele, but the reading is contested by other scholars; it is simply too difficult to reach a conclusion.[29]

But since the Tel Dan inscription refers to both a king of Israel, to whom we referred earlier, and a king of the house of David—and since we know that there are two entities involved in Yahweh worship, Israel and Judah—we reach the tentative conclusion that "house of David" relates in some way to the entity known as Judah. Perhaps those scholars who believe that David refers to the founder of a royal dynastic line are correct; perhaps he was the first king of Judah, from whom the others, Hezekiah and so on, are descended.

We still would like to know where "the city of Judah" is located—what place served as the capital of this kingdom? The city that attracts our attention more than any other is Jerusalem. The name appears in Sennacherib's prism inscription, mentioned earlier, with reference to Hezekiah, and thus it must have been the capital of Judah.[30] It is attested in an Aramaic letter from Elephantine in southern Egypt, near present-day Aswan, dated to the late fifth century B.C.E., in which the Jews of that community wrote to the high priest of Jerusalem.[31] From this we learn that the city served not only as the capital of Judah, but also as the religious center of the country. The name is not well attested in Hebrew inscriptions from the land of Israel itself, but we do have a few references that help. Above we referred to the burial inscription from Khirbet Bet Lei that most likely mentions Judah: the same inscription clearly mentions Jerusalem,[32] and a second inscription from the same site does also. Otherwise all that we possess is a single jar stamp from Lachish with the single word Y[R]ŠLM. None of this, of course, helps us locate the city, but here we must allow ourselves a little leeway, and take recognition of the living tradition of the Jews that the city of Jerusalem is located exactly where we know it to be. Indeed, excavations in the City of David section of Jerusalem have revealed prominent buildings, a well-developed water system, and other material remains, all pointing to a major urban center at the site.

To this point we have focused on the inscriptional evidence, which, as I indicated earlier, provides the most important material for the reconstruction of ancient Israelite history, giving us, for example, ample references to the names Israel and Judah, the god Yahweh, various kings, and more, with only occasional asides to other archaeological finds, such as the architectural remains at Arad and Jerusalem. We now must bring the wealth of other archaeological material into the picture in a more sustained fashion, for only by using *all* the evidence at our disposal will we be able to assemble the clearest picture. Let us start with the most recent period and work backward. As noted above, the Babylonian annals indicate that Nebuchadnezzar conquered the land of Canaan in the early sixth century B.C.E. Does the archaeological record show evidence of this conquest? The answer is clearly yes, as can be seen in such places as Jerusalem, Lachish, and elsewhere. Among the most famous demonstrations of the point appears in Yigal Shiloh's excavation of the City of David, where the burnt debris is clearly dated to the early sixth century B.C.E.

At Lachish we possess not only evidence for the burning of the city by the Babylonians in an archaeological context datable to c. 600 B.C.E., but also inscriptional evidence of prime importance. I refer to the famous Lachish Letters discovered in the 1930s, which I have mentioned until now only in passing.[33] These letters are military missives, small bits of inscribed pottery called ostraca, in which we learn about various attempts to withstand the Babylonian attack, efforts which naturally were desperate and in the end unsuccessful.

If we look at the period about one hundred years earlier, we find Assyrian documentation relating to the attack on Judah in 701 B.C.E. Again we turn our attention to the prism inscription of King Sennacherib, in which he describes how he laid waste to forty-six cities in Judah, and in which he famously boasts that he kept King Hezekiah "like a bird in a cage."[34] Interestingly, however, he never boasts of having conquered Jerusalem, the capital city. More famously, we possess the fabulous artwork from the palace walls of Sennacherib's royal abode, which portray the assault and destruction of Lachish and the exile of numerous Judaeans.[35] When we look at the archaeological record, we see the destruction of Lachish very clearly, as ably documented by David Ussishkin.

Moving back in time a few decades, we turn our attention to the Assyrian destruction of the northern kingdom of Israel. The annals of Sargon II provide details, including the number of people taken into exile.[36] We can confirm that this king's troops marched through Canaan, because fragments of cuneiform texts mentioning this king were found at both Samaria and Ashdod. In addition, the archaeological record shows a dramatic decrease in the population of Galilee and other regions in northern Israel after 721 B.C.E.

Above we noted that we do not know exactly where the city of Samaria is to be found. As already mentioned, we know that YHWH could be referred to as YHWH ŠMRN, and we know that the Assyrians referred to the king of Israel as "the Samarian." Presumably one of the large excavated tells in the northern part of the country provides the location for the city of Samaria, but which one? Three candidates emerge: Hazor in the far north, Megiddo guarding the Jezreel Valley, and Samaria in the central hill country. Large public buildings have been found at all three, but the best candidate of the three to emerge is indeed the city of Samaria in the central hill country. In this location one finds the largest public building in the region, clearly identifiable as a palace. And once again it is inscriptional evidence that seals the case for us. A sizable collection of ostraca was found at the site, which clearly must be a series of tax receipts, recording quantities of wine and oil and other commodities flowing into the city, indicating that Samaria was a government center.

Samaria is our best candidate for the capital city of Israel, but there is something at Hazor and Megiddo that attracts our attention. From a slightly earlier period, from the tenth century B.C.E., these two cities, along with a third city, Gezer, in the region of Judah, have identical city-gate complexes. And it is not only the design of the three city-gate systems that is the same, but perhaps more significantly their dimensions (Figure 1).[37]

FIGURE 1
Dimensions of the Three 10th-Century
City-Gate Complexes (in Meters)

	Megiddo	Hazor	Gezer
Length	20.3	20.3	19.0
Width	17.5	18.0	16.2
Entrance width	4.2	4.2	4.1
Wall width	1.6	1.6	1.6

We conclude that the two kingdoms, Israel and Judah, had close cooperation in the tenth century B.C.E., so much so that three of the largest cities of the two realms used the same Army Corps of Engineers, as it were, to construct their city gates.

Apart from the Merneptah Stele from c. 1210 B.C.E., the depiction of Shasu-Israelites on the walls of the Karnak temple from the same period, and the references to the Shasu of YHWH from about a century earlier, we possess no further epigraphic or pictorial evidence for Israel from before the tenth century B.C.E. There is, however, archaeological evidence that speaks to the origins of the people of Israel in the hill country of Canaan. Figure 2, based on the work of Israel Finkelstein, demonstrates that during the Late Bronze Age, that is, before 1200 B.C.E., the central hill country had very few settlements, but that during the Early Iron Age, that is, during the two centuries between 1200 and 1000 B.C.E., there is a burgeoning of settlements in the area.[38]

We move from 29 settlements in the Late Bronze Age (fifteenth through thirteenth centuries B.C.E.) to 254 settlements in the Iron I period (twelfth and eleventh centuries B.C.E.) to 520 settlements in the Iron II period (tenth through seventh centuries B.C.E.). Clearly, there is a new population emerging in the central hill country during the Iron Age.

Who were they? Can we identify their origins? The answer may be deduced from the nature of these settlements during this period. Archaeologists have noted that these sites are not real villages and certainly not cities, but instead have a specific oval-shaped formation, which leads scholars to call them elliptical sites. Furthermore, the interior of these ovals are empty, devoid of any construction: no houses, no buildings, simply empty. Who could have built settlements such as these? The layout—city planning would be too advanced a term here—reminds one of bedouin tent encampments. The bedouin construct their encampments in this fashion to create a pen or corral for their flocks, especially at night. During the

FIGURE 2

Number of Settlements in the Central Hill Country during the Late Bronze Age, Iron I, and Iron II

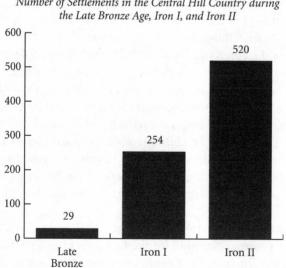

day, the sheep and goats are led to pasture by a team of shepherds, but at night only one or two shepherds are needed to guard an entire flock penned in by the surrounding tents. The elliptical sites in the central hill country presumably are of the same type, representing the sedentarization of pastoral nomads who have come off the desert fringe and have settled in the region.[39]

The overall picture forthcoming from this line of research provides the missing link, as it were, between two parts of our puzzle. Earlier we concluded, based mainly on Egyptian evidence, that in its early stages Israel was a pastoralist or bedouin people, identified by the Egyptians as part of the larger Shasu group. At a later stage we see recognizably Israelite names —that is, personal names reflecting worship of Yahweh—abundant in the central hill country of Canaan. These elliptical sites provide the bridge: the earlier Israelite pastoralists must have settled in the region, built settlements reminiscent of their desert-fringe origins, and only later developed villages and eventually cities in the central hill country. At some point, these pastoralists, who presumably were organized in a tribal system, must have moved to a new form of government, a monarchy—or to be more specific, two monarchies: one called Israel in the north, and one called Judah in the south.

There is one more item of interest here, and that is the analysis of the animal remains from the archaeological sites in the central hill country. Archaeologists today catalogue everything they find: the obvious things such as pottery, and such less obvious things as the animals' bones unearthed. An analysis of the animal bones found at these presumably Israelite sites reveals something very striking: the total absence or near total absence of any pig bones (see Figure 3).[40] This fact is especially remarkable in comparison with other sites in the general region. Sites on the coast (Ashkelon, Ekron, and Batash), which we can identify with the Philistines in the historical record, show pig bones accounting for between 8 and 18 percent of the total animal bones unearthed; and Heshbon in Transjordan, which we assume to be a Moabite site given its proximity to Dibon, the site at which the Mesha Stele was found, has about 5 percent pig bones. In light of these neighboring sites, the lack of pig bones in the central hill country sites (Izbet Sartah, Shiloh, Ebal, and Raddana) is truly astounding.

To summarize in chronological order: Israel begins as a Shasu or bedouin-type people, referred to for the first time in an Egyptian text, the Merneptah Stele. In time, the people move into the central hill country

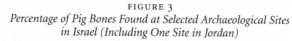

FIGURE 3
Percentage of Pig Bones Found at Selected Archaeological Sites in Israel (Including One Site in Jordan)

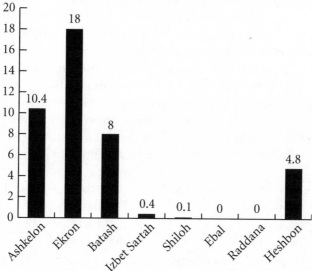

of Canaan. The first settlements there are of an elliptical type, suggesting their desert origins; we also note that these people abstained from eating pig. As time passed, the Israelites must have shifted from a tribal lifestyle to a monarchy; in fact, we have evidence of two monarchies, one in the south called Judah, with its capital in Jerusalem, whose royal line seems to have descended from the founding dynast named David, and one in the north called Israel, with its capital in Samaria, whose royal line seems to have descended from the founding dynast named Omri. The worship of the deity named YHWH shines through at every instance, in both of these kingdoms, though we also have one piece of evidence from each kingdom for a consort goddess named Asherah. The two kingdoms fought on the same side, apparently, in the middle of the ninth century B.C.E., against the kingdom of Aram to the north, as evidenced in the Tel Dan inscription. Slightly more than a century later, toward the end of the eighth century, the Assyrians arrived in the land, destroying the northern kingdom and attacking the southern kingdom as well. And a bit more than a century after that, in the early sixth century B.C.E., the Babylonians in turn unleashed their army in Canaan, which led to the destruction of Judah in general and the city of Jerusalem in particular.

If we lay the Bible on top of this evidence, the match is truly remark-able. The only aspect of the Bible's tale that is not clearly recognizable in the picture we have presented is the United Monarchy under David and Solomon.[41] This is not to say that that element of the Bible's narrative is fictional. Quite the contrary: since so much else of the biblical material is confirmed by our exercise, we have every reason to believe that the de-scriptions of David and Solomon in the books of Samuel and Kings also reflect actual history. In fact, one crucial text from the Bible illustrates this more than any other: 1 Kings 9:15, which informs us that Solomon built the three cities of Gezer, Hazor, and Megiddo. When we recall that it is specifically these three cities whose triple gates match so perfectly, all dated to the tenth century, it becomes nearly impossible to harbor any doubt about the historicity of the biblical material.

We began with the extreme statement that the Bible does not exist. Now that we have brought the Bible back into the picture here at the end of this enterprise, we may alter that comment and proclaim that cause for doubting the historicity of the Bible does not exist.[42] The minimalist agenda is simply that—an agenda—unsupported by facts, driven by ide-ology alone, and not to be countenanced.

NOTES

1. See, for example (and note the title of the book), the brief treatment by W. F. Albright, *The Biblical Period from Abraham to Ezra* (New York: Harper & Row, 1963). See the next two footnotes for a more comprehensive survey of an-cient Israelite history.

2. J. Bright, *A History of Israel* (Philadelphia: Westminster, 1959; second edition 1972; third edition 1981).

3. Bright, *History of Israel*; the most recent (fourth) edition (Louisville, Ky.: Westminster John Knox, 2000) includes an Introduction and Appendix by W. P. Brown.

4. A. Alt, *Die Landnahme der Israeliten in Palästina* (Leipzig: Reformationspro-gramm der Universität, 1925). An English version appeared in a collection of Alt's essays decades later: "The Settlement of the Israelites in Palestine," in *Essays on Old Testament History and Religion* (Garden City, N.Y.: Doubleday, 1966), 133–169.

5. The two names most commonly connected with the Peasant Revolt theory are G. Mendenhall, "The Hebrew Conquest of Palestine," *Biblical Archaeologist* 25 (1962): 66–87; and N. Gottwald, *The Tribes of Yahweh* (Maryknoll, N.Y.: Orbis, 1979).

6. For a recent statement, see S. D. Sperling, *The Original Torah* (New York: New York University Press, 1998), 41–60, especially the statements on pp. 54 and 57, with the prepositions "in" and "to" in italics, exactly as I have reproduced them here.

7. T. L. Thompson, *The Historicity of the Patriarchal Narratives* (Berlin: Walter de Gruyter, 1974); and J. Van Seters, *Abraham in History and Tradition* (New Haven, Conn.: Yale University Press, 1975).

8. M. W. Stolper, "Murashu, Archive of," in *Anchor Bible Dictionary* 4 (1992), 927–928, especially 928.

9. The scholars most associated with this view are N.-P. Lemche, *The Israelites in History and Tradition* (Louisville, Ky.: Westminster John Knox, 1998); and T. L. Thompson, *The Mythic Past: Biblical Archaeology and the Myth of Israel* (New York: Basic Books, 1999).

10. For more detailed accounts of the current debate between the maximalists and the minimalists, with a critique of the latter, see the two recent books by W. G. Dever: *What Did the Biblical Writers Know and When Did They Know It?* (Grand Rapids,Mich.: Eerdmans, 2001); and *Who Were the Early Israelites and Where Did They Come From?* (Grand Rapids, Mich.: Eerdmans, 2003).

11. The best collection of ancient inscriptions available in English translation is W. W. Hallo, ed., *The Context of Scripture*, 3 vols. (Leiden: E. J. Brill, 1997–2002), to be cited hereafter as *COS*. This work includes the entirety of the ancient Near East —that is, material not only from ancient Israel and its immediate environs, but from Egypt, Assyria, and Babylonia as well. In the remaining portion of this essay, I provide references to *COS* in the footnotes, to allow the reader to peruse the texts in English, along with the scholarly comments from the contributors to the three-volume set. If I do not cite *COS*, then the text under discussion simply is not included in this work, usually because the inscription is of a very minor nature. For the texts in the original Hebrew (and Moabite), including excellent photographs, see S. Ahituv, *Ha-ketav veha-Miktav* (Jerusalem: Bialik, 2005).

12. J. H. Tigay, *You Shall Have No Other Gods: Israelite Religion in the Light of Hebrew Inscriptions* (Atlanta, Ga.: Scholars Press, 1986).

13. For a sampling of seals and bullae, see *COS* vol. 2, 197–201.

14. *COS* vol. 2, 221.

15. *COS* vol. 3, 78–81.

16. *COS* vol. 3, 81–86 (for the reference to BYT YHWH, see Arad letter no. 18, p. 84).

17. *COS* vol. 2, 171–172.

18. *COS* vol. 2, 137–138.

19. *COS* vol. 2, –261-264 (with specific mention of Ahab on p. 263).

20. Notwithstanding the well-deserved fame of this artifact, on prominent display in the British Museum, it was not included in *COS* because it is mainly visual, with only brief captions accompanying the pictures.

21. *COS* vol. 2, 161–162, especially 162.

22. *COS* vol. 2, 40–41 (only the portion of the inscription that mentions Israel is included).

23. These very important panels remain *in situ* at the Temple of Karnak in Luxor. Once more we are dealing with artwork, with only a few captions, and thus *COS* does not contain this evidence.

24. *COS* vol. 2, 302–303.

25. *COS* vol. 3, 85 (Arad letter no. 40).

26. *COS* vol. 2, 179–180.

27. *COS* vol. 1, 467–468, especially 468.

28. *COS* vol. 2, 161–162, especially 162.

29. Thus, for example, the translation in *COS* vol. 2, 137–138 (see the end of the text on 138) does not include the words "house of David."

30. *COS* vol. 2, 302–303, in particular 303.

31. *COS* vol. 3, 128.

32. *COS* vol. 2, 180.

33. *COS* vol. 3, 78–81.

34. *COS* vol. 2, 303.

35. These magnificent panels are also on prominent display in the British Museum, where a separate room is dedicated to them.

36. *COS* vol. 2, 293–298, with the most detailed passages, including the number of people taken into exile (27,280 in one version, 27,290 in the other), on 295–296.

37. Data taken from W. G. Dever, *Recent Archaeological Discoveries and Biblical Research* (Seattle: University of Washington Press, 1990), 106 (for the layout of these gates, see p. 105).

38. I. Finkelstein, "The Rise of Early Israel: Archaeology and Long-Term History," in S. Ahituv and E. D. Oren, eds., *The Origin of Early Israel—Current Debate* (Beer-Sheva: Ben-Gurion University of the Negev Press, 1998), 7–64. Finkelstein's chart, on which Figure 2 is based, appears on p. 21.

39. I. Finkelstein, *The Archaeology of the Israelite Settlement* (Jerusalem: Israel Exploration Society, 1988). Line drawings of elliptical sites and photographs of bedouin encampments may be found on pp. 239–246.

40. Chart based on Finkelstein, "The Rise of Early Israel," 20.

41. I exclude from this statement the material in the book of Genesis, which describes the comings and goings of a family, not a nation. The historicity of these narratives needs to be judged on a separate basis. For my most recent statement on the patriarchal stories, see G. A. Rendsburg, "The Genesis of the Bible," in *The Blanche and Irving Laurie Chair in Jewish History*, Separatum published by the Allen and Joan Bildner Center for the Study of Jewish Life, Rutgers, The State University of New Jersey (2005), 11–30; available online at http://jewishstudies .rutgers.edu/faculty/grendsburg/genesis.pdf.

42. I realize that I have not dealt here with certain issues, most importantly the

Exodus and other matters related to earliest Israel. For a detailed treatment, see G. A. Rendsburg, "The Early History of Israel," in *Crossing Boundaries and Linking Horizons: Studies in Honor of Michael C. Astour on His 80th Birthday*, ed. G. D. Young, M. W. Chavalas, and R. E. Averbeck (Bethesda, Md.: CDL Press, 1997), 433–453.

Chapter 2

Bible, Archaeology, and the Social Sciences
The Next Generation

Elizabeth Bloch-Smith

Compared to the venerable discipline of biblical interpretation, which has been practiced for thousands of years, biblical archaeology is a relative newborn, only about eighty years old. Yet it offers fresh perspectives on the Bible, producing new information on virtually a daily basis and providing the realia of daily life that are often missing from the biblical text. Moreover, archaeology gives us evidence in the equivalent of an unedited form, so that in the best of cases we can determine the date and location of archaeological finds—a standard that is largely elusive for specific passages of the Bible.

Archaeologists bring methods and questions arising from the social sciences, including history, architecture, and anthropology, as well as, increasingly, the hard sciences to the study of ancient Israel. Taking a multidisciplinary approach, they also utilize written evidence, including the Bible, to elucidate material remains. Most American archaeologists do not dismiss the biblical text as ahistorical or unreliable; rather, they view it as an artifact with a long history that should be interpreted just as we would any other "heirloom" that has been preserved and reworked over time.

History of Biblical Archaeology

The first scientific excavations in the territory of ancient Israel were conducted by Sir William Flinders Petrie more than a hundred years ago. He tried to understand the nature of archaeological deposits and to excavate accordingly; he also articulated the principles of interpretation. Petrie's work laid the foundations for scientific excavation and the modern discipline of archaeology.

William Foxwell Albright harnessed this new, scientifically grounded discipline for theological purposes. His "Biblical Archaeology" had an essentially American agenda of countering challenges to the historicity of the Bible posed by literary-historical criticism.[1] Both his research agenda and the criteria for evaluating the finds were driven by a desire to verify biblical history. While director of the American Schools of Oriental Research Center in Jerusalem (1920–29, 1933–36), now called the Albright Institute of Archaeological Research, Albright supported excavation projects intended to elucidate biblical issues. These were largely funded by Christian institutions (mainly Protestant) and staffed by Christian clergy and seminarians as well as biblical scholars.[2] Albright's tenure as director there and as editor of the *Bulletin of the American Schools of Oriental Research* (1930–68) set the course for most American excavations in the region. Among his students were the field archaeologists G. Ernest Wright, Nelson Glueck (an American rabbi trained in the Reform movement), and Avraham Biran (working in Israel). Wright and Biran trained most of the American archaeologists working in Israel and Jordan today.

Albright's theological mantle fell to his student Wright, who continued to promote "biblical archaeology." As spokesperson for the Protestant "Biblical Theology Movement," Wright argued for the historicity of the Bible. Although his historical conclusions are no longer accepted, Wright's enduring legacy remains the introduction of the physical sciences, notably geology, into field projects that were focused on the Bible.[3]

A secular tradition of American excavation existed alongside this theologically inspired approach. Major research institutions, such as Harvard, the University of Pennsylvania, and the University of Chicago's Oriental Institute, sponsored and continue to sponsor excavations at important biblical sites but without a theological agenda. However, it has been seminary-funded, biblically inspired excavations that have had the greatest impact on the largely Christian lay audience and among seminary-trained American practitioners.[4]

Beginning in the 1970s American archaeologists shifted the focus from a biblical orientation to a more social-science–informed approach. Several factors contributed to this shift. American "new archaeology" nudged her more conservative biblical cousin toward a more anthropological and scientifically based orientation. The groundwork was laid by Lewis Binford's 1962 article "Archaeology as Anthropology," which advocated studying archaeological remains from social-scientific perspectives.[5] It was not until 1985 that the archaeologist Lawrence Stager effectively integrated social science inquiry and biblical archaeology in his seminal article on the family.[6] Drawing on conceptual categories of the social sciences, Stager created a paradigm for secular archaeologists' use of biblical texts. Thereafter, biblical archaeologists drew on various disciplines in order to elucidate culture in general, often focusing on social organization and changes that could be defined by quantifiable data. Now conceived as a science, archaeology freely drew from concepts and methods of her sibling hard and social sciences.[7] Theoretical work was further encouraged by political instability in the Middle East, which curtailed excavation just as Israeli antiquities laws rendered it more difficult to remove excavated materials from the country, even for study purposes. The shift from biblically inspired to scientifically informed archaeology is evident in William Dever's suggestion to abandon the designation "biblical archaeology" for the more inclusive term "Syro-Palestinian archaeology."[8] Dever sought to free field work from second-class status as the stepchild of biblical studies, to reestablish professional credentials within the wider discipline of archaeology, and to redefine "biblical archaeology" as a multidisciplinary program within Syro-Palestinian archaeology.

The previous generation of Israeli archaeologists was trained in biblically inspired excavation by Avraham Biran, a student of Albright's, Eliezer Sukenik, and Benjamin Mazar, a German-trained Assyriologist who had studied with Albright and excavated at Tell Beit Mirsim. Today, Israeli university archaeology labs are filled to overflowing with excavation finds, so the younger generation of Israeli archaeologists stresses excavation and analysis of material culture (archaeological finds) over the study of languages and literature, including the Bible. As a result, there is a growing rift, with Israelis agitating for higher standards of analysis of the finds and Americans advocating integration of theory and relevant languages and literature into the discussion. Because both of these are obviously desirable goals that raise professional standards, the current generation of archaeologists seeks to combine the two approaches.[9]

The expectation that archaeologists working on the Iron Age and the Persian Period will engage the hard sciences and social sciences as well as the Bible has intensified the problem of competent research. One result is a growing number of jointly authored works. For example, archaeologists pair with scientists for carbon dating, while American and Israeli archaeologists work together to combine their strengths in theory, text, and material culture. To demonstrate the ways in which this is taking place, we will look at three issues that are currently being debated—the beginnings of Israel, ancient Israelite identity, and the emergence of the Israelite state.

A Case Study: Early Israel

Recent contributions to biblical studies by social-science-informed archaeology have focused on early Israel. This research has been stimulated by current thinking about the nature of identity combined with new archaeological data. The Bible relates the history of the period from the alleged conquest and settlement of Canaan to the establishment of the state in the books of Joshua, Judges, Samuel, and Kings, which are collectively referred to as the Deuteronomistic History. Although there may have been earlier versions, these books were probably compiled during the Babylonian exile of the sixth and fifth centuries B.C.E., long after the events they describe.[10] Under Joshua's leadership, the united tribes of Israel conquered the entire land and killed or subjugated the indigenous peoples. After Joshua died, a series of tribal leaders, called "judges," led fluid alliances of tribes in battle. In imitation of other nations, the tribes called for a king to muster an army capable of repulsing hostile neighbors (2 Sam 8:19–20, 9:15–16). Samuel reluctantly anointed Saul to serve as the first king. Upon Saul's death, the elders of Israel journeyed to Hebron, where they anointed David, then king of Judah, to rule Israel and Judah together (2 Sam 5:1–5). David battled for territory and established Jerusalem as his capital city (2 Sam 5:6–9, 11). His son and successor, Solomon, captured additional territory, consolidated the kingdom, built an impressive palace and royal chapel in Jerusalem, and fortified provincial centers throughout the kingdom (1 Kings 6–9).

In order to identify the archaeological remains of this period, we need to determine the specific dates when these events allegedly took place. Traditionally, they have been ascribed to the Iron I period (ca. 1200–1000 B.C.E.). Until approximately ten years ago, archaeologists assigned remains to this period based on comparative material that was found in destruction levels attributed to King David and monumental constructions that were credited to Solomon. This approach presumed known dates for David and Solomon's reigns, plus the reliability of biblical accounts of David's wars and Solomon's building projects (1 Kings 9:15–19). However, the biblical account does not include dateable references, and its internal chronology is problematic.

Conservative American scholars draw on several converging lines of evidence, some of which were discussed in chapter 1, to address this problem: (1) a reference to a people "Israel" by the Egyptian pharaoh Merneptah at the end of the thirteenth century, (2) increasing settlement in the central highlands of Canaan beginning in the late thirteenth and early twelfth century, (3) the settlement of the Philistines (Sea Peoples) in the early twelfth century, and (4) the depiction of an Israelite king (Jehu?) paying tribute to Shalmaneser III in the Assyrian Black Obelisk from the mid-ninth century.[11] Using the chronological framework provided by these disparate data, scholars correlate the thirteenth-century reign of Pharaoh Rameses II with the biblical account of Israelite labor on the store cities of Pithom and Rameses (Exod 1:11) and begin the Israelite "settlement" in the late thirteenth and early twelfth century. The transition to the United Monarchy of Saul, David, and Solomon would then begin in the late eleventh or early tenth century.

Given this chronological framework, archaeological evidence challenges the Bible's historical account. Although numerous settlements were destroyed over a period of approximately 150 years,[12] not all the places mentioned in the Bible are included. Thus, archaeology does not confirm Joshua's conquests, and in the cases of Jericho, Ai, Hebron, and Arad it actually contradicts it. Instead of destroyed towns, archaeologists have found hundreds of small-scale settlements in the highlands north of Jerusalem and in Transjordan founded during the late thirteenth and early twelfth centuries.[13] Some new settlements were founded near Late Bronze Age sites (ca. 1600–1200 B.C.E.), most frequently along the edges of cultivated valleys. Numerous farmsteads and hamlets appear to have been self-sustaining, isolated settlements subsisting on a mixed economy of small-scale farming, herding, and stock-breeding, with few if any luxuries. The small rectangular houses typically had a ground floor divided into two or three spaces by pillars, demarcating space for sheep and goats and for domestic chores. A broad room at the back served for storage and perhaps eating and sleeping, except where there was a second floor. New homes generally covered 400 to 800 square feet, likely housing nuclear families of four or five individuals.[14] By comparison, houses at sites that had been occupied since the preceding Late Bronze Age were about twice as large.

Plant and animal remains testify to the diet and lifestyle of these highland settlers. The rising numbers of millstones, mortars and pestles, storage pits, silos, and agricultural terraces indicate increased sedentarization and agricultural activity. The inhabitants cultivated barley and wheat as well as olives and grapes, from which they produced oil and wine. Legumes, such as broad beans (ful), lentils, bitter vetch, chickpea, and peas provided vegetable protein. Their diet was sweetened by figs, dates, almonds, and possibly pomegranates in addition to grape syrup.[15] The settlers also herded sheep, goats, and cows, which would have provided meat, milk, fiber, and leather. Cattle served as draft animals, pulling wagons, carts, and plows.[16] The pottery repertoire consisted of a small selection of utilitarian forms mostly continuing local forms of the previous period and virtually all undecorated.[17] Their architecture, diet, material culture, livelihood, and language followed Late Bronze Age ("Canaanite") precedents and are indistinguishable from those of their non-Israelite neighbors.[18]

Ritual practices in the early Iron Age also continued Bronze Age traditions. Because of their location, two twelfth-century mountaintop shrines are presumed to be Israelite. On Mt. Ebal, where the Bible says Joshua built an altar (Deut 11:29, 27:4–8; Josh 8:30–32), a circular altar of fieldstones, six feet in diameter, was replaced by a rectangular stone altar measuring 24 by 27 feet. Bulls, sheep, goats, and young male fallow deer appear to have been sacrificed on both; except for the fallow deer, all of these animals are biblically sanctioned.[19] Likewise, the seven-inch-long bronze statuette of a bull that was found on the summit of a nearby ridge followed the indigenous practice of representing the deity through his attribute animal.[20] The deity, like the bull, was conceived of as strong and virile, and regarded with a mix of awe and fear. The bull was an accepted Israelite religious emblem, as demonstrated by Aaron's identification of the golden calf as "your god, O Israel, who brought you up out of the Land of Egypt" (Exod 32:4), Jeroboam's selection of bulls for his border temples in Dan and Bethel (1 Kgs 12:28), and the prophet Hosea admonishing Israelites for worshipping calves (Hos 8:5–6, 10:5–6).

Unfortunately, religious and nationalistic ideology continues to influence the interpretation of archaeological remains, as is evident in an argument over burials from the phase of highland settlement (Iron I ca. 1200–1000 B.C.E.).[21] Presuming that Israelite identity was sufficiently developed by that time to be manifest in a distinctive form of burial, Iron I highland burials that closely resembled "Canaanite" Bronze Age burials were consigned to the Late Bronze Age and those that conformed to later "Israelite" burials were attributed to the Iron II period (ca. 1000–586). That left virtually no burials in Iron I, leading to the conclusion that early Iron Age Israelites had interred their dead in simple, shallow graves, which could not be found because of erosion, predatory animals, and the archaeological

difficulties in locating isolated pits. Early Israel's aspiration to an egalitarian ideal provided the ideological rationale for adopting simple pit graves
for everyone.

In fact, not a single simple grave has been published. Surveys and excavations have recorded hundreds of Iron I highland burials, all in caves and
tombs that are indistinguishable from the earlier Late Bronze Age examples and consistent with the later Iron II burials. Rather than requiring the
disappearance of a deviant Iron I practice, the evidence demonstrates a
continuous trajectory: the early Israelites followed indigenous customs in
burial as in many other aspects of life.

Based strictly on archaeological remains, Israelites are indistinguishable from their non-Israelite highland neighbors. Without the biblical
testimony, we would not suspect that the newly settled population distinguished themselves from either their Bronze Age predecessors or their
non-Israelite contemporaries. We presume that these twelfth- and elev-
enth-century highland settlers considered themselves Israelites because
they lived in areas that were later part of the Israelite state.

Ethnicity and the Creation of Ethnic Identity

In approximately 1207 B.C.E., the Egyptian pharaoh Merneptah listed the
people "Israel" among vanquished foreign enemies.[22] Accepting the biblical text as essentially historical, "biblical archaeologists" presume that
there was a connection between Merneptah's Israel, biblical Israel, and at
least some of the population that founded the late thirteenth- and early
twelfth-century highland settlements. Since early Israelites are archaeologically indistinguishable from their neighbors, is it possible to ascertain
how they differentiated themselves from others?

Following the archaeologist Yohanan Aharoni, some archaeologists distinguish early Israelites from the indigenous "Canaanites" by finding traits
that characterize a territorially defined population.[23] In 1970, Aharoni
identified the collar-rim storejar as an exclusively Israelite pottery form.[24]
Pillared houses and the abstention from eating pig were later added to the
list of distinctive Israelite markers.[25] However, none of these features is exclusively Israelite: collar-rim jars and pillared houses are attested outside
of Israelite territory, and the diet of the indigenous highland population in
the preceding Late Bronze Age also lacked pig.[26] Moreover, the Bible never

mentions storejars or pillared houses, so their use is likely an environmental adaptation rather than an intentional marker of ethnic identity.

Ethnicity studies offer an alternative way to understand early Israel.[27] Shared interests often prompt unrelated clans to join forces. Such groups typically claim a common ancestry that provides a shared history and culture, enabling group members to identify one another and distinguish themselves from others. The group believes that some features, such as kinship, territory, and shared religion, existed from its inception ("primordial"); others are recognized as having arisen from changing circumstances ("circumstantial").

For early Israel, a short beard rather than a clean-shaven face (Lev 19:27; Deut 14:2), male circumcision (1 Sam 18:25–26; 31:4; 2 Sam 3:14), and refraining from eating pork (Lev 11:7–8; Deut 14:2) distinguished them from the Philistines, though not from their "Canaanite" highland neighbors. All three of these traits are supported by external evidence. Pictures from Medinet Habu at the time of Rameses III portray the Sea Peoples as clean-shaven, while Shalmaneser's mid-ninth-century Black Obelisk (admittedly later) depicts Israelites as bearded.[28] The Philistines (Peleset), whom the Bible denigrates as uncircumcised (1 Sam 18:25–26; 31:4; 2 Sam 3:14),[29] are omitted from Pharaoh Merneptah's list of the "[Sher]den, Shekelesh, Ekwesh, of the countries of the sea, who had no foreskins."[30] Finally, pig bones constituted 18 to 19 percent of the animal bones retrieved from the Philistine settlements of Ashkelon and Tel Miqne, proving that pig was a staple of the diet. This contrasts with the Late Bronze and Iron Age highland settlements, where only a single pig bone has been found at Late Bronze Age Shiloh and at Iron Age Ai and Raddana, demonstrating that pig wasn't consumed in the highlands by the Israelites or their predecessors.[31] Early Israelites resembled their highland neighbors, at least outwardly, in most respects—dress, facial hair and hairstyle, language, diet, house plan, pottery and other household possessions, livelihood, and even religious practices. However, they distinguished themselves from the Philistines, who were considered hostile enemies (notwithstanding David and Samson's brief liaisons), and were readily identifiable by their clean-shaven faces.

Ethnicity studies suggest that features may be added to or dropped from an ethnic group's account of itself over time.[32] Both artifacts and text demonstrate that Israelite identity and religion did not debut fully formed, but evolved over the centuries as existing elements were rejected

or reinterpreted and new features introduced in response to changing circumstances.[33] For example, the Mt. Ebal altar and the bull site demonstrate that sacrificial deer and bull-calf images were proscribed after having initially been accepted within Israel (2 Kgs 18:4; Exod 20:4). Changing
circumstances led to the incorporation and deletion of material from Israel's recorded "collective memory" (the Bible). The very process of writing and editing to enfranchise members of the growing Israelite people, a
process dubbed "narrativization," likely fostered cohesion and helped con-
solidate ethnic identity.[34]

Israelite traits recorded in the Bible, such as a short beard, circumcision, and abstaining from pork, would have been meaningful only in the
twelfth- to tenth- century context of the Philistines (or the Hellenistic period). Archaeology thus shows that the Israelites began to shape their collective memory by the tenth century. This refutes the argument of those
who claim that the Bible does not preserve material predating the seventh
century when the existing accounts were edited. Moreover, it suggests that
it was the Philistines and not the "Canaanites" (highland Semites) who
were the significant "other" for early Israel.

State Formation

Until relatively recently, scholars generally accepted the Bible as a faithful
record of Israel's increasing social and political complexity: beginning
with Abraham, families grew into clans that joined to form tribes led by
judges, which ultimately unified under a king to become a state. This progression followed the trajectory canonized in the 1960s: as egalitarian societies become stratified, social complexity evolves from band to tribe,
to chiefdom, and finally to state.[35] Archaeologically attested monumental
buildings, such as fortification walls, city gates, palaces, and stables, were
seen as indicating the socioeconomic complexity and political centralization associated with a "state."[36] As with the attempts to identify characteristics that differentiated Israelites from their neighbors, a list of traits for a
geographically defined population was interpreted as evidence of having
achieved statehood.

By the 1930s, excavators had identified the city gates, stables, and pillared buildings at Megiddo with Solomon's building projects listed in
1 Kings 9.[37] Thirty years later Yigael Yadin seemed to confirm that identification when he recognized similar gates at Hazor and Gezer; these fit the

biblical notation that Solomon had fortified Hazor, Megiddo, and Gezer (1 Kings 9:15).[38] This simplistic equation is now thrown into doubt by the discovery of similar gates at Philistine Ashdod and in later phases of the Israelite towns of Lachish and Tel Ira.[39]

To digress for a moment, the dating of remains popularly attributed to Kings David and Solomon, who are generally thought to have reigned in the tenth century, is currently the most contentious issue in archaeological circles. Israel Finkelstein proposed lowering all dates, beginning at about 1200 B.C.E., by fifty to one hundred years so that the monumental construction uncovered at Tel Jezreel would fit the biblical account associating the site with the mid-ninth-century Israelite King Ahab (1 Kings 21:1, 16; 2 Kings 9–10). This adjustment assigns city gates and walls, palaces, and stables to the reigns of the ninth-century kings Omri and his son Ahab rather than the tenth-century reign of Solomon (1 Kings 9).[40] Finkelstein bolstered his argument with revised dates for Philistine settlement in the region based on the appearance of their distinctive bichrome (decorated in black and red) pottery.[41] The reinterpreted evidence yielded a date approximately fifty years later than the traditionally accepted date, which supported the revised dating proposed for Tel Jezreel.

Noted archaeologists Amihai Mazar, Amnon Ben-Tor, Lawrence Stager, Shlomo Bunimovitz, and Avraham Faust have countered Finkelstein's proposal with additional comparative materials, carbon 14 dates from Tel Rehov, social and cultural factors inferred from archaeological remains, and the historical context presented in the Bible.[42]

Whoever turns out to be right, both sides acknowledge the need for impartial, scientific dating techniques as well as more refined distinction of pottery styles. Even carbon dating, for which a country-wide bank of dates has provided improved reliability,[43] still yields incompatible results; for example, dates from Tel Rehov substantiate the traditional "high chronology" while those from Tel Dor and Jezreel support Finkelstein's "low chronology."[44] Whatever the outcome of this debate, Finkelstein's challenge questions Solomon's accomplishments and casts the historicity of the biblical account into doubt.

Finkelstein measured Israel and Judah's progress toward statehood in terms of a series of archaeologically attested features that reflect growing economic, administrative, and political complexity: monumental buildings and inscriptions, large-scale centralized production, trade, and a settlement system of central towns with dependent villages and hamlets. On the basis of these criteria, he concluded that the northern kingdom of

Israel did not achieve "full-blown statehood" until the ninth century and
Judah not until the eighth century. The United Monarchy of David and
Solomon was therefore characterized as a possible "early" state, a transi-
tional stage on the road toward full-blown statehood.[45]

Again to his credit, Finkelstein's provocation stimulated a reevaluation
of the commonly held view, in this case of state formation. The traditional
view, articulated by Fried and Service, held that the development from
tribe to state correlated with a shift from a kin-based to a class-based society. Instead of assuming that centralized authority displaced the smaller
levels of political organization, most scholars now accept Øystein LaBianca's view that kin-based tribes can coexist with larger, class-based polities such as a state. Ancient Near Eastern societies, including Israel, are
now conceived in terms of a socioeconomic continuum that ranges from
the least complex structure, nomadic tribes, to the more complex sedentary chiefdoms and states, with a variety of gradations in between and
with various socioeconomic levels coexisting.[46]

Lawrence Stager and his students, J. David Schloen and Daniel Master,
and Bruce Routledge discuss Israelite statehood from the perspectives of
archaeological and literary evidence, along with the symbolic value of language and artifacts. Following LaBianca's lead, Master argues that tribes
and states can coexist. A study of modern Middle Eastern tribes supports
this view by showing that tribes can function within state organizations
and support an administrative apparatus of the size and complexity characteristic of a "state."[47] Following the groundbreaking studies of Stager
and Schloen, Master characterized Israelite society as a series of nested
(hierarchical) layers of authoritarian relationships. The father-son relationship provided the model for all levels of interaction, from the smallest
and least significant unit, the household, through the clan and tribe up to
the highest unit, the king. Master found Max Weber's characterization of
law and authority, a "patrimonial" regime, to fit Israel's social-political organization., Authority was bestowed by force of tradition or personal association rather than by virtue of charisma or qualification—no specific
qualifications were required. This "patrimonial" regime described the authority figures of ancient Israel, be they heads of households, patriarchs of
clans, or kings of state.[48]

Evidence that ancient Israel used this socio-political organization is
preserved in the Bible's political and judicial terminology. Fathers, "elders," and "kings" exercised authority in the Iron Age: fathers at the family
level, and elders at the local and state level in conjunction with kings at the

level of state. Thus, the Israelite kingdom consisted of nested (hierarchical), kin-based social units (family, clan, tribe, nation) and territorial units (household, town, tribal territory, state) ruled by force of kin-based tradition (father, elder, king).

In his work on Moab, Routledge argues that in addition to linguistic terms indicative of statehood, the concept of a "state" has to be physically manifest in order to concretize and propagandize. Routledge identifies select material expressions, including decorative Proto-Aeolic column capitals, "palaces" in royal or capital cities and, in Ammon and Moab, royal statues marked with divine emblems as symbols of statehood that were recognized in Israel, Judah, Ammon, Moab, and Edom.[49] Once again, dating Israelite monumental architecture will favor the transition to statehood either with Solomon in the tenth century or with the Omride kings in the ninth century.

What then can archaeologists say about the state of the Israelite state, or the state of the union, under David and Solomon? This question itself demonstrates how the social sciences have framed the discussion and infused it with social scientific terminology. By arguing for the "High Chronology," Lawrence Stager, Baruch Halpern, William Dever, Daniel Master, and Avraham Faust have left the United Monarchy, with its impressive trappings and propagandistic displays of political attainment, intact.[50] They provide the necessary chronological anchor by attributing the destruction of level IIB at the ancient city of Taanach to the military campaign of Pharaoh Sheshonq I (biblical Shishak) mentioned in both biblical (1 Kgs 14:25–58; 2 Chron 12:1–12) and Egyptian sources. Placing this destruction in 925 B.C.E. permits one to identify pottery styles that typify the tenth century. Armed with a tenth-century assemblage for comparative purposes, "High Chronology" supporters reclaim the Megiddo city gate as belonging to the period of Solomon. They also argue for rural resettlement, urbanization, and the development of regional administrative centers at the same time. Such concerted efforts would have been possible only under a coercive centralized authority, namely Kings David and Solomon. On the symbolic level, Stager notes that among the significant tenth-century centers, which include Megiddo, Taanach, Beth-Shean, Jezreel, Dor, Beth-Shemesh, and Yokneam, only Jerusalem boasted the insignia of statehood—a palace with associated temple complex.[51]

Following Routledge's reasoning, the Megiddo, Gezer, and Hazor fortifications and the Jerusalem palace and royal chapel would have signaled to neighboring polities Israel's high level political organization. Additionally, the ninth-century Tel Dan and Mesha inscriptions refer to the Davidic dynasty ("House of David"), demonstrating that Arameans and Moabites considered David the founding father of a political entity comparable to their own.[52] These inscriptions preserve foreign perceptions of the Judahite polity as a worthy enemy a century before Finkelstein thinks Israel achieved full or mature statehood.

However, the results of carbon dating support Finkelstein's "Low Chronology," robbing David and Solomon of the physical manifestations some researchers require for statehood. Moreover, the "High Chronology" may be undermined by Kevin Wilson's work questioning the historicity of the Sheshonq I topographical list for reconstructing his military campaign.[53] As the argument has been traditionally formulated, it is currently not possible to determine whether Israel achieved the degree of complexity considered indicative of statehood under Solomon in the tenth century or under later kings.

Conclusion

What do archaeology and the social sciences add to our understanding of ancient Israel and the Bible? Recent discussions have explored the emergence of Israel culturally, ethnically, and politically. These show that the Iron Age inhabitants of the central highlands shared many characteristics with their "Canaanite" neighbors and predecessors. The features by which they defined themselves actually set them apart from the Philistines rather than the "Canaanites." Regarding the transition to statehood, perhaps Schloen is correct in conceiving of statehood as a "state of mind," in which case no list of traits can suffice to categorize a political entity.[54] In the case of Israel, insight into the kingdom can be gained by examining the nature of authority, the factors that precipitated political development, and the means by which status was communicated. Even if Solomon was not a master builder, the population acknowledged his inherited authority as a son of David. Later generations attributed constructions to him because they considered him sufficiently powerful and resourceful to have fortified provincial centers. Future advances in dating may resolve the current differences of analysis and interpretation.

Both archaeological evidence and the Bible provide important information for reconstructing the history of ancient Israel; however, it is clear that biblical Israel and historical/archaeological Israel are not identical.

Biblical Israel is an ancient literary construct given form more than 2,000 years ago, while historical/archaeological Israel is a modern construct, a composite picture grounded in material remains, informed by biblical testimony, and fleshed out through insights produced by the social sciences. The archaeologically based reconstruction offered here is best considered a piece of a "road map," with alternate routes to consider and sights to watch for along the way.

NOTES

1. W. F. Albright, "The Impact of Archaeology on Biblical Research—1966," in *New Directions in Archaeology*, ed. D. N. Freedman and J. C. Greenfield (Garden City, N.Y.: Doubleday, 1969), 1–4; P. Machinist, "William Foxwell Albright: The Man and His Work," in *The Study of the Ancient Near East in the Twenty-First Century*, ed. J. S. Cooper and G. M. Schwartz (Winona Lake, Ind.: Eisenbrauns, 1996), 385–403; S. Gitin, "The House that Albright Built," *NEA* 65 (2002): 5–10.

2. W. G. Dever, "Biblical Archaeology," in *The Oxford Encyclopedia of Archaeology in the Near East*, ed. E. M. Meyers (New York: Oxford University Press, 1997), 315–19.

3. G. E. Wright, *Biblical Archaeology* (Philadelphia, Pa.: Westminster, 1957); E. Campbell, "Wright, George Ernest," in *The Oxford Encyclopedia of Archaeology in the Near East*, 350–52.

4. W. Dever, *Recent Archaeological Discoveries and Biblical Research* (Seattle and London: University of Washington Press, 1990), 20.

5. L. Binford, "Archaeology as Anthropology," *American Antiquity* 28 (1962): 217–25.

6. L. Stager, "The Archaeology of the Family in Ancient Israel," *BASOR* 269 (1985): 1–35.

7. A. Joffee, "New Archaeology," in *The Oxford Encyclopedia of Archaeology in the Near East*, 134–38.

8. W. Dever and S. Paul, *Biblical Archaeology* (Jerusalem: Keter, 1973). Ziony Zevit categorizes professional and institutional reasons both for and against changing the name ("Biblical Archaeology versus Syro-Palestinian Archaeology," in *The Future of Biblical Archaeology: Reassessing Methodologies and Assumptions*, ed. J. Hoffmeier and A. Millard [Grand Rapids, Mich., and Cambridge, U.K.: Eerdmans, 2004], 3–19).

9. Most Europeans shun biblical-period sites in Israel. One current exception is the joint German-Swiss-Finnish expedition to Tel Kinrot.

10. I. Provan, *Hezekiah and the Book of Kings* (BZAW 172; Berlin and New York: de Gruyter, 1988).

11. J. Hoffmeier, "The (Israel) Stela of Merneptah (2.6)," and K. L. Younger Jr.,

"Black Obelisk (2.113F)," in *The Context of Scripture*, ed. W. Hallo (Leiden, Boston, and Köln: Brill, 2000), vol. 2, Monumental Inscriptions from the Biblical World, 40–41 and 269–70.

12. Hazor stratum XIII, Megiddo stratum VIIB, Beth Shan stratum VII, Bethel, Beth Shemesh stratum IV, Gezer stratum XV, Timnah, Tell Beit Mirsim stratum C, Tel Halif, and Lachish stratum VII, but also Aphek (the Egyptian residency), Ashdod stratum XIV, Tel Miqne/Ekron stratum VIII, and Haror strata K3 and B7. The evidence is conveniently summarized in Amihai Mazar, *Archaeology of the Land of the Bible, 10,000–586 B.C.E.* (Anchor Bible Reference Library; New York and London: Doubleday, 1990), 329–34; R. Younker, "The Iron Age in the Southern Levant," in *Near Eastern Archaeology: A Reader*, ed. S. Richard (Winona Lake, Ind.: Eisenbrauns, 2003), 369–70.

13. I. Finkelstein, *The Archaeology of the Israelite Settlement* (Jerusalem: Israel Exploration Society, 1988).

14. Based on ethnographic studies that calculate roofed square meters allocated per person and censuses of hill country Arab villages in the late 1800s and early 1900s; I. Finkelstein, *Archaeology of the Israelite Settlement*, 268–69, n. 22.

15. O. Borowski, *Agriculture in Iron Age Israel* (Boston: American Schools of Oriental Research, 2002), 87–128.

16. O. Borowski, *Every Living Thing: Daily Use of Animals in Ancient Israel* (Walnut Creek, London, New Delhi: Altamira, 1998), 231–33.

17. For a full discussion and bibliographic references see Elizabeth Bloch-Smith and Beth Alpert Nakhai, "A Landscape Comes to Life: The Iron Age I," *NEA* 62 (1999): 75–76.

18. Bloch-Smith and Nakhai, "A Landscape Comes to Life," 62–92, 101–27, esp. 70–78.

19. A. Zertal, "An Early Iron Age Cultic Site on Mount Ebal: Excavation Seasons 1982–1987, Preliminary Report," *Tel Aviv* 13–14 (1986–87): 105–66, esp. 151–61; and "'Go to the Land of the Perizzites and the Giants': On the Israelite Settlement in the Hill Country of Manasseh," in *From Nomadism to Monarchy: Archaeological and Historical Aspects of Early Israel*, ed. I. Finkelstein and N. Na'aman (Jerusalem and Washington, D.C.: Yad Izhak Ben-Zvi, Israel Exploration Society and Biblical Archaeology Society, 1994), 47–69, esp. 61–65

20. A. Mazar, "The Bull Site: An Iron Age I Open Cult Place," *BASOR* 247 (1982): 26–37.

21. R. Kletter, "People without Burials? The Lack of Iron I Burials in the Central Highlands of Palestine," *IEJ* 52 (2002): 28–48; A. Faust, "'Mortuary Practices, Society and Ideology': The Lack of Iron Age I Burials in the Highlands in Context," *IEJ* 54 (2004): 174–90; E. Bloch-Smith, "Resurrecting the Iron I Dead," *IEJ* 54 (2004): 77–91.

22. J. Hoffmeier, "The (Israel) Stela of Merneptah (2.6)," in *The Context of Scripture*, vol. 2, Monumental Inscriptions from the Biblical World, 41.

23. I. Finkelstein, *The Archaeology of the Israelite Settlement;* W. Dever, "Cultural Continuity, Ethnicity in the Archaeological Record, and the Question of Israelite Origins," *Eretz-Israel* 24 (1993): 22*–33*, "Ceramics, Ethnicity, and the Question of Israel's Origins?" *BA* 58 (1995): 200–13, "Will the Real Israel Please Stand Up? Archaeology and Israelite Historiography: Part 1," *BASOR* 297 (1995): 61–80, *What Did the Biblical Writers Know and When Did They Know It? What Archaeology Can Tell Us about the Reality of Ancient Israel* (Grand Rapids, Mich.: Eerdmans, 2001); I. Finkelstein and N. Silberman, *The Bible Unearthed: Archaeology's New Vision of Ancient Israel and the Origin of Its Sacred Texts* (New York: Free Press, 2001).

24. Y. Aharoni, "New Aspects of the Israelite Occupation in the North," in *Near Eastern Archaeology in the Twentieth Century: Essays in Honor of Nelson Glueck,* ed. J. Sanders (New York: Doubleday, 1970), 264–65.

25. W. Dever, *What Did the Biblical Writers Know and When Did They Know It?;* I. Finkelstein and N. Silberman, *The Bible Unearthed;* Z. Zevit, *Religions of Ancient Israel: A Synthesis of Parallactic Approaches* (New York: Continuum, 2001).

26. B. Hesse, "Husbandry, Dietary Taboos, and the Bones of the Ancient Near East: Zooarchaeology in the Post-Processual World," in *Methods in the Mediterranean: Historical and Archaeological Views on Texts and Archaeology,* ed. E. Small (Leiden, New York: Brill, 1995), 217–30; B. Hesse and P. Wapnish, "Can Pig Remains Be Used for Ethnic Diagnosis in the Ancient Near East?" in *Archaeology of Israel: Constructing the Past, Interpreting the Present,* ed. N. Silberman and D. Small (JSOTSupp 237; Sheffield: Sheffield Academic, 1997), 238–70. Avraham Faust has a forthcoming book on the topic, *Israel's Ethnogenesis: Settlement, Interaction, Expansion and Resistance.*

27. I. Finkelstein, "Ethnicity and Origin of the Iron I Settlers in the Highlands of Canaan: Can the Real Israel Stand Up?" *BA* 59 (1996): 198–212, and "Pots and People Revisited: Ethnic Boundaries in the Iron Age I," in *The Archaeology of Israel,* ed. N. Silberman and D. Small, 216–37. For a bibliography of the literature on ethnicity see Bruce MacKay, "Ethnicity and Israelite Religion: The Anthropology of Social Boundaries in Judges" (Ph.D. dissertation, University of Toronto, 1997).

28. *Medinet Habu VIII; I. Earlier Historical Records of Ramesses III* (Chicago: University of Chicago Press, 1930), plates 37, 39, 44; J. Pritchard, *The Ancient Near East in Pictures: Relating to the Old Testament* (Princeton, N.J.: Princeton University, 1954), figures 351 and 352.

29. Also the men of Shechem (Gen 34:14).

30. J. Breasted, *Ancient Records of Egypt,* vol. 3, "The Nineteenth Dynasty" (1906; reprinted New York: Russell & Russell, 1962), 249, §588.

31. B. Hesse, "Husbandry, Dietary Taboos, and the Bones of the Ancient Near East," 217–30; B. Hesse and P. Wapnish, "Can Pig Remains Be Used for Ethnic Diagnosis in the Ancient Near East?" 238–70.

32. For a fuller treatment of this topic, see E. Bloch-Smith, "Israelite Ethnicity

in Iron I: Archaeology Preserves What Is Remembered and What Is Forgotten in Israel's History," *JBL* 122 (2003): 401–25.

33. M. Smith, *The Early History of God: Yahweh and the Other Deities in Ancient Israel* (San Francisco: Harper & Row, 1990), 7–12.

34. S. Cornell, "That's the Story of Our Life," in *We Are a People: Narrative and Multiplicity in Constructing Ethnic Identity,* ed. P. Spickard and W. Burroughs (Philadelphia: Temple University Press, 2000), 43–44.

35. M. Fried, *The Evolution of Political Society* (New York: Norton, 1967); E. Service, *Primitive Social Organization* (New York: Norton, 1962).

36. D. Master, "State Formation Theory and the Kingdom of Ancient Israel," *JNES* 60 (2001): 117–31; A. Mazar, "Remarks on Biblical Traditions and Archaeological Evidence concerning Early Israel," in *Symbiosis, Symbolism, and the Power of the Past: Canaan, Ancient Israel, and Their Neighbors from the Late Bronze Age through Roman Palaestina,* ed. W. Dever and S. Gitin (Winona Lake, Ind.: Eisenbrauns, 2003), 85–98.

37. Stratum IV; P. L. O. Guy, *New Light from Armageddon* (Oriental Institute Communications; Chicago: University of Chicago Press, 1931), 44–48; R. S. Lamon and G. M. Shipton, *Megiddo I. Season of 1925–34 Strata 1–5* (Chicago: Oriental Institute Publications, 1939), 59.

38. Y. Yadin reassigned the gate and ashlar palaces to the tenth-century Solomonic Strata VA-IVB and the pillared buildings to the ninth-century Omride stratum IVA (*Hazor—The Head of All Those Kingdoms* [Schweich Lectures, 1970; London: British Academy, 1972], 147–64).

39. D. Ussishkin, "Notes on Megiddo, Gezer, Ashdod, and Tel Batash in the Tenth to Ninth Centuries B.C.," *BASOR* 277/278 (1980): 71–91.

40. I. Finkelstein, "The Arch of the United Monarchy: An Alternate View," *Levant* 28 (1990): 177–87.

41. For example, Megiddo VIA, Arad XII, and Beer-Sheva VII would date to the tenth century, while Megiddo VA-IVB, Arad XI, and Beer-Sheva V move to the ninth century.

42. L. Stager, "The Impact of the Sea Peoples (1185–1050 BCE)," in *The Archaeology of Society in the Holy Land,* ed. T. Levy (London: Leicester University, 1990), 332–48; S. Bunimovitz and A. Faust, "Chronological Separation, Geographical Segregation, or Ethnic Demarcation? Ethnography and the Iron Age Low Chronology," *BASOR* 332 (2001): 1–10.

43. I. Sharon, "'Transition Dating'—A Heuristic Mathematical Approach to the Collation of Radiocarbon Dates from Stratified Sequences," *Radiocarbon* 43 (2001): 345–54; I. Sharon and A. Gilboa, "Early Iron Age Radiometric Dates from Tel Dor: Preliminary Implications for Phoenicia and Beyond," *Radiocarbon* 43 (2001): 1343–51; idem., "An Archaeological Contribution to the Early Iron Age Chronological Debate: Alternative Chronologies for Phoenicia and Their Effects on the Levant, Cyprus, and Greece," *BASOR* 332 (2003): 7–80; I. Sharon, A. Gilboa,

and E. Boaretto, "¹⁴C and the Early Iron Age Levantine Chronology: Where Are We Really At?" paper presented at the 2nd European Conference on the Synchronization of Civilizations in the Eastern Mediterranean, 2000; Vienna, April 28–June 1, 2003.

44. Sharon and Gilboa, "An Archaeological Contribution to the Early Iron Age Chronological Debate," 7–80; I. Finkelstein and E. Piasetzky, "Comment on ¹⁴C Dates from Tel Rehov: Iron-Age Chronology, Pharaohs and Hebrew Kings,' " *Science* 302 (2003): 568b; A. Mazar and I. Carmi, "Radiocarbon Dates from Iron Age Strata at Tel Beth Shean and Tel Rehov," *Radiocarbon* 43 (2001): 1333–42; H. J. Buins, J. van der Plicht, and A. Mazar, "¹⁴C Dates from Tel Rehov: Iron-Age Chronology, Pharaohs and Hebrew Kings," *Science* 300 (2003): 315–18.

45. I. Finkelstein, "State Formation in Israel and Judah: A Contrast in Context, A Contrast in Trajectory," *NEA* 62 (1999): 35–52.

46. M. Rowton, "Urban Autonomy in a Nomadic Environment," *JNES* 32 (1973): 201–15; idem., "Enclosed Nomadism," *JESHO* 17 (1974), 1–30; P. C. Salzman, "Introduction: Processes of Sedentarization as Adaptation and Response," in *When Nomads Settle*, ed. P. Salzman (New York: Praeger, 1980), 1–19; J. M. Miller, *Archaeological Survey of the Kerak Plateau* (Atlanta, Ga.: Scholars Press, 1991), 5–8; Ø. LaBianca, *Sedentarization and Nomadization: Food System Cycles at Hesban and Vicinity in Transjordan* (Berrien Springs, Mich.: Andrew University Press, 1990), 10–21; Ø. LaBianca and R. Younker, "The Kingdoms of Ammon, Moab and Edom: The Archaeology of Society in Late Bronze/Iron Age Transjordan (ca. 1400–500 BCE)," in *The Archaeology of Society in the Holy Land*, ed. T. Levy, 399–411. The most sophisticated recent treatment of the topic is Bruce Routledge's book, *Moab in the Iron Age: Hegemony, Polity, Archaeology*.

47. D. Master, "State Formation Theory and the Kingdom of Ancient Israel," *JNES* 60 (2001): 117–31; D. Master, "Reconstructing the Tenth Century in Ancient Israel," in *100 Years of American Archaeology in the Middle East: Proceedings of the American Schools of Oriental Research Centennial Celebration, Washington, DC, April 2000*, ed. D. Clark and V. Matthews (Boston: ASOR, 2003), 215–29; M. Weber, *Economy and Society*, vol. 2, ed. G. Roth and C. Wittick (Berkeley: University of California Press); P. Khoury and J. Kostiner, "Introduction: Tribes and the Complexities of State Formation in the Middle East," in *Tribe and State Formation in the Middle East*, ed. idem (Berkeley: University of California Press, 1990), 3–4.

48. D. Master, "State Formation Theory and the Kingdom of Ancient Israel," 128; cf. L. Stager, "The Archaeology of the Family in Ancient Israel," 1–35; J. D. Schloen, "The Patrimonial Household in the Kingdom of Ugarit: A Weberian Analysis of Ancient Near Eastern Society" (Ph.D. dissertation, Harvard University, 1995).

49. B. Routledge, "Evolution Is as History Does: On State Formation in Iron Age Transjordan," in *100 Years of American Archaeology in the Middle East*, ed. D. Clark and V. Matthews, 244–48.

50. Lawrence Stager lecture, "The Crisis of the Tenth Century BCE," at the Gruss Colloquium in Judaic Studies conference, "Text, Artifact, and Image: Revealing Ancient Israelite Religion," April 28, 1998; B. Halpern, *David's Secret Demons: Messiah, Murderer, Traitor, King* (Grand Rapids, Mich., Cambridge, U.K.: Eerdmans, 2001), esp. 460–78; W. Dever, *What Did the Biblical Writers Know and When Did They Know It?* esp. 124–31; D. Master, "State Formation Theory and the Kingdom of Ancient Israel," 117–31; A. Faust, "Mortuary Practices, Society and Ideology," 174–90; and A. Faust, "Abandonment, Urbanization, Resettlement and the Formation of the Israelite State," *NEA* 66 (2003): 147–61.

51. L. Stager, "The Patrimonial Kingdom of Solomon," in *Symbiosis, Symbolism, and the Power of the Past: Canaan, Ancient Israel, and Their Neighbors from the Late Bronze Age through Roman Palaestina*, ed. W. Dever and S. Gitin (Winona Lake, Ind.: Eisenbrauns, 2003), 63–67 and 410.

52. B. Routledge, "Evolution Is as History Does," 240; K. A. D. Smelik, "The Inscription of King Mesha (2.23)," and A. Millard, "The Tell Dan Stele," in *The Context of Scripture*, ed. W. Hallo, vol. 2: Monumental Inscriptions from the Biblical World, 137–38 and 161–62.

53. K. Wilson, "The Campaign of Pharaoh Shoshenq I into Palestine" (Ph.D. dissertation, Johns Hopkins University, 2001); K. Wilson, "The Campaign of Pharaoh Shoshenq I in Palestine," http://www.bibleinterp.com/articles/Wilson-Campaign_of_Shoshenq_I_1.htm.

54. J. D. Schloen, "The Iron Age State as a State of Mind: A Response," in *100 Years of American Archaeology in the Middle East*, ed. D. Clark and V. Matthews, 283–92.

Part II

New Approaches to the Bible

Chapter 3

Literary Approaches to Biblical Literature
General Observations and a Case Study of Genesis 34

Adele Berlin

Literary approaches to the Bible go back to ancient times, although many people have the impression that they are a modern invention. One need only think of early Christian allegorical readings or rabbinic Midrash to realize that the use of literary strategies to interpret the Bible has a very long history. Ancient and medieval exegetes regularly developed their exegesis (interpretation) around what we would consider literary phenomena, like the repetition of words and phrases, the sequencing of narratives, plot symmetries, and the portrayal and development of characters. And I expect that literary approaches, in one form or another, will be with us as long as the Bible is read, for they are part and parcel of biblical interpretation.

New and ever-changing, though, is the mode of the literary inquiry. As assumptions change about the nature of a text and how its meaning may be discerned, so do the questions posed and the analytic tools used to answer them. The territory subsumed under "literary approaches to the Bible" is vast, even if confined to the contemporary scene, and it resists easy categorization. This chapter will therefore offer a selective view of this enterprise, highlighting what I see as its more significant recent trends. The discussion will be structured around three rubrics: (1) comparative literature, (2) the influence of literary theory and criticism, and (3) from interpretation to the history of interpretation. These rubrics should not be construed as a chronological progression, and they are not entirely separable; they simply provide a convenient way to divide up the territory.

Before we proceed, let me offer a broad definition of what literary approaches are and what they are trying to accomplish. The overarching purpose of a literary inquiry is a better understanding of the text—its construction, its forms of expression, its meaning and significance, and/or its relationship to non-textual events or to other texts.

The text is a vehicle of representation. Literature is a verbal construction of a world, analogous to the visual construction of the world in art. It may represent the real world (in which case it may appear historical even when it is not), or a non-real world. A literary interpretation of the Bible probes the Bible's construction of the world and analyzes the forms of expression through which that world is constructed. It examines biblical modes of discourse, literary conventions and assumptions, and context. It seeks to show how the Bible imagines the world and what message that image conveys. I would say that whenever we ask what the text means or how it creates meaning, whenever we engage in an act of interpretation, we are, in some way, using a literary approach. This definition may seem overly broad, but nothing less can encompass all in the past and the present that falls under the heading of literary approaches.

Comparative Literature: Is the Bible like Other Literatures or Is It Unique?

Some of the earliest interpreters of the Bible lived in the Greco-Roman world and were, quite naturally, influenced by Greco-Roman literature, both because it was familiar to them and because it was held in such high esteem. Unlike the Israelites or the Jews of antiquity, the Greeks not only wrote literature, but also talked about how to write it. Given their penchant for abstract thinking, they discussed literature in a theoretical way, ascertaining what constituted good form, appropriate content, and convincing rhetoric. The Greek model became the gold standard, but the results when this model was applied to the Bible caused some consternation, for biblical literature did not always seem to follow Greek rules. For quite a number of years, through the Middle Ages and into the Early Modern period (Renaissance), Greek literature was the standard against which the Bible was measured. And if not Greek literature, then other vernacular literatures (most notably Arabic, Italian, and English).[1] Inevitably, comparing these literatures with the Bible generated a certain amount of anxiety about how the Bible would fare in the comparison. Did the Bible work the same way as other literatures? Did it fall short of other literary works? Or was it the greatest literature ever written? The tendency among biblical scholars was, not surprisingly, to conclude that the Bible was the best, even when, or perhaps especially when, it departed from more usual literary practices. From this long and complex history I have chosen one particularly dramatic expression of this tendency, typical of its time. It was written in 1772 by the Yale theologian Timothy Dwight. For Dwight, the distinctiveness of biblical literature is its glory, its claim to genius. He says of the biblical authors that

> Unencumbered by Critical manacles, they gave their imagination an unlimited range . . . and in every period, snatched the grace which is beyond the reach of art, and which, being the genuine offspring of elevated Genius, finds the shortest passage to the human soul. With all this license no writers have so few faulty passages. "But" says the Critic "they don't describe *exactly according to our rules*." True sir: and when you can convince me that *Homer and Virgil*, from whom you gather those rules, were sent into the world to give Laws to all other authors; when you can convince me that every beauty of fine writing is to be found, in its highest perfection, in their works, I will allow the beauties of the divine writers to be faults. 'Till that can be demonstrated, I must continue to admire the most shining instances of Genius, unparallel'd in force, or sublimity. . . .²

For Dwight, the classical model was the epitome of literature, but the Bible answered to a higher authority.

By the twentieth century, the glorification of the Bible's aesthetic superiority had receded (although it remains an occupational hazard), as had the epitomization of the Greek model. Comparisons with Greek literature, however, remained useful. A high-water mark in the early development of modern literary approaches to the Bible is Erich Auerbach's comparison of the narrative styles in Homer and the Bible. Homeric narrative style, he found, foregrounds every event and every detail, developing each point in full, often creating a lengthy diversion from the main plot. Biblical narrative does just the opposite, highlighting the main action as economically as possible and leaving the rest in obscurity, unexpressed, thereby creating the sense that it is "fraught with background." Auerbach summed up these differences:

> It would be difficult, then, to imagine styles more contrasted than those of these two equally ancient and equally epic texts. On the one hand [in Homer], externalized, uniformly illuminated phenomena, at a definite time and in a definite place, connected together without lacunae in a perpetual

foreground; thoughts and feeling completely expressed; events taking place in leisurely fashion and with very little of suspense. On the other hand [in the Bible], the externalization of only so much of the phenomena as is necessary for the purpose of the narrative, all else left in obscurity; the decisive points of the narrative alone are emphasized, what lies between is nonexistent; time and place are unidentified and call for interpretation; thoughts and feeling remain unexpressed, are only suggested by the silence and the fragmentary speeches; the whole, permeated with the most unrelieved suspense and directed toward a single goal . . . remains mysterious and "fraught with background."[3]

Auerbach's study would be seen, in retrospect, as the beginning of the study of biblical narrative poetics, but that did not happen until several decades later, when the field called narratology (the study of the structure and workings of narrative) grew popular among literary scholars and was applied to the Bible by those knowledgeable enough to do so, most famously Robert Alter and Meir Sternberg. More on narrative poetics later.

Meanwhile, before new literary theories reached them, biblical scholars became acquainted with newly discovered and deciphered bodies of literature from the ancient Near East. Here was a more appropriate group of texts than the Greek classics against which to read the Bible, texts from the East rather than the West, and from the same time or an earlier one.[4] The peoples of the ancient Near East were mentioned in the Bible itself; they were Israel's predecessors and neighbors, and their literature informed the biblical writings. Now biblical literature began to appear typical, rather than idiosyncratic. Many of its forms, motifs, and images were part of a common Near Eastern literary stock. The Flood story turned out to be an oft-told tale throughout Mesopotamia and Asia Minor; proverb collections like those in the book of Proverbs were discovered in Egypt and Mesopotamia, some strikingly similar to their biblical counterparts; and the psalmists appeared to have had forerunners among the poets of Ugarit. Even the covenant between God and Israel, that most biblical of concepts, owes its literary structure, and even its conceptual framework, to the influence of ancient vassal treaties—international treaties between the king of an empire and less powerful kingdoms that swore allegiance to him. These treaties served as loyalty oaths, binding the vassal exclusively to the suzerain, stipulating the vassal's obligations, and listing the divine punishments that would result from any infraction of the treaty. In like fashion the Torah spells out the binding force of the covenant, the obligations of Israel to God (the laws), and the penalties for disobedience (the curses in Leviticus 26 and Deuteronomy 28).

In the Bible, the political vassal treaty became a powerful religious metaphor, the loyalty oath par excellence, not to a human king but to the divine king, God. This fit nicely with the religion of Israel since, unlike the gods of Mesopotamia, the God of Israel demanded exclusive fidelity from his worshippers. The God of Israel was, in this regard, more like a Mesopotamian king than like a Mesopotamian god. A citizen of Mesopotamia, or of anywhere in the ancient world outside of Israel, could worship many gods but must be loyal to only one king. It is no accident, then, that the Bible so often speaks of God using kingship imagery.

The suzerain-vassal form is especially prominent in Deuteronomy, a book that preserves more of the classic treaty structure than any other book in the Bible.[5] Moreover, parts of Deuteronomy were composed in Judah during the Neo-Assyrian period and resemble treaties from this period, especially the Vassal Treaties of Esarhaddon, the Neo-Assyrian king (reigned 681–669 B.C.E.; the treaties are dated to 672). At that time the relationship between Judah and Assyria was tense; Judah was often on the verge of being conquered by Assyria. Would Judah become a vassal of Assyria or would it remain independent? Given that political context, modern scholars see a more pointed use of the vassal-treaty form in Deuteronomy. Deuteronomy is not merely substituting religion for politics; it is making a political statement as well as a religious one. Bernard Levinson puts it in these words:

> At a number of points, the authors of Deuteronomy seem consciously to have patterned their covenant after this treaty tradition, which they could have known either directly or in Aramaic translation. From this perspective, Deuteronomy represents a counter-treaty: Its authors turned the weapon of imperialism into a bid for freedom, shifting its oath of loyalty from the Assyrian overlord to their divine sovereign.[6]

This statement typifies current literary approaches in contrast to older ones. Whereas earlier scholars were satisfied with the simple identification of a genre or literary form, current scholars seek a more nuanced understanding of how a particular form may be employed in a specific case. Additionally, as we can detect in Levinson's words, current literary interest focuses on matters of the cultural or ethnic identity and/or on the relationships of power among different groups (usually groups of different ethnicity, gender, or social class).[7] We will see more examples of this later, when we discuss the story of Dinah.

While ancient Near Eastern literature clearly has a lot to contribute to the understanding of early biblical writings, not all parts of the Bible emerged from the cultural world of Egypt and Mesopotamia. When it comes to the later parts of the Bible, Greek literature enters the picture again, but not in the same way that it did for earlier scholars. A significant amount of the Bible was written or edited in the Persian and Greek periods (from 539 B.C.E. until the second century B.C.E.). This is also the time of the flourishing of classical Greek literature—drama, philosophy, and historiography—that occurred beginning in the fifth and fourth centuries B.C.E. (There is little actual literature from Persia from this period; most of the written documents are inscriptions or archival material.) Greek literature, of which there is an abundance, serves as the context for late biblical writings much as ancient Near Eastern literature serves for earlier writings. This is most evident in the books of Esther and Daniel.

In the course of writing a commentary on the book of Esther, I delved into Greek literature from the Persian period, including Herodotus and other historiographers as well as dramatists.[8] The Greeks wrote quite a bit about the Persians, the dominant world power of the time, and they described them with stereotypical images and motifs. They portray the Persian king and his court as decadent, with luxurious trappings, much drinking of wine, and government spies to warn about plots on the king's life. They decry the hierarchy and the bureaucracy, typical of the large Persian empire but absent in the small Greek city-states, and they disapprove of the fawning of inferiors over superiors, so alien to their more democratic views. On the other hand, they admire the superb communication system, connecting all parts of the empire, and the importance of law and legal procedure. These same stereotypical motifs figure prominently in Esther. Many scholars took this as proof of the historical accuracy of Esther. But Esther, with its many exaggerations, coincidences, and historical improbabilities, is so clearly a work of fiction that at best one can say that its background is accurate, as one might say of a historical novel. The point I want to make is a literary one: Esther should be seen as typical of the literature of its day. The book emerged from a literary context in which Persians were described in certain conventional ways, and it partakes of those conventions.[9]

I do not argue that there was a direct connection between the Greek writings and Esther (as Levinson does for Deuteronomy and the Assyrian vassal treaties), but rather that such conventions as they both share were in the air, part of the cultural baggage of the ancient world. I do not know if the author of Esther had read Herodotus.

That the author of Daniel read Herodotus, however, is precisely the point argued recently by Paul Niskanen.[10] In its "predictions of the future," Daniel contains much information about Antiochus IV, most of it confirmed by extrabiblical sources. But the end of chapter 11 contains an apocalyptic vision of Antiochus's final campaign to Egypt followed by his death in a cataclysmic battle. These events do not correlate with known historical sources. For this reason, scholars conclude that the author of Daniel lived and wrote during the time of Antiochus IV, and knew of events up to and including the Maccabean revolt; but he made up later events in order to bring the life of Antiochus to a close. But why, asks Niskanen, did the author compose this particular account with these particular elements? Niskanen suggests that the author did not make up the story from scratch, but modeled it after the story of another king, the Persian king Cambyses, as recounted by Herodotus in Book 3 of *The Histories*. Niskanen finds much in the portrait of Antiochus that correlates with Herodotus's portrait of Cambyses, including the king's madness and his sacrilegious disregard for law. The deaths of both kings is presented as divine retribution for their violations of the religious law of their subject peoples. Moreover, argues Niskanen, it is entirely likely that the educated Jewish author of Daniel knew Greek and had read Herodotus. If Niskanen is correct, we have here an example of direct literary borrowing.

Whether the relationship between Greek and biblical literature was direct or indirect, biblical scholars must take into account the Greek literary world no less than the ancient Near Eastern literary world, for both are literary contexts from which biblical literature emerged and with which it interacted. The comparison of the Bible with other ancient literatures continues to be a productive mode of analysis.

Not all comparisons were with ancient literatures. Scholars throughout history compared features of biblical poetry to their own vernacular poetries. For instance, attempts were made to discover in biblical poetry Arabic quantitative meters or English accentual meters. These efforts met with no lasting success. Biblical poetry never quite fit the model of other poetry, except in the basic universals of all poetry—terseness and the high frequency of imagery.

Literary scholars of the mid-twentieth century had more success comparing biblical prose narrative with modern fiction. Literary criticism provided tools which, when applied to the Bible, revealed never-before-noticed aspects of plot and character. Narrative poetics soon followed, with its attention to the analysis of discourse.[11] Biblical narrative prose appeared to follow many of the same or comparable rules as contemporary prose fiction. But that leads into the next rubric, for literary theory, more than the comparativist spirit, was driving the study of biblical narrative.

The Influence of Literary Theory and Criticism: Modernism and Postmodernism

While the influence of literary theory on the study of the Bible dates from classical times, it gained new momentum in the 1970s, when a few prominent literary scholars, like Robert Alter and Frank Kermode, turned their attention to the Bible, with exciting results. They were soon joined by biblical scholars, and from this marriage of literary scholars and biblical scholars was born a new approach to the Bible. It is sometimes called "the Bible as Literature," or, more aptly, "literary approaches to the Bible."

These literary approaches set themselves in opposition to historical criticism, or source criticism (once called "literary criticism"), which had been the reigning method among biblicists. While historical critics sought to get behind the text to its pre-textual and early textual origins, literary critics concentrated on the final product, the text as it now stands (a diachronic vs. a synchronic approach); historical critics assumed the text to be a conglomeration of sources, but literary critics approached it as a coherent unity; historical critics sought the one correct meaning, but literary critics opened the possibility of many meanings and of different kinds of meaning. Nevertheless, historical criticism should not be written out of a discussion of literary approaches, because, as I will later suggest, it has become more important to the literary study of the Bible than ever before.

As one new literary theory or school followed another, each, in turn, was applied to the Bible: New Criticism, Formalism, Structuralism, Reader-Response Criticism, Feminism, and various types of Postmodernism.[12] The applications proved fruitful. New observations were made about the fabric of biblical discourse, the patternings of words and structures, and narrative poetics (the way a story is told, its compositional techniques). Then new questions were raised about the representation and role of women, the power-structures reflected in the texts, and the ideology of texts and readers. All this brought with it a much greater awareness of the process of interpretation, of how meaning is made by texts and/or by readers. The notion that a text has a single correct meaning was challenged and replaced by the notion that there are potentially a multitude of meanings. A text read from one perspective might mean something different if read from another perspective. The Bible could be, and indeed has been, read differently at different times by different people. If ambiguity within a text was the darling of the New Critics, the multiplicity of meanings is the fair-haired child of the Postmodernists.

There is no single literary approach or method. Literary inquiry is a congeries of methods and reading strategies, sometimes conflicting, that are not easily integrated into a coherent program. Attesting to this fact is *The Cambridge Companion to Biblical Interpretation,* which contains four separate chapters relating to literary interpretation: "Literary Readings of the Bible," "Poststructuralist Approaches: New Historicism and Postmodernism," "Political Readings of Scripture," and "Feminist Interpretation." These chapter titles give a sense of where postmodern literary interests lie. Because of the popularity of narratology during the last decades of the twentieth century, narrative dominated the modern and postmodern literary-critical scene in biblical studies, with poetry a distant second and legal discourse almost entirely absent.[13] Now, however, the scope has widened and non-narrative sections of the Bible are also receiving attention.[14]

I will not enter the thicket of abstruse literary theory to define the various schools or movements within the modern or postmodern (or poststructuralist) camps. Nor will I attempt to survey the enormous bibliography of modern and postmodern literary studies of the Bible. It is more useful, I think, to select one pericope and follow it through various interpretive permutations. For my case study I have chosen Genesis 34, the Story of Dinah. The evolution of literary interpretations of this story exemplifies the development of literary approaches to the Bible.

The Story of Dinah, as it is often called, recounts an episode in which Dinah, the daughter of Jacob and Leah, is apparently seduced and/or abducted by Shechem, a Hivite neighbor. Shechem, having slept with Dinah, then falls in love with her and wants to marry her. Jacob is silent on the matter, but his sons are outraged at the prospect. Nevertheless, they proceed with marriage negotiations, including the stipulation that all the Hivite men will be circumcised. This is a pretext on the brothers' part, and when the Hivites are in pain from the circumcision, Simeon and Levi,

Dinah's brothers, kill the Hivite men and rescue Dinah from Shechem's house. Jacob is not pleased, but the brothers insist that they have saved their sister's honor.

This story is sometimes called "The Rape of Dinah," but since not everyone agrees that Dinah was raped,[15] I prefer the more neutral title "The Story of Dinah." But even this title is misleading because the story is really more about Jacob and his sons, Simeon and Levi, than about Dinah (just as the so-called "Binding of Isaac" in Genesis 22 is about Abraham, not his son; and the "Story of Amnon and Tamar" in 2 Samuel 13 is really more about Absalom). But perhaps our story is not about individuals at all. Stephen A. Geller, bypassing the question of the main character and pointing to what he thinks the story is about, calls it "The Sack of Shechem," thereby highlighting the place, not the characters.

Already we see that it will not be easy to determine what this story is about. As I proceed, keep in mind the following questions and the different answers to them that will be proffered: (1) What point does the story want to make? (2) How should the sexual encounter between Dinah and Shechem be explained? (3) Who is the hero of the story?

The Locus of Meaning: Is the Meaning in the Text or in the Reader?

I begin with Meir Sternberg, who devoted a chapter to our story in his 1985 book, *The Poetics of Biblical Narrative*.[16] Sternberg's thesis is that the Bible is a foolproof composition and that any competent reader will discern its message. How does one become a competent reader? One reads Sternberg's book. It is intended to make us competent readers by revealing the Bible's narrative poetics, about which Sternberg writes brilliantly. Narrative poetics is the wording and structures of the narrative, the building-blocks of the discourse by means of which the plot and characters are conveyed. Narrative poetics becomes the basis for Sternberg's interpretation of the story.[17]

A corollary of Sternberg's foolproof composition thesis is that a biblical narrative, by virtue of its foolproof composition, can persuade the reader of the correctness of its position even when that position runs counter to normal expectation. The normal response of the reader of Genesis 34, posits Sternberg, would be to condemn the actions of Simeon and Levi, who enter into a bad-faith negotiation with the Hivites and then massacre them—a punishment far out of proportion to the offense committed by one of their members. But, says Sternberg, the narrator views the two brothers as the heroes, and convinces the reader to do so as well. The narrator could have done this less obliquely but he chose, according to Sternberg, to make his task of persuasion more challenging by introducing some balance, some sympathy for all the characters. Sternberg reasons that "the more difficult he makes the task of persuasion . . . the more difficult it will become for us to withstand its guidance."[18]

Sternberg points to a number of specific instances in which the narrative garners sympathy for Simeon and Levi. He finds that these two brothers look good in contrast to Jacob, to the other brothers, and to the Hivites. In the first four verses, Dinah is repeatedly referred to as the daughter of Jacob, thereby positioning Jacob as the person responsible for her, yet when Jacob hears that his daughter has been defiled, he does nothing; he keeps silent until his sons come home. The sons, by contrast, are enraged, and it is they, not the father, who seek to defend the honor of the family.

One may side with the Hivites on two counts—that Shechem fell in love with Dinah and that the entire community of Hivites was willing to undergo circumcision, as Simeon and Levi stipulated. But, suggests Sternberg, the Hivites lose the reader's sympathy when they cast the agreement as a financial deal, forgetting that the issue for the brothers is a matter of honor. Then, out of the blue, in verse 26 we learn that Dinah had all the while been in Shechem's house and that Simeon and Levi, after killing all the male Hivites, take Dinah out of Shechem's house. Sternberg accuses the Hivites of having taken Dinah as a hostage, perhaps to use her to blackmail her relatives into a marriage arrangement, an action that fully justifies the brothers' deceit in making the agreement with the Hivites. Simeon and Levi are, in Sternberg's view, on a rescue mission, not a wanton massacre.

Sternberg also differentiates Simeon and Levi from the other brothers; the latter plunder the town, seizing goods and human booty, while Simeon and Levi do not. Finally, at the end of the story, Jacob confronts Simeon and Levi for having angered the Canaanite neighbors, who may attack the weaker Israelites. But Simeon and Levi are given the last word: "Should our sister be treated like a whore?" This question would seem to indicate that family honor trumps friendly relations with the neighbors. It also points Sternberg toward the meaning of the story as a whole. He says that the concern of Simeon and Levi has been "to redress the wrong done to their sister and the whole family, which includes *the prevention of an exogamous marriage*."[19] We will return to the idea of exogamous marriage later.

Sternberg was attacked vociferously by Dana Nolan Fewell and David

M. Gunn in a 1991 article.[20] They reject his notion of foolproof composition in favor of the possibility of multiple interpretations, or conflicting competent readings. Basing their analysis on the same narrative poetics—that is, the same techniques of storytelling—they arrive at a different interpretation. They do not evaluate Jacob's silence negatively, arguing that it derives from caution and concern for the well-being of the family. They question whether Dinah was held hostage, interpreting her presence in Shechem's house as an act of her own free will, a choice she has made based on Shechem's newfound love for her. Fewell and Gunn see Simeon and Levi not as the idealists that Sternberg sees, but as self-centered and vengeful, defending their own honor, not the honor of their sister. For Fewell and Gunn, the offense committed is against Dinah, not against the male members of the family, and they fault Simeon and Levi for failing to understand this.

Their literary approach does not permit them to ask what the author's purpose was in telling this story; they can only venture to discuss the ways readers can read it. So they dismiss the idea that the story is about exogamous marriage and read it instead as a story about "rights vs. responsibility." To Fewell and Gunn, Sternberg's reader holds normative values that hinge on an ethics of rights, while Fewell and Gunn's reader "responds with an ethics of responsibility, where relationships, care, and consequences shape moral choices."[21] They speak of conflicting responsibilities rather than competing rights. They therefore admire Jacob, whose initial silence and final criticism of the brothers they see as a sign of sensitivity and concern for consequences, as opposed to the brothers, who insist on their rights no matter what the consequences.

I doubt that either Sternberg or Fewell and Gunn would entirely convince today's readers, but they are usefully set side by side to show how different assumptions lead to different results. The two main issues that separate Sternberg from Fewell and Gunn are: (1) How much of the meaning is made by the text and how much by the reader. For Sternberg, all meaning resides in the text; his is a text-oriented approach. For Fewell and Gunn all meaning resides in the reader; theirs is a reader-oriented approach. (2) Whose meaning we are searching for: the meaning the story had for an ancient Israelite, or the meaning(s) it has for today's reader. Sternberg aims for the first while Fewell and Gunn can only aim for the second. As Fewell and Gunn explain elsewhere, "Instead of seeking the one legitimate meaning, namely what the text . . . meant in its 'original context,' we recognize that texts are multivalent and their meanings radically contextual. . . ." They prefer to "read these narratives as we might read modern novels or short stories, constructing a story world in which questions of human values and beliefs . . . find shape in relation to our own (and our readers') world(s)."[22] In other words, Fewell and Gunn see the Bible in the light of today's values while Sternberg aims to uncover the values of the biblical narrator/author. In addition, Sternberg claims that his is an objective reading while Fewell and Gunn claim that no reading can be objective.

These differences between Sternberg on the one hand and Fewell and Gunn on the other mark the divide between modernism and postmodernism. As David Gunn says elsewhere:

> I used to think that the dividing line in biblical scholarship was that between "historical criticism" and "literary criticism." But that is patently not the case. The divide is between modern and postmodern. Put very baldly, it is the difference between a project that reaches for the unity, stability, and truth of the text, and one that seeks the fractures, instabilities, and multivalences of a text which "itself" is protean. Meir Sternberg's poetics . . . are modern.[23]

Needless to say, Fewell and Gunn are postmodern.

The question of whether meaning resides in the text or in the reader is ultimately irresolvable. Many biblical scholars, tired of the debate, acknowledge some truth in both positions: both the reader and the text contribute to the interpretive process. As I put it in an earlier essay, "readers bring something to their reading of a text . . . but . . . the text influences how it is read."[24] Furthermore, Gunn's neat distinction between modernism and postmodernism is not as absolute as it may sound. Later postmodernism made room for investigating meaning not only for today's reader but for any reader on the long timeline of biblical interpretation. That includes the "first" reader as well as all subsequent readers. One may begin to speak of early postmodernism and later postmodernism(s). The former, exemplified by Fewell and Gunn on Genesis 34, focuses on the modern reader and is unconcerned with the historical context of the story. Later postmodernism, especially New Historicism (to be discussed shortly), focuses on the ideologies of the text in its historical context. As we will soon see, to get into the mindset of the text is once again a respectable endeavor to certain postmodernists, as it always has been to historically oriented biblical scholars.

The Horizon of Interpretation: Contextuality

When Fewell and Gunn made the point that meaning is "radically contextual," they had in mind the context of the reader. But "contextual" can also mean the literary or textual context—what surrounds the story, the larger framework in which it is embedded. Neither Sternberg nor Fewell and Gunn look beyond the Dinah story to consider how the story relates to its context in Genesis, in the Torah, or in the entire Bible.[25] Increasingly, scholars read a pericope not in isolation but as part of a larger body of related texts whose interconnections they explore. Meaning is generated through contextual interpretation; a comparison of one text with another helps us to see that text in a new light.[26] The comparison of text A with text B will suggest one interpretation, while a comparison with text C will show it in a completely different light. For example, reading the Dinah story in light of the story of Amnon and Tamar in 2 Samuel 13[27] will produce quite a different interpretation than will reading it in light of the endogamous marriages of the patriarchs in Genesis, or in light of Deuteronomy's absolute ban on the Canaanites,[28] or Ezra's ban on foreign wives, or other events that took place at Shechem.[29] The contextual horizon may be as narrow as the surrounding chapters of the Jacob cycle[30] or as broad as the entire Hebrew Bible, or even beyond (which brings us back to the "comparative literature" approach discussed earlier).

The choice of the comparative text is the modern interpreter's choice. To read one text in light of another text is to use contextuality as a hermeneutic strategy. Occasionally, though, the Bible introduces its own internal reference—it alludes to one text in another, thereby setting up an interpretive context. Increasingly, the Bible is seen as a masterpiece of interlocking texts, wherein one part refers to, echoes, or otherwise confronts another part. These related phenomena are often collected under the term "inner biblical interpretation."[31] Interestingly, the observation about the Bible's intertextuality, its process of engagement with earlier parts of itself, which is a very literary way of looking at things, coincides with some source-critical views about the nature of the biblical text.[32] A source critic informed by literary approaches, David M. Carr, puts it as follows: "ancient Near Eastern (including biblical) authors were much more inclined than we are to build on earlier texts, incorporating, combining, and expanding them into a new and complex whole."[33] Here is a sign that some newer forms of literary criticism are reconnecting with historical criticism.

The Bible's internal reference to Genesis 34 is in Genesis 49:5–7. Not everyone is convinced that these verses are actually alluding to the Dinah story, but they were understood this way by some ancient readers.[34] I tend to see an allusion here, probably by the same author who wrote Genesis 34 (as opposed to a later author interpreting an earlier story). Given the present shape of Genesis, where we read Genesis 34 before Genesis 49, Genesis 49 can hint at Simeon and Levi's past deeds cryptically because they have been spelled out some chapters earlier. Without Genesis 34, the reference to weapons, lawlessness, slaying, and fierce anger in Genesis 49 would be obscure or unintelligible.

> Simeon and Levi are a pair;
> Their weapons are tools of lawlessness.
> Let not my person be included in their council,
> Let not my being be counted in their assembly.
> For when angry they slay men,
> And when pleased they maim oxen.
> Cursed be their anger so fierce,
> And their wrath so relentless.
> I will divide them in Jacob,
> Scatter them in Israel.

These verses are part of Jacob's deathbed speech to his sons, foretelling their destinies. In actuality, of course, this is poetic hindsight—a retrojection of later tribal allotments and fortunes into the mouth of the father of those tribes. Since Jacob is speaking, it is not surprising that his attitude here coincides with his attitude in Genesis 34: in both places the action of the brothers is condemned, and in Genesis 49 it is used to explain why neither Simeon nor Levi ultimately had land allotments.[35] Does that mean that we should understand Genesis 34 as Genesis 49 does—that Jacob was right and that Simeon and Levi were wrong? Certainly the implication is that the author of Genesis 49 would like us to. (Oddly, none of the literary studies of our story are bothered by this.)

If we conclude that the author of Genesis (or the author of these two pericopes now situated in Genesis) meant for us to condemn Simeon and Levi, we must ask why. How does this evaluation of the two brothers fit into Genesis as a whole? It has long been suggested by biblical exegetes that the actions of Simeon and Levi in the Dinah story, like the mention of Reuben's lying with his father's concubine in Gen 35:22, disqualify Jacob's three oldest sons from the prerogatives of the firstborn, leaving Judah, son number four, first in line. In other words, these stories about eponymous sons, understood to be stand-ins for the tribes bearing their names, explain why Judah becomes the most prominent tribe.[36]

New Historicism: Reading for Ethnicity and Gender

Issues of identity, particularly those relating to gender or ethnicity, have captured the spotlight in contemporary literary studies, especially in New Historicism and/or Cultural Studies.[37] These two related approaches are similar in their efforts to discover the cultural, social, political, or religious institutions and ideology embedded in the text. New Historicists see the text as a reflection of the institutions and/or ideology from which it arose, and they aim to reveal those institutions or ideologies that inform the text. New Historicism as applied to the Bible, in the words of Robert Carroll, "seeks to construct a cultural poetics of the Bible."[38] That is to say, biblical texts are to be read for what they can tell us about the Bible's religious and political ideologies and institutions.

This is a move back to a more text-centered approach than early postmodernists (like Fewell and Gunn) advocated. The ideology of the current reader is not of major concern here; it has been replaced by the ideology of the text. New Historicism, unlike New Criticism, views the text as a historical artifact. It is not a detached independent object, but grew out of a particular historical moment. The important historical moment for the New Historicist is the time when the text was created, not the time the text purports to be describing. New Historicists would not use the Dinah story to reconstruct the early history of the patriarchs and their Canaanite neighbors; they would not see it, as earlier scholars did, as a record of an early conflict involving the tribes of Simeon and Levi in the region of Shechem. Rather, they ask how and why the Israelite past was being presented at the time the story was written. In other words, how is the story using the past to talk about the present?

But when was the story written? Here a would-be New Historicist encounters the perpetual problem of biblical studies: how to date a text. And suddenly, historical criticism and redaction criticism, those old efforts to date texts and to construct their textual history, formerly disdained by literary scholars from New Criticism to early postmodernism, once again become relevant to literary interpretation. The old historical modes of biblical scholarship and the new literary modes are drawing closer together.[39]

Let us look at a few studies I gather loosely under the rubric of New Historicism or Cultural Studies. Stephen A. Geller, in a 1990 essay, declares our story to be one iteration of two related themes that form part of the dominant religion of the Bible, especially in Deuteronomic theology: the prohibition of intermarriage with Canaanites and the demand for their total extermination.[40] Deuteronomy 7:1–5 words it strongly:

> When the Lord your God brings you to the land that you are about to enter and possess, and He dislodges many nations before you—the Hittites, Girgashites, Amorites, Canaanites, Perizzites, Hivites, and Jebusites . . . and the Lord . . . delivers them to you and you defeat them, you must doom them to destruction; grant them no terms and give them no quarter. You shall not intermarry with them; do not give your daughters to their sons or take their daughters for your sons. For they will turn your children away from Me to worship other gods. . . . Instead, this is what you shall do to them: you shall tear down their altars, smash their pillars, cut down their sacred posts, and consign their images to the fire.

Exodus 34:11–16 expresses similar thoughts, warning against making a covenant with the inhabitants of the promised land and against taking wives from among their daughters, lest they become a snare to the Israelites, leading them to whore after other gods; and commanding the Israelites to tear down the altars, pillars, and posts.

Geller reads the story on two levels: the narrative level and the typological level. Typological readings are usually associated with Christian exegesis of the Old Testament as foreshadowing the New Testament, but typology is an interpretive strategy used by the rabbis, too, where it is referred to by the phrase *ma'aseh 'avot siman lebanim*, "the deeds recounted of the fathers are indicative of what will occur to their descendents."[41] Typological interpretation is even found within the Bible itself.[42] In typological interpretation, persons or events are viewed as figures that are historically real themselves, but that also prefigure later persons and events.

On the narrative level, this story is an episode in the family history of Jacob, a story of crime and punishment. On the typological level, the more significant level for Geller, it foreshadows events in the national life of later Israel, specifically the Josianic reforms in 621 B.C.E., famous for their eradication of idolatrous practices (note the eradication of the altars, pillars, and posts in Deuteronomy 7 and Exodus 34). By this time the real Canaanites were long gone; "Canaanite" had become an abstraction, a code word for all that was religiously alien to Israel. The Canaanites (Hivites) in our story, says Geller, represent the Judean opponents of Josiah's reform —the heretical priests of the *bamot*, the outlawed places of sacrifice, and their followers. As "Canaanites" they are also associated with licentious sexual practices, another feature of the Bible's portrait of Canaanites. And as the Bible construes it, sexual relations with Canaanites lead Israel to apostasy. Geller finds sexual licentiousness in Shechem's behavior. The invitation to intermarriage that follows is even closer to the very thing against which Deuteronomy warns.

Geller interprets the story as a polemic from the time of Josiah. Yairah Amit, who also reads typologically, dates the story to the time of Ezra and finds in it a hidden polemic against the Samaritans.[43] Like Geller, Amit does not take "Canaanites" literally. For her they represent the Samaritans, the group whom the returning Judeans opposed and in contrast to whom they constituted their Judean/Jewish identity. For both Geller and Amit, a typological interpretation trumps a literal interpretation. The significance of the story is in the way the remembered or invented past serves the ideological agenda of an author writing either during the late Judean monarchy or in postexilic times. In both explanations "Canaanite" stands for "the other," those from whom Israel differentiates itself as it defines its identity.

Taking an altogether different tack focusing on sex as a social marker of power and authority, and using a feminist anthropological approach bolstered by examples from Greek and Roman literature, Helena Zlotnick finds that Genesis 34 is not about a crisis generated by a rape, but about a clash between two marital strategies or ideologies: arranged marriage and abduction marriage.[44] Jacob and his family had the tradition of arranged marriages, but Shechem's action is a case of abduction marriage. The strategy of abduction marriage is known from stories in the classical world, often in foundational stories, and so Zlotnick concludes that "the episode of Dinah's 'rape' proved as critical as were the rapes of the Sabine women for the foundation of the Roman state, and of Lucretia for the demise of the Roman monarchy and the rise of the Republic."[45] As an Israelite foundation story, "[t]he affair of Dinah put an end to any ideology of coexistence in patriarchal Canaan."[46] Zlotnick does not date the story, but she, like Geller and Amit, sees it as speaking to the issue of Israelite identity.

While Zlotnick's identification of Dinah's "rape" as abduction marriage may at first sound far-fetched, it receives support from another recent study, made independently by Joseph Fleishman, who concluded that abduction marriage is the best explanation of Shechem's actions.[47] Fleishman does not employ a feminist or an anthropological approach, and he gets his proof from ancient Near Eastern legal texts and from biblical and rabbinic material, not from classical sources as Zlotnick does.

Abduction marriage explains some points that are otherwise less satisfactorily explained. It supplies the reason that Dinah remained in the house of Shechem, from which her brothers "rescue" her. According to this interpretation, they are not rescuing a rape victim but annulling an abduction marriage. Abduction marriage also leads us to reconsider the meaning of the punch-line that closes the story: "Should our sister be treated like a whore?" The issue is not sexual looseness, or even premarital sex per se, but the authority of the family to regulate marriages. The term *zonah*, generally translated "prostitute," refers to a woman who engages in a sexual relationship outside of a formal union.[48] The brothers do not consider abduction marriage to be a legal marriage. Shechem acted as though Dinah were independent and accessible, like a prostitute, a woman not under the authority of a father, brother, or husband. Abduction marriage denies Dinah's family any authority over her, and is therefore an insult to the honor of the family. That is what angers Simeon and Levi.

But why is not Jacob angry and insulted? Complicating the conflict between marriage strategies, in Zlotnick's view, is the guest-host relationship that obtains between Jacob and the Hivites. Jacob, a newcomer to the area, is the guest of the Hivites, the native residents; he and his hosts are bound by the accepted rules of the guest-host relationship, involving reciprocity and voluntary association. This guest-host relationship becomes strained as a result of the abduction marriage, clearly offensive to the Israelites and perhaps not the norm among the Hivites either. Zlotnick explains Jacob's silence not as callous indifference (as Sternberg does), or as concerned restraint (as Fewell and Gunn do), but as his inability to reconcile marriage by abduction with the Hivites' obligation as hosts. What is Jacob, as a guest, to do when his hosts have imposed a type of marriage arrangement that is anathema to his own family? Zlotnick interprets the offer of marital and economic exchanges later in the story as the Hivites' attempt to repair the damaged guest-host relationship, a relationship that Jacob apparently would have liked to preserve but that his sons rendered null and void.

Geller, Amit, and Zlotnick all demonstrate, in one way or another, the current interest in gender, ethnicity, identity, and power. Zlotnick concentrates on gender while Geller and Amit are more concerned with ethnic distinctions. These three studies find the significance of our story in what it says about the establishment of Israel's identity, an identity shaped in contrast to a Canaanite identity (whether "Canaanite" is taken literally or symbolically). Increasingly, ethnic identity is becoming the focus of much biblical interpretation. The Bible, especially the Torah, is, after all, the primary locus of the expression of Israel's identity: its past, its values and worldview, and its place among the nations of the world. The Bible tells Israel who it has been and who it should be.

Let me sum up the answers to the three questions I posed earlier. Interpretations of the Dinah story, including some not presented here, yield the following results:

1. The main point of the story has to do with
   a. how the tribe of Judah came to dominate.
   b. the question of exogamous vs. endogamous marriage.
   c. the Bible's anti-Canaanite polemic.
   d. an anti-Samaritan polemic.
   e. the early history of Israel's relations with its neighbors.
   f. Shechem as a place with positive or negative associations.
2. The sexual encounter between Dinah and Shechem involves
   a. a rape.
   b. consensual premarital sex.
   c. abduction marriage.
3. The hero of the story is
   a. Jacob.
   b. Simeon and Levi.
   c. Dinah.
   d. the story does not make this clear.

These "answers" are mutually exclusive, but each can be justified within its own interpretive system. To ask which answer is the correct one is to go back to the mind-set in which there can be only one right answer. If the history of biblical interpretation teaches us anything, it is that there have always been many interpretations of a biblical text. And, as literary theory has shown, the interpretation will depend on who is doing the interpreting and for what purpose. All interpretation is contextual.

The better question now is, to borrow Yvonne Sherwood's words, "which interpretative trajectories (if any) have the right to define, and contain the text."[49] The issue is not what the text means, but who controls its interpretation; who sets the agenda, who makes the rules, who confirms the validity of the results. This question itself is very postmodern in its search for where power lies. And its answer is that exclusive power lies with nobody, for postmodernism seeks to break the hold that any institution claims to have on the text or its interpretation.

Let me go one step further and suggest that postmodernism has not only affected how we understand meaning, but, directly or indirectly, how we understand the nature and evolution of the biblical text. Here I will synthesize the results of historical criticism (how the text originated and how it evolved before its final form) and the newer approach of inner biblical interpretation. Historical criticism shows that the text is composed of earlier components combined and redacted several times over to form new compositions. Inner biblical interpretation reveals the presence, throughout the Bible, of a dynamic process of reinterpretation, wherein earlier traditions are alluded to, reformulated, updated, and interpreted (for example, the use of the Torah in Psalms, or Chronicles' rewriting of Samuel-Kings). The Bible, then, gives witness to a process that renders the notion of "original meaning" meaningless. The meaning of the earliest sources of the Bible is buried in an overlay of layers of subsequent meaning. Authors, editors, or redactors never intended for the earliest meaning to survive. They overwrote it, because they wanted to promote their own take on ancient traditions. J, the Yahwist source according to historical critics, presumably our earliest source, was already re-using even earlier, nearly unidentifiable sources that he (*pace* Harold Bloom, who proposed that J was a woman) reshaped. Then P, the Priestly source, came along and reworked J. D, the Deuteronomic source, independently did its own large rewrite job. When all of this got combined into the Torah, the final product, the Torah as a whole, took on yet another interpretive life as the raw material for subsequent rewritings and reinterpretations within the Bible and beyond. Seen from a postmodern perspective, source criticism combined with inner biblical interpretation make the biblical authors look downright postmodern.[50]

The question now is no longer "What did the text originally mean?" but rather, "What did the text mean in a given source, or in a specific time and place?" This is yet another sign of a convergence between historical criticism and its erstwhile enemy, literary criticism. Ironically, current postmodernism makes source criticism once again relevant, even indispensable, to the literary study of the Bible. Healing the earlier fractures between the literary-oriented and the history-oriented approaches to the Bible will benefit both. Indeed, there are indications of a rapprochement between these two modes of biblical interpretation.[51]

From Interpretation to the History of Interpretation

Until this point we have been discussing modern and postmodern exegesis: how contemporary scholars interpret the Bible. Postmodernists, theoretically at least, do not privilege contemporary interpretations, for these are no more valid than the interpretations that have come before. Having established that meaning is not one but many, postmodernists may seek as many meanings as possible, because, in a certain sense, the meaning of a pericope is the sum of all the meanings that have been assigned to it. Postmodernists therefore are ready to step back to see how pre-moderns interpreted the Bible (something that exegetes for most of the twentieth century avoided). The door to more serious engagement with the history of interpretation has now opened.

Other factors were independently at work to ignite interest in the history of interpretation, especially its early history—namely, the study of inner biblical interpretation and the rise of interest more generally in the Second Temple period (or the Greco-Roman period, roughly the fourth century B.C.E. through the first century C.E.). This is the time when the Bible was achieving canonical status and when many biblical interpretations were either preserved or created. Some are found within the Bible itself, but more are documented in the Qumran scrolls, the Apocrypha and Pseudepigrapha, Hellenistic Jewish writers like Philo and Josephus, and the New Testament, and slightly later in rabbinic and early Christian writings.[52] Moreover, unlike the biblical texts, these extrabiblical texts are datable with relative certainty and within narrow parameters, so we are on firmer ground when we discuss their historical context. Here we have identifiable readers or groups of readers who left us explicit evidence of their interpretations.

Interpretations of the Dinah story are well-documented for the Second Temple period, and they have generated a large body of recent secondary literature that cannot be reviewed here.[53] Suffice it to say that early interpreters went out of their way to justify the actions of the brothers and to vilify the Hivites. Simeon and Levi were acting upon God's command for vengeance, or were guided by an angel, or had a heavenly sword; the Hivites deserved to be destroyed because they were rapists, immoral pagans, and failed to extend proper hospitality to strangers. The opponents of Jewish intermarriage become the heroes, for since Ezra endogamous marriage had become an important issue in the definition of Jewish identity. In addition to promoting current ideas of Jewish identity, these interpretations eliminate the moral ambiguity of the story and turn it into a smooth, unproblematic tale of Jewish heroism against a foreign enemy. The Hellenistic Jewish writers retell the story, as they do other biblical stories, as part of a larger agenda to justify the Bible and biblical Jewish behavior that might otherwise sound primitive or unjust to a reader steeped in Greek cultural values. (Modern readers have an analogous problem.)[54] That does not necessarily mean that these interpreters were making up their interpretations from whole cloth; they may have been drawing on more ancient traditions of interpretation. But by the same token, there seems little doubt that they are shaping the meaning of the story to the needs and tastes of their times.[55] Interpretation always takes place in a historical context.

How does this interest in early biblical interpretation intersect with literary approaches to the Bible? Like early postmodernism, on the one hand, it replaces interest in the text with interest in its interpreters and their interpretations. It averts its gaze from the biblical text and focuses instead on the reader, the ancient interpreter, as the maker of meaning. On the other hand, like New Historicism and Cultural Studies, the study of early interpretation is rooted in a historical context, and its overarching goal (while generally unstated) is to write a "cultural poetics" of early interpretation.

Besides, the study of the history of interpretation provides an antidote for the postmodernist frustration of never being able to pin down the meaning of a text. If we can never know what a text means, we can at least find satisfaction in knowing what a given interpreter thought it meant, and in figuring out why he thought so.

The contemporary act of interpreting and the study of past interpretation form a complementary pair of literary approaches to the Bible. Both are occupied with the recovery of ideology. The first inquires into the ideology of the biblical text; the second examines the ideology of the interpreters. Another way to say it is that the first is concerned with how the Bible constructs its meaning of the world, and the second with how interpreters construct their meaning of the Bible.

NOTES

1. Modern vernacular literatures would be important in the twentieth century, but for a different reason: new literary theories were built on them (notably English, Russian, and French).

2. *A Dissertation on the History, Eloquence, and Poetry of the Bible* (New Haven, Conn.: printed by Thomas and Samuel Green, 1772), 4–5; quoted in *The Hebrew Bible in Literary Criticism,* ed. Alex Preminger and Edward L. Greenstein (New York: Unger, 1986), 2. Dwight (1752–1817) served as President of Yale College from 1795 until his death.

3. Erich Auerbach, *Mimesis: The Representation of Reality in Western Literature,* translated from the German by Willard R. Trask (Princeton, N.J.: Princeton University Press, 1957; first published in 1946), 9.

4. At this same time, the dating of many parts of the Bible was being revised downward, so that biblical texts were thought to be more ancient and closer in time to the ancient Near Eastern texts.

5. Moshe Weinfeld, *Deuteronomy and the Deuteronomic School* (Oxford: Clarendon, 1972), 66.

6. Bernard Levinson, "Deuteronomy," in *The Jewish Study Bible,* ed. Adele Berlin and Marc Zvi Brettler (New York: Oxford University Press, 2004), 358. For a fuller discussion of this point, see his "Textual Criticism, Assyriology, and the History of Interpretation: Deuteronomy 13:7a as a Test Case in Method," *JBL* 120 (2001): 36–41 and *Deuteronomy and the Hermeneutics of Legal Innovation* (New York and Oxford: Oxford University Press, 1997), 147. Moshe Weinfeld observes that even when used as religious metaphors, the treaty-language did not lose its political import and that political faithlessness had long been identified with religious faithlessness. He notes that the religious reforms of Hezekiah and Josiah were expressions of both religious and political emancipation (*Deuteronomy and the Deuteronomic School,* 84–85).

7. In this regard it is interesting to note the relationship of Meir Sternberg's 1998 book, *Hebrews Between Cultures: Group Portraits and National Literature* (Bloomington: Indiana University Press, 1998) to his *Poetics of Biblical Narrative* (Bloomington: Indiana University Press, 1985). He calls the second book a companion volume rather than a sequel, and he explains the relationship of the two as moving "from the poetics of narrative as a drama of reading to the poetics of culture as a drama of (inter)group imagining" (*Hebrews Between Cultures,* xxii). This statement is a conscious reflection of the general movement from the poetics of narrative to the poetics of culture.

8. Adele Berlin, *Esther* (Philadelphia: Jewish Publication Society, 2001), xxviii–xxxii.

9. This conclusion was anticipated by the famous historian Arnaldo Momigliano, who said in 1965: "No doubt many of the features of the books of Judith and Esther can be explained in terms of international storytelling with a Persian background; and the same is true of several stories in the first Books of Herodotus . . ." (*Essays in Ancient and Modern Historiography* [Chicago and London: University of Chicago Press, 1994], 27). For a more complete discussion on the fictional, indeed farcical, nature of Esther see A. Berlin, *Esther,* xvi–xxviii.

10. Paul Niskanen, "Daniel's Portrait of Antiochus IV: Echoes of a Persian King," *CBQ* 66 (2004): 378–386. See also Paul Niskanen, *The Human and the Divine in History: Herodotus and the Book of Daniel* (Journal for the Study of the Old Testament Supplement Series, 396; London and New York: T&T Clark International, 2004).

11. Scholars associated with the study of biblical narrative in the 1970s and 1980s include Robert Alter, Shimon Bar-Efrat, Adele Berlin, David Gunn, Frank Polak, and Meir Sternberg.

12. For more on these terms see the essay adapted by Adele Berlin and Marc Zvi Brettler, "The Modern Study of the Bible," in *The Jewish Study Bible*, especially pp. 2090–2096; Carl R. Holladay, "Contemporary Methods of Reading the Bible," in *The New Interpreter's Bible* (Nashville, Tenn.: Abingdon Press, 1994), 1.125–149, esp. 136–149; Mark Allan Powell, *The Bible and Modern Literary Criticism, A Critical Assessment and Annotated Bibliography* (New York and Westport, Conn.: Greenwood Press, 1992); John Barton, ed., *The Cambridge Companion to Biblical Interpretation* (Cambridge: Cambridge University Press, 1998).

13. For a good survey of the work done on biblical narrative see David Gunn, "Hebrew Narrative," in *Text in Context*, ed. A. D. H. Mays (Oxford: Oxford University Press, 2000), 223–252. It is interesting to note that Gunn's article does not discuss what biblical narrative is, but rather what has been written about it. By contrast, W. G. E. Watson's article on poetry in the same volume is a description of biblical poetry, with little sense of how the study of poetry has developed.

14. Among the best examples are Carol A. Newsom, *The Book of Job: A Contest of Moral Imaginations* (Oxford and New York: Oxford University Press, 2003); Yvonne Sherwood, *The Prostitute and the Prophet: Hosea's Marriage in Literary-Theoretical Perspective* (Sheffield: Sheffield Academic Press, 1996); Francis Landy, *Paradoxes of Paradise: Identity and Difference in the Song of Songs* (Sheffield: Almond, 1983); Tod Linafeldt, *Surviving Lamentations: Catastrophe, Lament, and Protest in the Afterlife of a Biblical Book* (Chicago: University of Chicago Press, 2000); and Baruch Schwartz, *Torat ha-kedushah: 'iyunim ba-hukah ha-kohanit sheba-Torah* (Jerusalem: Magnes and Hebrew University, 1999).

15. Those who question whether Shechem raped Dinah include Lyn Bechtel, "What if Dinah Is not Raped? (Genesis 34)," *JSOT* 62 (1994): 19–36; Joseph Fleishman, "Shechem and Dinah—in the Light of Non-Biblical and Biblical Sources," *ZAW* 116 (2004): 12–32; Richard Elliott Friedman, *Commentary on the Torah* (San Francisco: HarperSanFrancisco, 2001), 116; Tikva Frymer-Kensky, *Reading the Women of the Bible* (New York: Schocken, 2002), 181–183; Mayer Gruber, "A Re-examination of the Charges against Shechem Son of Hamor," *Bet Mikra* 157 (1999): 119–127; John van Seters, "The Silence of Dinah (Genesis 34)," in *Jacob—commentaire à plusieurs voix de Gen 25–36; mélanges offerts à Albert de Pury*, ed. Jean-Daniel Macchi and Thomas Römer (Geneva: Labor et Fides, 2001), 239–247; Ellen J. van Wolde, "Love and Hatred in a Multiracial Society: The Dinah and Shechem

Story in Genesis 34 in the Context of Genesis 28–35," in *Reading from Right to Left: Essays on the Hebrew Bible in Honour of David J. A. Clines,* ed. J. C. Exum and H. G. M. Williamson (Sheffield: Sheffield Academic Press, 2003), 435–449. Most recently, Hilary Lipka has added her voice to this camp (*Sexual Transgression in the Hebrew Bible* [Sheffield: Sheffield Phoenix, 2006], 184–199). I agree that whatever took place, it was not rape in the modern sense. Early feminist readings distorted the picture by placing too much emphasis on Dinah and on the sexual nature of the crime. I view Dinah much as I view Bathsheba in 2 Samuel 11—a female character necessary to a plot whose action is motivated by a sexual act, but not an important character in her own right nor the focus of the story's significance. I am therefore not troubled by her "silence." For a different view see the works by Susanne Scholz (*Rape Plots: A Feminist Cultural Study of Genesis 34* [New York: Peter Lang, 2000]; "Through Whose Eyes? A 'Right' Reading of Genesis 34," in *Genesis* (The Feminist Companion to the Bible, Second Series, ed. A. Brenner; Sheffield: Sheffield Academic Press, 1998), 150–171; "Was It Really Rape in Genesis 34? Biblical Scholarship as a Reflection of Cultural Assumptions," in *Escaping Eden: New Feminist Perspectives on the Bible,* ed. Harold Washington, Susan Graham, and Pamela Thimmes (New York: NYU Press, 1999), 182–198. The idea that Dinah was raped is still maintained by some scholars; see Yael Shemesh, "Rape Is Rape Is Rape: The Story of Dinah and Shechem (Genesis 34)," *ZAW* (forthcoming, 2007).

16. Meir Sternberg, *The Poetics of Biblical Narrative* (Bloomington: Indiana University Press, 1985), 445–475.

17. Sternberg's assumption that any competent reader, knowledgeable about narrative poetics, will discern the text's meaning is obviously faulty when one realizes that a number of scholars, including Fewell and Gunn and also Yairah Amit (Sternberg's student), all use the same analysis of narrative poetics but reach quite different conclusions about the story's meaning. See below.

18. Meir Sternberg, *The Poetics of Biblical Narrative,* 467.

19. Meir Sternberg, *The Poetics of Biblical Narrative,* 472, my italics.

20. Danna Nolan Fewell and David M. Gunn, "Tipping the Balance: Sternberg's Reader and the Rape of Dinah," *JBL* 110 (1991): 193–211. Sternberg responded the following year in "Biblical Poetics and Sexual Politics: From Reading to Counterreading," *JBL* 111 (1992): 463–488.

21. Danna Nolan Fewell and David M. Gunn, "Tipping the Balance," 209.

22. David M. Gunn and Danna Nolan Fewell, *Narrative in the Hebrew Bible* (Oxford: Oxford University Press, 1993), p. 9.

23. David M. Gunn, "Hebrew Narrative," in *Text in Context,* 226.

24. Adele Berlin, "The Role of the Text in the Reading Process," *Semeia* 62 (1993): 143. Robert P. Carroll makes a similar statement ("The Reader and the Text," in *Text in Context,* 24). Carroll is not unsympathetic to reader-oriented strategies and is definitely in favor of a plurality of readings, but he cautions: "I

would however not want to advocate too strongly a reader-response ideology for all reading strategies. Texts deserve greater distance, more respect and engagement than reader-response approaches would allow. Without some oppositional element provided by texts over against the reading self the text will be swamped by the overwhelming subjectivities of readers. There must be space for the text to contribute something to the hermeneutic process."

25. Sternberg takes a tentative step in this direction when he mentions the issue of exogamous marriage. Paul Noble also criticizes both studies for their failure to discuss the broader meaning of the story ("A 'Balanced' Reading of the Rape of Dinah: Some Exegetical and Methodological Observations," *Biblical Interpretation* 4 [1996]: 174–175). But Noble also rules out the idea of exogamous marriage (p. 183), preferring to see the story as about crime and punishment (pp. 187 and 195). In my view, he has not progressed beyond Fewell and Gunn in this matter.

26. This is not a new way of generating meaning; rabbinic Midrash relies heavily on contextual interpretation.

27. David Noel Freedman, "Dinah and Shechem, Tamar and Amnon," in *Divine Commitment and Human Obligation*, ed. John R. Huddlestun (Grand Rapids, Mich.: Eerdmans, 1997), 1.485–495.

28. Stephen A. Geller, "The Sack of Shechem," *Prooftexts* 10 (1990): 1–15.

29. Carol Meyers mentions the possibility that the story may reflect the special position of the city of Shechem as both a congenial and troublesome place in premonarchic Israel ("Dinah," *ABD* 2. 200). It is the site of the covenant gathering in Joshua 24 and the site of Abimelech's abortive attempt to establish a monarchy, resulting in the destruction of the city (Judges 9). It is also the burial-place of Joseph and the first capital of the Northern Kingdom.

30. Ellen J. van Wolde reads the story in the context of Genesis 28–35 ("Love and Hatred in a Multiracial Society"). She concludes that in this context, Genesis 34 is a story about monotheism and mono-ethnicity and that the mono-ethnic position is grounded in a monotheistic position. Her reading strategy forms a comparison with Sternberg and with Fewell and Gunn. Like Sternberg, van Wolde finds that the narrative invites the reader to side with Simeon and Levi. But her own values are closer to those of Fewell and Gunn, so she is not happy about the point the story is making. Fewell and Gunn find the story's values to be in line with their own values; indeed, they see the story as promoting their own values. Van Wolde, on the other hand, finds ancient values within the story but is then critical of those values; she perceives a tension between the story's values and her own. (Stephen Geller does the same, as do numerous feminist expositions that judge the treatment of women in ancient texts by today's standards.)

31. The major work in this area is Michael Fishbane, *Biblical Interpretation in Ancient Israel* (Oxford: Clarendon, 1985). Developing the idea from his teacher, Nahum Sarna, Fishbane demonstrated that later parts of the Bible often interpret

earlier parts. His aim was to show that the types of interpretation known from rabbinic sources were already inherent in the Bible itself. For an overview see Benjamin D. Sommer, "Inner-biblical Interpretation," in *The Jewish Study Bible,* 1829–1835.

32. I use the term "intertextuality" gingerly here, conscious of the critique of Thomas R. Hatina, "Intertextuality and Historical Criticism in New Testament Studies: Is There a Relationship?" *Biblical Interpretation* 7, no. 1 (1999): 28–43. Hatina criticizes the misuse of this term by biblical scholars, especially New Testament scholars examining allusions in the New Testament to the Hebrew Bible. They use the term pragmatically, as a substitute for "allusion," and are generally unaware of the complex meaning it has in poststructuralist theory, from which it came. Hatina sees little in common between biblical historical critics and poststructuralists. His article contains a very good discussion of intertextuality. The type of intertextuality I have in mind here is more thoroughgoing than merely allusion, but it does not bear all the freight of the poststructuralist sense of the term.

33. David M. Carr, *Reading the Fractures of Genesis: Historical and Literary Approaches* (Louisville, Ky.: Westminster John Knox, 1996), 16.

34. James L. Kugel, *The Bible As It Was* (Cambridge, Mass.: Belknap, 1997), 234, points out that 4 Macc 2:19–20 took Genesis 49 as an allusion to Genesis 34. He words his statement craftily and noncommittally, saying that Genesis 49 "seemed to interpreters to shed light on the true significance of this incident. For while the story of Dinah is not explicitly mentioned elsewhere in the Hebrew Bible, interpreters from earliest times found an allusion to it at the end of the book of Genesis. . . ." We don't know whether or not Kugel himself sees an allusion to the Dinah story in Genesis 49.

35. The Levites were assigned to divine service and therefore did not have private agricultural holdings; the tribe of Simeon was absorbed into the tribe of Judah. Compare the poem in Deuteronomy 33, which praises Levi as the priestly tribe (with no reference to Genesis 34) and omits Simeon altogether.

36. Source critics identify both passages as belonging to J, a Judean source. David M. Carr (*Reading the Fractures of Genesis,* 304), a source critic informed by literary approaches, concludes that both Genesis 34 and 49:5–7 are part of the work of a pro-Judean author who reshaped earlier material in the Jacob and Joseph stories for the purpose of promoting the tribe of Judah by disqualifying earlier-born sons of Jacob, including Simeon and Levi.

37. I use these terms in a broad and benign sense, without the radical political overtones that accompanied their birth. As with other avant-garde movements, their popular acceptance tames them.

38. "Poststructuralist Approaches, New Historicism and Postmodernism," in *The Cambridge Companion to Biblical Interpretation,* 57. See also the remarks of Sternberg cited in note 7.

39. David M. Carr makes a different but related observation: "Already this survey suggests a potential convergence between recent postmodern synchronic studies and recent diachronic studies. Just as diachronic studies are focusing more on illuminating the present form of the text, synchronic studies are displaying increasing interest in the very textual disunity that was often the mainstay of transmission history" (*Reading the Fractures of Genesis*, 11).

40. Stephen A. Geller, "The Sack of Shechem," 1–15. Geller's work resembles van Wolde's in its general conclusion about mono-ethnicity and in its author's revulsion toward ancient values, but it is much more nuanced and developed, and historically contextualized.

41. Stephen A. Geller, "The Sack of Shechem," 2.

42. Michael Fishbane, *Biblical Interpretation in Ancient Israel*, 350–379.

43. Yairah Amit, *Hidden Polemics in Biblical Narrative*, trans. Jonathan Chipman (Leiden: E. J. Brill, 2000), 189–217. For a related view, see Bernd Jørg Diebner, who does not date the story to the time of Ezra but asks how it would have been read at that time ("Gen 34 und Dinas Rolle bei der Definition 'Israels,'" *Dielheimer Blätter zum Alten Testament* 19 [1984]: 59–76).

44. Helena Zlotnick, *Dinah's Daughters, Gender and Judaism from the Hebrew Bible to Late Antiquity* (Philadelphia: University of Pennsylvania Press, 2002), 33–48.

45. Helena Zlotnick, *Dinah's Daughters*, 26.

46. Helena Zlotnick, *Dinah's Daughters*, 41–42.

47. Joseph Fleishman, "Shechem and Dinah—in the Light of Non-biblical and Biblical Sources," *ZAW* 116, no. 1 (2004): 12–32; see also Joseph Fleishman, "Why Did Simeon and Levi Rebuke their Father in Genesis 34:31?" *JNSL* 26, no. 2 (2000): 101–116.

48. S. Erlandsson, "*znh*" in *Theological Dictionary of the Old Testament*, ed. G. Johannes Botterweck and Helmer Ringgren (Grand Rapids, Mich.: William B. Eerdmans, 1980), 4.100.

49. Yvonne Sherwood, *A Biblical Text and Its Afterlife: The Survival of Jonah in Western Cultures* (Cambridge: Cambridge University Press, 2000), 3.

50. Jeremy Cohen, in tracing the career of a single verse from the Bible through medieval exegesis, makes a related observation: "the role of interpretation in the formation of the biblical text is for this book a methodological premise. . . . A historical study of biblical interpretation may not casually presume that at the moment of its composition a scriptural text possessed a clear, indisputable meaning from which all subsequent understanding of that text departed. It is difficult if not impossible to determine whether a text ever had an original, uninterpreted meaning; more often than not, the qualitative distinction between this meaning and later, interpretative expositions is untenable. The extant text of the Bible itself derives from several lengthy processes of transmission, reflection, and revision; it

never did have a single, absolute value that the historian can recover" ("*Be Fruitful and Increase, Fill the Earth and Master It*," *The Ancient and Medieval Career of a Biblical Text* [Ithaca and London: Cornell University Press, 1989], 11).

51. See F. Dobbs-Allsopp, "Rethinking Historical Criticism," *Biblical Interpretation* 7, no. 3 (1999): 235–271. Dobbs-Allsopp stresses the ongoing importance of historical criticism to the literary study of the Bible and wants to rethink traditional historical criticism from a postmodern perspective.

52. See James Kugel, *The Bible As It Was*. This is not actually a new area of study, but it had been eclipsed by the focus on the original meaning of the text and by a general lack of regard in academic circles for pre-modern interpretation. With the more recent acceptance and valuation of multiple interpretations, including ancient (or "pre-critical") ones, and a growing interest in the process and development of interpretation, the way was open for the study of these ancient interpretations. In terms of the history of biblical studies, this marks a move away from the early stages of the formation of the Bible (its origin and pre-textual sources) to the later development of biblical writings, after a body of them had gained some authority in the community and were therefore studied, interpreted, and echoed in new compositions. For overviews see Devorah Dimant, "Use and Interpretation of Mikra in the Apocrypha and Pseudepigrapha," in *Mikra: Text, Translation, Reading, and Interpretation of the Hebrew Bible in Ancient Judaism and Early Christianity*, ed. Martin Jan Mulder (Assen: Van Gorcum; Philadelphia: Fortress Press, 1988), 379–420, esp. 396–399; and Hindy Najman, "Early Nonrabbinic Interpretation," in *The Jewish Study Bible*, 1835–1844.

53. The summary in Tikva Frymer-Kensky, *Reading the Women of the Bible* (New York: Schocken, 2002), 341 is useful and has served as the basis for some of my remarks here. James Kugel offers excerpts of the texts and brief explanations (*The Bible As It Was*, 233–244). For in-depth studies of specific writings, see Tjitze Baarda, "The Shechem Episode in the Testament of Levi: A Comparison with Other Traditions," in *Sacred History and Sacred Texts in Early Judaism: A Symposium in Honor of A. S. van der Woude*, ed. J. N. Bremmer and F. Garcia Martinez (Kampen: Pharos, 1992), 11–73; John J. Collins, "The Epic of Theodotus and the Hellenism of the Hasmoneans," *HTR* 73 (1980): 91–104; Louis H. Feldman, "Philo, Pseudo-Philo, Josephus, and Theodotus on the Rape of Dinah," *JQR* 94 (2004): 253–277; James L. Kugel, "The Story of Dinah in the Testament of Levi," *HTR* 85 (1992): 1–34; Judith H. Newman, "Judith 9 and Genesis 34," in *Praying by the Book: The Scripturalization of Prayer in Second Temple Judaism* (Atlanta, Ga.: Scholars Press, 1999), 123–138; S. R. Pummer, "Genesis 34 in the Writings of the Hellenistic and Roman Periods," *HTR* 75 (1982): 177–188; and Angela Standhartinger, "'Um zu Sehen Die Töchter des Landes' Die Perspektiv Dinas in der Judisch-Hellenistichen Diskussion üm Gen. 34," in *Religious Propaganda and Missionary Competition in the New Testament World: Essays Honoring Dieter Georgi* (Leiden: E. J. Brill, 1994), 89–116.

54. See Louis H. Feldman, "Philo, Pseudo-Philo, Josephus, and Theodotus on the Rape of Dinah," 253–277.

55. How much of early interpretation reflects the interpretive tradition of the author and how much reflects his own ideology remains a question. Kugel stresses the former, while Feldman argues for the latter.

Chapter 4

Feminist Approaches to the Hebrew Bible

Esther Fuchs

When I first began to publish essays on gender and the Hebrew Bible there were but a handful of publications on this subject, mostly in the history of religion.[1] Little did I imagine that within two decades the topic would burgeon into a sub-field within biblical studies, complete with conflicting interpretive theories and methods as well as a full gamut of interdisciplinary approaches, ranging from literary criticism to history, from sociology to theology, from anthropology to narrative theory. Three major commentaries on women in the Bible have appeared since the subject emerged as a legitimate area of scholarly study, including a dictionary of named and unnamed women, and a number of entries in encyclopedias and reference books.[2] In addition, there are a number of anthologies, including a volume on feminist theories and methods, as well as introductions and readers.[3]

The interest in gender and the Bible has become all the more intense since the early 1990s with the recognition of the role played by racial, ethnic, sexual, national, and religious differences among feminist readers.[4] In the United States, the religious authority or status of the Bible has generated a spate of publications among theologians as well, for whom the question affects practices, such as ordination and inclusion in leadership positions, as well as educational, ritual, and administrative activities in various denominations in Christianity and Judaism.

Despite the sudden wealth of publications, little has been done to map out a history of contemporary feminist theoretical thinking about the Hebrew Bible.[5] Few have been the attempts to sort out the various feminist approaches, how they evolved, and their lines of contention and of convergence. Alice Bach's *Women in the Bible: A Reader* reprints frequently used scholarly articles side by side without trying to classify them by category, discipline, focus, theory, or method.[6] Some feminist scholars have interpreted specific passages, chapters, and even biblical books without tracing their assumptions to previous scholarship or offering a context in relation to contemporary scholarship.[7] This practice has a longstanding tradition within biblical studies, where interpreting specific textual passages is considered to be an achievement in and of itself, regardless of its relation to previous work. As a result, the field is rife with insightful and important and creative commentaries on biblical texts, but not necessarily with theoretical thinking about methods or assumptions.

Understanding feminist histories and theories of interpretation is crucial, not only to give credit to pioneering efforts, but also to offer useful paradigms for those involved in the field as well as for those who attempt to enter it. The most prominent theories that dominate the field today emerged in the late 1970s and early 1980s. At the risk of simplification and recognizing that various approaches have been used by various scholars at various times, I will propose that three major approaches dominate the contemporary feminist study of the Hebrew Bible.

The first focuses on women's historical experiences and literary expressions, on women's authentic cultures and voices. Those engaged in this approach search for traces of women's activities and influences, exhume forgotten customs and traditions, explore the textual celebration and validation of women, and emphasize passages that reflect the historical or rhetorical power of women. This approach, therefore, includes depictions of women as deities and leaders, prophets and embodiments of wisdom; and ways in which women have changed history, created their own rituals and practices, and followed their goddesses whether as marginal practices or in the dead center of male monotheism. As a result, those who treat the Bible this way are likely to find textual evidence for the historical equality and power of women, arguing that some passages were composed by women and that some expressions are distinctly feminine. To the extent that male domination has been found in the Bible, they argue that it is the result of post-biblical cultures and interpretations. This approach then focuses on female activity, its priority, superiority, and pervasiveness in ancient Near Eastern civilizations. Attempts to focus on female images of God and on ancient Near Eastern goddesses and their presence in or influence on the Hebrew Bible in essence elaborate this approach. Wherever this approach has been used, it always requires reconstructive work—

reconstructing women's histories or their experience. Foremost among those who follow this approach are Phyllis Trible, Carol Meyers, Ilana Pardes, and Tikva Frymer Kensky.

Closely related are those who accept the premise that the Bible was composed by and about men but argue that it offers a diverse and complex representation of ancient women's lives. Women's roles transcend simple stereotypes, offering a diversity of images and a variety of authentic voices. In historical terms, this approach argues that women emerge both as influential leaders and as submissive followers. In literary terms, it claims that women are both venerated and denigrated, both central and marginal.

Those who take this point of view concede that male-centered perspectives were not only imposed on the Bible by later commentaries and elaborations, but were also manifestations of ancient Near Eastern civilizations that no longer exist. They therefore emphasize the long history of the Bible's composition, the various sources, layers, authorships and the fluidity and diversity of the ideologies that inspired it. As a result, they find both women's and men's voices, both female and male cultures and traditions in the Bible, even while admitting that women's culture, power, and voice were to some extent muted by the Bible's masculine context and framework. This approach emphasizes that the biblical text is in the eyes of its beholders, that it is open to any and all interpretations and perspectives.

The scholars who take this point of view write from various viewpoints, sometimes even in a single book, implying that one can choose different approaches to the same material. In historical terms, they insist on change and diversity across periods and classes; in literary terms they tend to focus on the reader rather than the text and to shift attention away from the author. Refusing theoretical coherence and methodological consistency, they tend to accord equal significance to all approaches, including creative, midrashic, and imaginative, explaining masculine bias as a result of historical context and evolution. Foremost among the practitioners who follow this path are Phyllis Bird, Mieke Bal, Athalya Brenner, and Susan Ackerman.

The third and final approach begins from the premise that the Bible was not merely composed, edited, transmitted and canonized by men, but is also a patriarchal compilation, giving voice to patriarchal institutional practices and endorsing the social and symbolic supremacy of men. Unlike those who see the Bible as a literary product of a particular time and place, these critics see it as having invented and created the sexual categories and hierarchies that its many readers take for granted. Unlike those who maintain that the biblical narrative is descriptive and inclusive, comprehensive and diverse, they argue that the Bible endorses desirable forms of behavior and that it has contributed to the way contemporary womanhood is defined in both religious and secular contexts. This approach is, therefore, based on skepticism as to the Bible's innocence, on criticism of any gender bias, and on opposition to the superiority of one gender above the other. Historically speaking, it sees the Bible not merely as a product of male-centered culture, but as one of the texts that actively created this culture, having disrupted and replaced previous cultures in which women were regarded as deities, as potential leaders, and as equals. This approach understands the diversity and plurality of female roles in the Bible as a shallow façade that hides a "false consciousness" of the ruling class in which women are marginalized as secondary characters and supporting agents in a male-centered history. The feminist critic who analyzes "positive" and "negative" representations of women poses the question "positive for whom?" or "for what?" Unlike those taking the other two points of view, who see female voices or traditions as sources of female empowerment, the feminist critic asks why these particular voices or traditions have been included and what possible uses the patriarchal narrator might have had for them. This radical skepticism is an intellectual stance that refuses to take the way female characters are presented at face value. Rather than seeing women as actors in a male drama, be it historical or literary, the feminist critic asks how gender has shaped this drama and how gender politics illuminates the very structure of biblical narrative. Rather than constructs floating in a male world, women are the fulcrum from which this world is reexamined. Feminist criticism considers the Bible as itself a patriarchal interpretation of the ancient world, therefore just as subject to inquiry as are modern and contemporary commentaries on the Bible.

Although this may appear contradictory, feminist criticism is often misunderstood as "negative" or "rejectionist"; however, the feminist critic does not reject the Bible, though she may criticize it. The patriarchal slant of the text is not a reason to reject it, but rather its greatest value and significance. The feminist critic seeks to question her own social and ideological role as a woman in the western world. In this sense, the reading she does is not of the Bible, but rather of herself. It is small wonder that critics who began to write from a feminist premise turned their attention to modern Western culture, art, and film. I see my work as feminist criticism and would include Cheryl Exum, Alice Bach, and Claudia Camp as well as Ilona Rashkow, Gale Yee, and Lillian Klein in that category as well.

Twenty or thirty years ago, practically nothing was written on the biblical narrative from a feminist theoretical perspective. The only feminist literary approach to the Hebrew Bible available at the time was Phyllis Trible's *God and the Rhetoric of Sexuality.* Trible was explicit about her theological goals:

> Focusing on texts in the Hebrew Scriptures, I have sought a theological vision for new occasions. But I do not propose thereby to offer a comprehensive program for doing biblical theology. Nor do I claim that the perspectives given here dominate the scriptures. Instead, I have accented what I consider neglected themes and counterliterature. Using feminist hermeneutics, I have tried to recover old treasures and discover new ones in the household of faith. Though some of these treasures are small, they are nonetheless valuable in a tradition that is often compelled to live by the remnant.[8]

For Trible, then, a feminist exoneration of the Hebrew Bible is an assertion of Christian faith as much as it is an attempt to assert that feminism as such is not necessarily an anti-biblical or anti-Christian position. By reading references to women as significant and "positive," she sought to bring feminism and the Bible into a collaborative alliance, one that held much promise and hope for women of faith.[9]

It is possible that Trible's defense of the Hebrew Bible was articulated as a response to Mary Daly's theological rejection of Christianity in *Beyond God the Father.*[10] Trible argued her case by focusing on select texts, notably on Genesis 2–3. By providing the original Hebrew meaning of *adam* as a generic noun meaning "humankind" rather than "man" and by insisting that *ezer kenegdo* (Gen 2:18) does not mean subservient helpmate but rather equal partner, Trible sought to "depatriarchalize" or exonerate the Bible of the charge of patriarchal bias. She found female imagery in biblical references to God. In a manner reminiscent of the Christian understanding of the New Testament as repairing and redeeming the "Old Testament," she suggested that the few remaining problematic elements in the Genesis story were reversed and redeemed by the books of Ruth and the Song of Songs. In a later book, Trible argued that female victims are portrayed with empathy and that God is often on their side.[11]

In 1982, I sought to introduce a nonreligious approach to a text I understood as great literature, though great literature biased and problematic from a feminist perspective.[12] As literary approaches to the Bible began to multiply, I sought to combine them with a feminist approach. Looking at the figure of Deborah from the book of Judges, for example, I did not ask historical questions about what it was that permitted women to emerge as leaders during the pre-monarchic period; rather, I asked how this leader fit in the text and how she compared to the male judges that preceded and followed her—in other words, how she was represented by the male narrator, whose gender I understood to be inseparable from his art. Where Trible saw resolutions, my reading of Ruth introduced problems: Whose purpose was Ruth serving by her loyal friendship with Naomi? Was it not the patrilineal continuity of her husband's family that she set out to restore? When celebrating her as a heroine, are we asked to value women's friendship or to validate patriarchal structures? Religious leadership and access to divine truth and authority as embodied by the male God are denied to both Ruth and Esther, who are seen as agents in the greater saga of protecting the family and the national units. My approach, then, differed from Trible's in looking at biblical heroines critically.

Reading against the grain challenged the approach articulated by Phyllis Bird in her pioneering essay "Images of Women in the Old Testament."[13] Bird and the scholars who followed her in the 1990s argued that the Hebrew Bible is too diverse for feminists to stand in judgment of its attitude toward women.[14] She argued that the Hebrew Bible draws on sources that are descriptive and prescriptive, positive and negative, limiting and liberating, celebratory and punitive of women. Her historical reading of the Hebrew Bible projected its problematic aspects into a distant past, attributing its alleged diversity to a long history of composition. She understood the Bible as reflecting an ancient society in which women were subordinate. Challenging the concept of objective and unbiased history, I suggested that rather than reflecting reality, the Bible establishes what is real. It is not merely male-centered (that is, reflective of a male society), but also patriarchal, in the sense that it seeks to establish male supremacy and authority as a fundamental principle, ordained by God, decreed by nature, and determined by historical events.

In order to be effective, ideology must always hide its origin, its investments, and its interests; therefore, it is pointless to expect its signature to be obvious. My article "Who is Hiding the Truth? Deceptive Women and Biblical Androcentrism" exposed the ideological investments of repeated associations of women with deception, demonstrating how religious doctrine and patriarchal ideology are inextricable from each other.[15] Unlike

Bird, who distinguished between descriptive and prescriptive texts, between "novellas" like Ruth and Esther or myths like Genesis 2-3 and legal codes, I insisted that we take the ideas of biblical narrative seriously, subjecting them to careful analysis in much the same way that we do the text's aesthetic or literary features.[16] Though later accused of reading the text too rigidly or simplistically, I in fact set out to add yet another dimension to the biblical text's poetic complexity—its sexual politics.

In "The Literary Characterization of Mothers and Sexual Politics in the Hebrew Bible" I further challenged the assumption that we can approach the biblical narrative as merely a literary work of art rather than as an ideological text.[17] Stories in which a birth is announced as a test case show that the repeated presentation of barren women who miraculously become pregnant after the announcement by a divine (male) messenger and then happily give birth to male sons is not simply a literary convention, as Robert Alter argued, nor a "positive" manifestation of biblical femininity, but rather a sophisticated political construct that serves the interests of a particular group or class.[18] Feminist insights into the power relations between men and women in patriarchal societies expose the political investments of what is repeated, what is left out, whose words are reported, and what details are provided.[19] For example, as soon as they give birth, thereby securing patrilineal continuity, mother figures frequently disappear from the narrative. Rather than differentiating between "good" and "bad" images of women, we have to ask the question "good for whom (*cui bono*)?" Valuing mothers is not in and of itself a symptom of approval or a trace of ancient feminism. Motherhood insures the viability of patrilineal genealogies in a precarious world. It is, therefore, vital to the functioning of biblical patriarchy, which promotes women to the extent that they contribute to or promote its success.

My reading of the biblical text refused to exempt it from modern critical examination on the basis of its being ancient or historical. Instead, I believe that the interaction of language and power is precisely the hallmark of the Bible as great ancient literature and that it is precisely this relationship that feminist criticism ought to examine. Most importantly, we must pay attention to the way mother figures are used in broad male genealogical sagas, how female speeches are embedded in contexts having to do with procreation, the ways in which direct dialogues between the male deity and female subjects are suppressed, how female characters enter and exit right before and after delivering sons, and the differences between how male and female characters are characterized.

In my view, patriarchal ideology played as prominent a role in shaping the biblical narrative as did the monotheistic ideology that Meir Sternberg has exposed.[20] A failure to appreciate the consistent differences between the presentation of males and that of females runs the risk of perpetuating the problem.[21] "Objective" literary critics often hide or suppress the continuity between their male-centered interpretation and that of the biblical narrators.

In an article titled "Deception and Women: A Response," Edwin M. Good declared that my interpretation had the potential to undermine the religious authority of the Bible:

> If [Fuchs] is right that (1) the Bible is androcentric and (2) androcentrism is an unacceptable construction of the world—and I believe she is right on both counts—then the Bible has ceased to be either an adequate ground of authority for religious truth or an adequate source of religious insight. If it has lost validity in either sense, because it is at best partial in its construction of the world, then Biblical authority is dead, and feminism has killed it. Feminism has done what Deism could not do, what liberalism could not do, what many modern efforts to modify Christianity's sense of the basis of this truth failed to do.[22]

While Good is right about the subversive implications of feminist critical reading, he (like Cullen Murphy) takes the religious definition of the Bible for granted. His concern is with the Bible's status as a source of "religious truth" or "religious insight." Religion as such, however, is an interpretation of reality, rather than a manifestation of reality, fact, or truth as such. To claim that an interpretation is "truth" or "insight" is a religious claim. It is not an objective description of a religious document, but rather accepts what such documents purport to be. Those who understand religion as a hierarchical structure based on concepts of authority and power may indeed find a feminist approach threatening, and those who understand "truth" in absolute terms may find a feminist approach objectionable. But those who see religion as a basically poetic and mystical interpretation of human life and the Bible as a literary text welcome feminist criticism as a powerful interpretive lens that rejects authority, hierarchy, and all forms of fundamentalism.

In the late 1980s Mieke Bal questioned the application of feminist critique to an ancient text like the Bible, because she saw it as moralistic, anachronistic, and ideological.[23] Her position rests on postmodern rejections of political criticism in general in accordance with their opposition to single or total conceptions of truth.[24] Using contemporary literary theories as a point of entry into the biblical text, she argued for the legitimacy of any and all literary readings of the Hebrew Bible. Shifting the emphasis from the biblical text to the reader's ideology and subjectivity, she suggested that the Bible is too diverse to be read from any one political perspective. Bal's approach inadvertently re-enshrines the traditional, even religious reluctance to question the Bible, even though she subtitled her first book as a feminist literary reading (albeit without offering a definition for that term).

In *Lethal Love: Feminist Literary Readings of Biblical Love Stories* Bal argued that interpretation often depends on the interpreter's models,[25] rejecting the concept and even the possibility of searching for meaning. At the end of the book she rejects any coherent interpretation of women as simply dangerous lovers or "lethal" partners. Though she concedes that the Bible as a whole is patriarchal, she rejects the very notion of wholeness and the possibility of generalization. Bal's radical relativism and pluralistic approach rejects any and all coherent interpretation, thus undermining the need and logic of feminist struggle for social change. "Through a patient elaboration of the set of critical terms, a critique of previous readings, and the construction of my own, I came up with the answer: the point is that there is none, at least not a single one; the point of literary analysis is that there is no truth, and that this contention can be reasonably argued."[26]

In *Murder and Difference: Gender, Genre and Scholarship on Sisera's Death* Bal presents "gender" as only one among several perspectives that may be used to interpret a text.[27] She argues that using this particular approach can help identify the gender of the speaker in the biblical text. For example, while the narrator of Judges 4 is male, the poem of Deborah in Judges 5 is spoken by a female. By refusing to consider the social, historical and political basis of the conceptual pair "male/female," Bal treats these terms as unchangeable givens. Her description of feminine and masculine genres is problematic. According to her, feminine genres tend to be concentrated around the village and the family, to be poetic, and to offer few details. Masculine genres tend to focus on adventures outside, to be epic, and to offer many details.[28] These literary categories re-enshrine traditional sexual stereotypes. Toward the end of the book, in a surprising reference to historical context, Bal raises the question of Jael's violence against Sisera: "However, in a society in which the women are 'in the tent' and in which their position is utterly circumscribed, the number of moments when they have power over a man can be counted on the fingers of one hand. The confrontation of Jael with the enemy of her people unleashes in the mind the possibility of a reversal of roles."²⁹ Deviating from her linkage of gender and genre in the book of Judges, Bal suggests that Jael's violence expresses the pent up and suppressed energy of the women restricted by biblical patriarchy. In *Death and Dissymmetry,* she develops this interpretation even further in order to explain the peculiar analogy between passive and submissive victimized daughters on the one hand and violent ruthless women who wreak havoc on men on the other. Using psychoanalytic definitions of femininity, Bal suggests that violent women embody the suppressed mothers in the book of Judges, who furiously unleash their vengeance on men who seek to victimize their daughters. In so doing, she reduces the historical background of the book of Judges to the Freudian family romance of angry mothers lashing out at violent fathers for having mistreated their passive daughters. Nevertheless, she articulates a critique of modern historians who impose traditionally patriarchal concerns about war and politics on the book of Judges.

The first comprehensive effort to present a female-centered view of the Bible using historical rather than literary criticism was published by Carol Meyers in 1988. In *Discovering Eve: Ancient Israelite Women in Context,* she set out to reconstruct the historical past or ancient Near Eastern context "behind" the biblical text.³⁰ In her theoretical introduction Meyers argues that while ancient Israel may have been patrilineal, it was not necessarily a hierarchical or patriarchal society where women were subordinated.³¹ Tracing lineage and allocating property did not necessarily entail the subordination of women. The agricultural economy of the villages that survived the tough conditions of the Palestinian hill country during the late Bronze Age (1550–1200 B.C.E.) required the active participation of women. In Meyers's view, Genesis 2-3 reveals the productive as well as reproductive roles of women in this ancient economy, roles that were crucial to the survival of the Israelite peasant-pioneers. Because the family household was the central social unit prior to the establishment of a monarchy, women's contribution to its functioning and survival was nothing less than crucial. This contribution was closely related to the socializing, religious, and educational responsibilities by means of which women shaped the next generation. Meyers, therefore, infers that the relationship between men and women in monarchic Israel must have been egalitarian and complementary, in contrast to the hierarchical relationship that was a product of the centralization of power resulting from the emergence of royal authority and the construction of the Temple in the tenth century B.C.E. While the royal, religious, military, and political bureaucracies may have affected the lives of the urban upper class, agrarian life continued to depend on strong independent and autonomous women, the ancient Eves or the majority of Israelite women. Meyers argues then that the actual restrictions on women began in a much later period—shortly before the exile or even later under Greco-Roman influence, rather than in ancient Israel.

In the early 1990s Ilana Pardes shifted the historical search for submerged or erased female traditions to a literary search for female power as expressed in scattered verses and paragraphs in the Hebrew Bible. Much in the tradition of Trible's unearthing of a "counterliterature," Pardes sought to unearth female—if not feminist—"countertraditions" in the Hebrew Bible.[32] Her method focused on ancient Near Eastern mythologies rather than history (terms she tends to use interchangeably), albeit without hypothesizing a previous period of female ascendancy. These "countertraditions" suggest strata of repressed femininity and traces of repressed ancient goddesses.[33] Pardes recaptures these repressed female voices by attending to textual detail, filling in gaps, and imagining a relationship with a female deity, in short by providing mythological or narrative contexts for texts where the Bible itself is too brief or elliptical. Thus she spells out the variety of ways in which Miriam is characterized, the sympathetic sides of Rachel, and the erotic longings in the Song of Songs by demonstrating the relationships between various voices. In a manner reminiscent of the way in which Trible had presented the Song of Songs as reconciling or harmoniously resolving the story of creation, Pardes reads the story of Ruth as an "idyllic revision" of the contest between Leah and Rachel, and the Song of Songs as an "idyllic revision" of the problematic marital bond between God and the nation of Israel as presented by the prophets. In the speeches where Eve and Rachel name their children, Pardes finds a lost female tradition. Though she accepts that Rachel is not as fully characterized a literary character as Jacob, Pardes nevertheless argues that the text treats Rachel's hopes and dreams as well as it does Jacob's dream.[34] In the enigmatic episode involving Zipporah and God's angel (Exodus 4) she finds traces of a tradition of female saviors and echoes of the submerged myth of the Egyptian goddess Isis. Though she claims to follow Mieke Bal, Pardes is much closer to Trible than she is willing to concede. She focuses strictly on female "countertraditions," without connecting them with the patriarchal perspective they disrupt or in which they are embedded.

The early 1990s saw not only the reemergence of efforts to find positive traditions of women in Israelite history and biblical literature, but also a resurgence of feminist criticism. J. Cheryl Exum, who in the 1980s had approached biblical women as positive role models, as saviors, heroines, and venerable contributors to a miraculous plot of survival and redemption, changed her mind toward the end of the decade and began to read the text more suspiciously. In one of her earlier articles about biblical mothers, she emphasized the importance and significance of the matriarchs in Israelite history and in the biblical narrative. In Genesis, they enabled the Israelites to achieve God's promise, emerging at strategic points to move the plot forward. The mothers of Exodus were crucial to the success of Moses.[35] Exum's transition to a feminist interpretation became more explicit when she reread the biblical mothers in light of the concept of patriarchal ideology. In the preface to her book *Fragmented Women: Feminist (Sub)versions of Biblical Narratives* she put it as follows: "In androcentric texts like the Bible, women are often made to speak and act against their own interests. This being the case, the central organizing question of this book is: what androcentric agenda do these narratives promote?"[36] One of her discoveries was that "over and over, that agenda was motivated by male fear and desire in response to women's sexuality and the resultant need of patriarchy to control women."[37] Extending earlier analyses that had found narrative gaps, marginalization, and the silencing of women, Exum suggested that such strategies should be read as patriarchal acts of literary rape.[38] Thus, she proposed that we read the stories of Jephthah's anonymous daughter, Saul's daughter Michal, and even of Bathsheba as enacting textual violence or figurative rape against the female characters.[39] Not only is Michal victimized by her father's intrigues, but she also falls victim to David's political machinations; above all, however, her story is submerged, fragmented, and truncated by the biblical narrator in such a way as to reveal relentless literary violence.[40] Exum reads the story of Samson's women in Judges 13-16 as exemplifying the patriarchal polarization of the "good woman" (Samson's mother) and the "bad woman" (the three Philistine "whores" who expedite his demise). While the good women are characterized by motherhood and nurturing, sexuality and sensuality characterize the evil ones.[41] It is these latter who obtain forbidden knowledge or power over men. Representing Samson's "whores" as dangerous foreigners in contrast to his righteous mother encourages women to become lawful and loyal mothers. Adding a psychoanalytic edge to her feminist critical method, Exum interprets the stories of the endangered matriarchs in Genesis as symptoms of patriarchal fear and desire: the fear of losing one's wife as sexual object and exclusive possession, and the desire (and fear) of sharing that very possession with other men. She extends the political analysis of the biblical narrative by including psychoanalytic explanations for the silencing, truncating, and marginalizing of women characters.

A self-proclaimed "oppositional critic," Alice Bach elaborates a feminist approach to the Hebrew Bible by applying reader-oriented theory to the critique of patriarchal ideology. To do this, she asks how a feminist reader would resist Alter and Sternberg's descriptive literary reading of the biblical stories.[42] Thus if the narrator presents the perfect wife as sedentary and loyal to her husband, Bach proposes that we see her ominous counterpart, the "strange woman," as seeking to overthrow the limitations of the patriarchal regime. Read from the viewpoint of Potiphar's wife, the story of seduction and betrayal in which she takes part becomes the account of a woman who transgressed the social conventions that inhibit female sexuality by opening her house and her mouth to a strange man.[43] According to Bach, these misogynous narrative strategies are intensified in later interpretations of the Joseph story, which attempt to exonerate the perfect male hero, Joseph, at the expense of his wily female counterpart. Bach also finds submerged thematic associations between female sexuality and death in the way post-biblical portrayals of Esther and Judith show them using their beauty, speech, and wine to undermine male adversaries. Examining modern film representations of the Bathsheba and Tamar stories, she resists the continuing association of female sexuality with the deadly results to those who succumb to it. According to Bach, the late nineteenth-century European obsession with the deadly Salome, the ultimate femme fatale of the New Testament, serves as a cultural retaliation against early feminism and interprets the vicious and voracious Salome of European paintings and Hollywood productions as symptomatic of "the male fear of the courtesan as killer."[44]

The reader who wishes to extricate herself from the grip of the male imagination must not lose sight of the political interests of the way these figures are represented and the power investments of a male regime whose goal is to subdue the sexually expressive and socially independent woman. According to Bach, then, power is an integral part of the narrator's point of view and of the final contours of the text. It cannot be set aside or ignored or even added to an exploration of women's authentic voices or traditions. Those voices and traditions are impossible to detect in a document that is so thoroughly framed by a male-centered vision of reality and history. For Bach, the Hebrew Bible is an expression of the historical victory of patriarchy; only by reading against the grain can a woman reader today hope to fully grasp the extent to which authentic female power has been defeated.[45]

Almost diametrically opposed to Bach's critical stance is Susan Ackerman's effort to recover the variety of important roles occupied by women. Taking her cue from Mieke Bal, Ackerman finds in the Hebrew Bible, notably in the book of Judges, a diversity of female types, which she believes played a central role within the "larger arenas of Israelite theological belief and ritual practice."[46] Ackerman connects these to ancient Near Eastern myths as well as to subsequent New Testamental accounts. Thus, she sees the barren mother type already in the Canaanite epic of Aqhat as well as in the virgin birth of Mary.[47] Unlike feminist critics who focused on male intervention in the act of procreation, Ackerman focuses on the story of birth and the possible destruction of the son, as well as on the various ways in which the son's death is thwarted or miraculously enacted in the apparently more enlightened biblical materials. Ackerman also examines the woman warrior type embodied by Deborah, Jael, and, in later literature, Judith, tracing the lethal associations of military and erotic power to the Canaanite war goddess Anat, Baal's female ally (1550–1200 B.C.E.). For Ackerman, demoting the goddess to human form does not represent the kind of theoretical and methodological problem it represented for feminist historians of religion like Judith Ochshorn and Gerda Lerner.[48] She is more interested in the continuities and changes in such representations than in the political implications of the war goddess's transformation into a woman warrior.[49] Ackerman reconstructs Jael and Deborah as ritual functionaries or religious leaders, assigning religious authority and power to them as well as to other female characters in Judges (e.g., Jephthah's daughter, Manoah's wife, Michah's mother) in much the same way that Carol Meyers did in her reconstruction of the pre-monarchic period.[50] In Ackerman's view, references to idolatrous queen mothers are historical evidence not of female heresy but of a thriving religious practice upheld by leading Israelite women who followed the Queen of Heaven in her various guises. She sees Sisera's mother as a powerful queen mother who enjoyed both political and economic privileges. Her awaiting the arrival of her son by a window evokes Asherah, the Canaanite goddess who was worshipped by several queen mothers even during the monarchy (e.g., Ma'acah, Nehushtah, Bathsheba). The Hebrew Bible, then, according to Ackerman, records both the mythologies and the histories of both images and lives of the women of ancient Israel. "It is, if anything, a book not of 'either/or' but of 'both/and,' a book that both glorifies the deeds of men and embraces the tales of women."[51]

This optimistic conclusion is precisely the problematic point of entry for Claudia Camp, who sees women's religious roles as occasions for analysis and criticism, not celebration. In her view, the Hebrew writers constructed their national narrative by obfuscating and denying women's religious authority. Like Cheryl Exum, Claudia Camp made a transition from finding female-centered portrayals to feminist critique.[52] She suggests that the "strange woman" (*isha zara*) was a focus of biblical opprobrium, not only because of her foreign origin and suspicious sexuality, but also because of the tradition of ancient wisdom and her religious authority as a member of a priestly caste. Camp links the woman trickster in Proverbs to the women in the stories about Samson and Solomon, who reflect the fascination with and fear of strange women as a source of wisdom, erotic power, and potential death. According to Camp, treating biblical women as "other" is part of the ideology of priestly and ritual purity which emerged most clearly in the post-exilic period. "Through the Strange Woman paradigm, the symbolic components of 'true Israelite' identity—right nationality, right deity, right sex—are brought into relationship with the construction of 'true' (= priestly) leadership—right lineage, right cult, right gender."[53] It is woman not just as sexually different, but also as ethnically and nationally different that represents the background against which we should understand the strict prohibitions against foreign wives, especially in Ezra and Nehemiah. Camp inverts the image of the "foreign" and "strange" woman, examining the concept of religious holiness that is embedded in and embodied by the ancient Near Eastern and even postexilic woman who did not follow the biblical doctrines, laws, and codes of propriety.

As the 1990s drew to an end, the feminist approach to the Hebrew Bible gained momentum. Feminist critiques today often combine the category of gender politics with postcolonial, psychoanalytic, and Marxist criticism in order to question the basic assumptions of biblical and western culture.[54] African, Latin American, and East Asian feminists, who bring different questions to the biblical texts, are opening up an especially exciting perspective.[55] The contemporary embrace of multiplicity and diversity has created a new space for approaches that distinguish themselves as "different" or idiosyncratic.

While I affirm the validity of diverse feminist approaches, I do not intend here to endorse a kind of nihilistic "anything goes" approach to the Hebrew Bible. Rather, I have tried to present a theoretical overview of the methods that feminist readers applied, often without acknowledging the pioneering efforts and radical differences among us. It is important that our openness to multiple approaches not turn feminism into a toy in our world, where diversity is the hallmark of the manufactured desires of the marketplace; rather, I hope that it opens a genuine debate about feminist theory and method.[56] This debate may perhaps begin with what I have called "points of resonance."[57] Rather than fragmenting scholarly discussion into academic "cliques," we should be mapping out points of agreement and disagreement. The point of debate and conversation is not to deny our theoretical differences but to create bridges and alliances that will enable us to speak with each other across our theoretical, religious, national, political, and ideological differences. The goal is not to create a uniform or homogeneous feminist scholarship, but rather to develop a diverse and energetic field that avoids repetition by remembering the past and boldly facing the divide that continues to separate many of us from the equally diverse yet still male-dominated world of biblical studies.[58] A plurality of critical voices differs greatly from the over-saturated marketplace diversity of scholarly approaches in which feminist theory is at risk of being added as yet another one of several new flavors to be stirred into the consensus that preceded its revolutionary appearance two decades ago.

NOTES

1. For example, Mary Daly, *Beyond God the Father: Toward a Philosophy of Women's Liberation* (Boston: Beacon Press, 1973); Rosemary Ruether, ed., *Religion and Sexism: Images of Women in Jewish and Christian Traditions* (New York: Simon and Schuster, 1974); Carol Christ and Judith Plaskow, *Womenspirit Rising: A Feminist Reader in Religion* (San Francisco: Harper and Row, 1979).

2. See Carol Newsom and Sharon Ringe, eds., *The Women's Bible Commentary* (Louisville: Westminster and John Knox Press, 1992); Athalya Brenner, ed., *A Feminist Companion to the Bible* (Sheffield: Sheffield Academic Press, 1993–1995); Elisabeth S. Fiorenza, ed., *Searching the Scriptures* (New York: Crossroads, 1993); Carol Meyers et al., eds., *Women in Scripture: A Dictionary of Named and Unnamed Women in the Hebrew Bible, the Apocryphal/Deuterocanonical Books and the New Testament* (Boston: Houghton Mifflin, 2000).

3. Adela Y. Collins, ed., *Feminist Perspectives on Biblical Scholarship* (Chico: Society of Biblical Literature, 1985); Letty M. Russell, ed., *Feminist Interpretation of*

the Bible (Philadelphia: Westminster Press, 1985); Peggy L. Day, ed., *Gender and Difference in Ancient Israel* (Minneapolis: Fortress Press, 1989); Mieke Bal, ed., *Anti-Covenant: Counter-Reading Women's Lives in the Hebrew Bible* (Sheffield: The Almond Press, 1989); Alice Bach, *The Pleasure of Her Text* (Philadelphia: Trinity Press, 1990); Alice Laffey, *An Introduction to the Old Testament: A Feminist Perspective* (Philadelphia: Fortress Press, 1988); Athalya Brenner and Carole Fontaine, eds., *Reading the Bible: Approaches, Methods and Strategies* (Sheffield: Sheffield Academic Press, 1997).

4. For example, Kwok Pui-lan, *Discovering the Bible in the Non-Biblical World* (New York: Maryknoll, 1985). See also *The Postmodern Bible,* by the Bible and Culture Collective (New Haven, Conn.: Yale University Press, 1995).

5. By "feminism" I refer to the idea that women are human beings. As a theory, or cluster of theories, feminism refuses any interpretation of sexual, physiological, or behavioral differences between the sexes as proof of inadequacy or inferiority in either sex. Systematic interpretations of the history of feminist criticism of the Hebrew Bible include Katheryn Pfisterer Darr, *Far More Precious than Jewels: Perspectives on Biblical Women* (Louiville: Westminster, 1991) and Pamela J. Milne, "Toward Feminist Companionship: The Future of Feminist Biblical Studies and Feminism," in *Reading the Bible: Approaches, Methods and Strategies,* ed. Athalya Brenner and Carole Fontaine (Sheffield: Sheffield Academic Press, 1997), 39–60. By contrast, an ongoing effort to classify approaches to the New Testament have been undertaken by Elisabeth S. Fiorenza, see for example, *Sharing Her Word: Feminist Biblical Interpretations in Context* (Boston: Beacon Press, 1998).

6. Alice Bach, ed., *Women in the Bible: A Reader* (New York: Routledge, 1999).

7. See for instance Lillian Klein, who has not made explicit her use of my definition of sexual politics in the Bible.

8. *God and the Rhetoric of Sexuality* (Philadelphia: Fortress Press, 1978), xvi.

9. Elisabeth Schussler Fiorenza sought to achieve a similar theological goal by using the method of historical reconstruction in her book, *In Memory of Her* (New York: Crossroad, 1983).

10. Mary Daly, *Beyond God the Father: Toward a Philosophy of Women's Liberation* (Boston: Beacon Press, 1973).

11. See Phyllis Trible, *Texts of Terror: Literary-Feminist Readings of Biblical Narratives* (Philadelphia: Fortress Press, 1984).

12. "Status and Role of Female Heroines in the Biblical Narrative," *The Mankind Quarterly* 23, no. 2 (1982): 149–160, reprinted in Alice Bach ed. *Women in the Hebrew Bible: A Reader,* 77–84. For an elaboration of my approach along male-related typologies, such as the mother, wife, sister, and daughter, see my *Sexual Politics in the Biblical Narrative: Reading the Hebrew Bible as a Woman* (Sheffield: Sheffield Academic Press, 2000).

13. "Images of Women in the Old Testament," in *Religion and Sexism: Images*

of Woman in the Jewish and Christian Tradition, ed. Rosemary Radford Ruether (New York: Simon and Schuster, 1974), 41–88.

14. See for example, Susan Niditch, "Portrayals of Women in the Hebrew Bible," in *Jewish Women: A Historical Perspective* (Detroit, Mich.: Wayne State University Press, 1998), 25–45; Tikva Frymer-Kensky, "The Bible and Women's Studies," in *Feminist Perspectives on Jewish Studies,* ed. Lynn Davidman and Shelly Tenenbaum (New Haven and London: Yale University Press, 1994), 16–39.

15. "Who Is Hiding the Truth? Deceptive Women and Biblical Androcentrism," in *Feminist Perspectives on Biblical Scholarship,* ed. Adela Yarbro Collins (Chico, Calif.: Society of Biblical Literature, 1985), 137-144.

16. Phyllis Bird, "Images of Women in the Old Testament," 75–77. See for additional subsequent essays her book *Missing Persons and Mistaken Identities: Women and Gender in Ancient Israel* (Minneapolis: Fortress Press, 1997).

17. Esther Fuchs, "The Literary Characterization of Mothers and Sexual Politics in the Hebrew Bible," in *Feminist Perspectives on Biblical Scholarship,* 117–136. Reprinted in *Narrative Research on the Hebrew Bible (Semeia* 46), ed. Miri Amihai, George Coats and Anne M. Solomon (Atlanta: Society of Biblical Literature, 1989), 151–168.

18. Robert Alter, "How Convention Helps Us Read: The Case of the Bible's Annunciation Type-Scene," *Prooftexts* 3, no. 2 (1983): 115–130. See also *The Art of Biblical Narrative* (New York: Basic Books, 1981). On mothers as "positive" images in the Bible, see John H. Otwell, *And Sarah Laughed* (Philadelphia: The Westminster Press, 1977).

19. Kate Millet, *Sexual Politics* (New York: Ballantine, 1969).

20. Meir Sternberg, *The Poetics of Biblical Narrative: Ideological Literature and the Drama of Reading* (Bloomington: Indiana University Press, 1985); James G. Williams, *Women Recounted: Narrative Thinking and the God of Israel* (Sheffield: Almond Press, 1982).

21. See my articles "Marginalization, Ambiguity, Silencing: The Story of Jephthah's Daughter," *The Journal of Feminist Studies in Religion* 5, no. 1 (spring 1989): 35–46; "'For I Have the Way of Women': Deception, Gender and Ideology in Biblical Narrative," in *Reasoning with the Foxes: Female Wit in a World of Male Power (Semeia* 42), ed. J. Cheryl Exum and Johanna W. H. Bos (Atlanta, Ga.: Society of Biblical Literature, 1988), 68–83; "Structure and Patriarchal Functions in the Biblical Betrothal Type-Scene: Some Preliminary Notes," *Journal of Feminist Studies in Religion* 3, no. 1 (spring 1987): 7–14; "Contemporary Biblical Literary Criticism: The Objective Phallacy," in *Mappings of the Biblical Terrain: The Bible as Text,* ed. Vincent L. Tollers and John Maier (London and Toronto: Bucknell University Press, 1990), 134–142.

22. Edwin M. Good, "Deception and Women: A Response," in *Reasoning with the Foxes,* 132. This alarmist interpretation reemerges in Cullen Murphy's *The*

Word According to Eve: Women and the Bible in Ancient Times and Our Own (New York and Boston: Houghton Mifflin, 1998). Murphy presents my approach as follows: "According to one feminist commentator, Esther Fuchs, of the University of Arizona, who avowedly has little use for the Bible, deceptiveness is a motif that runs through most [biblical] narratives involving women, both condemnatory and laudatory ones." The characterization of my approach as "rejectionist" reveals the religious mindset of those who see the Bible as a given rather than itself a literary interpretation open to critical reading.

23. Mieke Bal, "Tricky Thematics," in *Reasoning with the Foxes*, 133–155.

24. Linda J. Nicholson, ed., *Feminism/Postmodernism* (New York and London: Routledge, 1990); Chris Weedon, *Feminist Practice and Poststructuralist Theory* (Oxford and Cambridge: Blackwell, 1987).

25. Mieke Bal, *Lethal Love: Feminist Literary Readings of Biblical Love Stories* (Bloomington and Indianapolis: Indiana University Press, 1987), see especially 10–36.

26. *Lethal Love*, 132.

27. Mieke Bal, *Murder and Difference: Gender, Genre and Scholarship on Sisera's Death* (Bloomington and Indianapolis: Indiana University Press, 1988).

28. *Murder and Difference*, 125.

29. *Murder and Difference*, 131.

30. Carol Meyers, *Discovering Eve: Ancient Israelite Women in Context* (New York: Oxford University Press, 1988).

31. *Discovering Eve*, 24–46.

32. Ilana Pardes, *Countertraditions in the Bible* (Cambridge: Harvard University Press, 1992). Pardes takes Bal to task for equating feminism with modernity. See *Countertraditions*, 27.

33. Ilana Pardes, "Preliminary Excavations," *Countertraditions*, 1–12.

34. Ilana Pardes, *Countertraditions*, 60–78.

35. J. Cheryl Exum, " 'Mother in Israel': A Familiar Story Reconsidered," in *Feminist Interpretation of the Bible*, ed. Letty M. Russell (Philadelphia: The Westminster Press, 1985), 73-85.

36. J. Cheryl Exum, *Fragmented Women: Feminist (Sub)versions of Biblical Narratives* (Valley Forge, Pa.: Trinity Press International, 1993), 11–12.

37. J. Cheryl Exum, *Fragmented Women*, 12.

38. Esther Fuchs, "Marginalization, Ambiguity, Silencing: The Story of Jephthah's Daughter," *Journal of Feminist Studies in Religion* 5, no. 1 (1989): 35–46.

39. J. Cheryl Exum, *Fragmented Women*, 16–41, 170–201.

40. J. Cheryl Exum, *Fragmented Women*, 42–60.

41. J. Cheryl Exum, *Fragmented Women*, 61–93.

42. Alice Bach, *Women, Seduction, and Betrayal in Biblical Narrative* (Cambridge: Cambridge University Press, 1997), 13–33.

43. Alice Bach, *Women, Seduction, and Betrayal*, 53.

44. Alice Bach, *Women, Seduction and Betrayal,* 260.

45. Alice Bach, "Man's World, Women's Place: Sexual Politics in the Hebrew Bible," in *Women in the Hebrew Bible: A Reader,* ed. Alice Bach (New York and London: Routledge, 1999), xiii–xxvi.

46. *Warrior, Dancer, Seductress, Queen: Women in Judges and Biblical Israel* (New York: Doubleday, 1998), 9. This title evokes the diversity of women's roles in much the same way a previous book by Alice Ogden Bellis sought to do in *Help-mates, Harlots, Heroes: Women's Stories in the Hebrew Bible* (Louisville, Ky.: Westminster Press, 1994).

47. *Warrior, Dancer, Seductress, Queen,* 181–215.

48. Judith Ochshorn, *The Female Experience and the Nature of the Divine* (Bloomington: Indiana University Press, 1981); Gerda Lerner, *The Creation of Patriarchy* (Oxford and New York: Oxford University Press, 1986).

49. Susan Ackerman, *Warrior, Dancer, Seductress, Queen,* 27–88.

50. See also Jo Ann Hackett, "Rehabilitating Hagar: Fragments of an Epic Pattern," in *Gender and Difference in Ancient Israel* (Minneapolis: Fortress Press, 1989), 12–27.

51. Susan Ackerman, *Warrior, Dancer, Seductress, Queen,* 202.

52. Claudia V. Camp, *Wisdom and the Feminine in the Book of Proverbs* (Sheffield: Almond Press, 1985); *Wise, Strange and Holy: The Strange Woman and the Making of the Bible* (Sheffield: Sheffield Academic Press, 2000), 13–35.

53. Claudia V. Camp, *Wise, Strange and Holy,* p. 229.

54. Ilona N. Rashkow, *Taboo or not Taboo: Sexuality and Family in the Hebrew Bible* (Minneapolis: Fortress Press, 2000); Gale A. Yee, *Poor Banished Children of Eve: Woman as Evil in the Hebrew Bible* (Minneapolis: Fortress Press, 2003). But see also a "purely" feminist critique in Lillian Klein, *From Deborah to Esther: Sexual Politics in the Hebrew Bible* (Minneapolis: Fortress Press, 2003).

55. "Feminist and Womanist Criticism," in *The Postmodern Bible,* by the Bible and Culture Collective (New Haven, Conn.: Yale University Press, 1995), 225–271.

56. Teresa L. Ebert, *Ludic Feminism and After: Postmodernism, Desire, and Labor in Late Capitalism* (Ann Arbor: The University of Michigan Press, 1996).

57. Esther Fuchs, "Points of Resonance," in *On the Cutting Edge: The Study of Women in Biblical Worlds* (New York: Continuum, 2004), 1–21.

58. On the gap between feminist criticism and biblical studies, see Adele Reinharz, "Feminist Criticism and Biblical Studies," in *Reading the Bible: Approaches, Methods and Strategies,* 30–38.

Part III

Ancient Practice

Chapter 5

The Laws of Biblical Israel

Raymond Westbrook

Laws and Law Codes

The most famous law code associated with the Bible is the Ten Commandments, but the Torah (Pentateuch) contains many more commandments —613 in all, according to Rabbinic tradition. Like the Ten Commandments, most of them regulate relations between humans and God, for example dietary rules, rules of personal purity, sacrifices and dedications by individuals, or priestly duties and cultic rules regarding the community as a whole. Other rules in the Torah prescribe purely ethical behavior, like helping one's neighbor, providing charity, or not oppressing the poor. Only about 60 provisions are what we would regard nowadays as law. They are rules that establish rights and duties as between individuals, with regard to marriage, inheritance, property, contract, crime and tort, etc. They cover disputes that can be tried in a human court and give solutions that are enforceable by the normal machinery of justice.

These 60 laws are unevenly spread through the second to the fifth books of the Torah. They are embedded in three of the literary sources that scholars have identified in that segment of the Bible, which are thought to have been written at different times during the first millennium B.C.E. (although their exact dating is a matter of great dispute). Nearly half of the 60 laws are to be found in chapters 21 and 22 of Exodus, in a context usually associated with the Elohist (E) source. An equal number are found in the book of Deuteronomy, mostly concentrated in chapters 21 and 22, but with scattered examples from chapter 15 to chapter 25. Deuteronomy is considered to be an independent source. For the rest, a smattering of laws are found at various points in Leviticus, mostly incidental to regulations regarding purity or priestly functions, and three laws are expounded at length in Numbers. The latter two books contain what is called the Priestly (P) source.

The bulk of the laws in the Torah are thus concentrated in two main clusters. The first, in Exodus 21 and 22:1–16, is usually called the Mishpatim and is part of a larger unit referred to as the Covenant Code (Exod 20:22–23:33). It forms a solid block that is followed, after some transitional provisions (Exod 22:17–19), by a series of ethical rules, moral exhortations and cultic regulations. The second cluster, in Deuteronomy 21 and 22, has a central block that is divided by a group of ethical rules (Deut 22:1–12) and other provisions scattered among mostly ethical and exhortatory material. The pervasive moral rhetoric of Deuteronomy is attached even to everyday laws: for example, legal sanctions are adorned with admonishments such as "you will purge the evil from among you, and all Israel will hear and be afraid" (Deut 21:20).

My concern to separate out laws from other normative or exhortatory material is not just the imposition of a modern category upon ancient sources. The laws already had a separate existence in antiquity. They represent a special type of literature that has remarkably close parallels among Israel's neighbors, both in style and in content. Indeed, the parallels to an external source are the closest of any literary genre in the Bible.

The external source in question is the so-called "law codes." The most famous example is Codex Hammurabi (CH) from Babylonia of the eighteenth century B.C.E., but the texts of no fewer than ten other codes, in whole or part, have been recovered, widely scattered in time and space. Seven are from the Near East and are written in cuneiform script. Of these, two are in Sumerian, from the cities of Ur (Codex Urnamma—CU) and Isin (Codex Lipit-Ishtar—CL) in southern Mesopotamia dating to the twenty-first and nineteenth centuries respectively, one in Akkadian from Eshnunna (CE), a city to the north of Babylon and dated about thirty years earlier than CH, one from Assyria dating between the fourteenth and eleventh centuries (Middle Assyrian Laws—MAL) and one in Hittite from the Hittite capital Hattusha in Anatolia (Hittite Laws—HL) covering a slightly earlier time span. Finally, a small excerpt of a code comes from sixth-century Babylonia (Neo-Babylonian Laws—NBL).[1] Outside the Near East we have in Greek an excerpt from the laws of Drakon, ruler of Athens in the seventh century, and a large code from Gortyn (Crete), dated to the sixth century.[2] A Roman code called the Twelve Tables is traditionally dated to the fifth century.[3] The Greek and Roman codes are usually ignored by biblical scholars, but they share the same characteristics as the Near Eastern codes; they come from the Mediterranean region not very far from Israel, and they are a lot closer in time to the biblical sources than are most of the cuneiform codes.

All of these law codes are strikingly similar in form. Their salient characteristic is the *casuistic* sentence, namely, a conditional clause stating the circumstances of a hypothetical case, followed by a clause stating the legal consequences. For example: "If a man knocks out the eye of a man, his eye shall be knocked out" (CH 196).

The content of all of the codes is everyday law as would be practiced in the courts. The similarity in content, however, runs even deeper. Many of the same cases keep recurring in different codes, not always with identical facts or with the same solution, but close enough to show that they drew upon the same situations and the same legal principles. For example, the case of an adulterer caught in the act is found in the Middle Assyrian Laws, the Hittite Laws, and the Gortyn Code, with variations in the punishment inflicted, but all with some discretion in punishment allowed to the husband. The punishment of theft by payment to the owner of a multiple of the thing stolen is found in Codex Hammurabi, the Hittite Laws, and the Twelve Tables.

If we look at the biblical laws, we find that they fit perfectly into the same pattern. They are for the most part casuistic in form and contain many cases found in a number of law codes. In the Mishpatim we find multiple payments for theft, but also many other examples, such as the case of a man who suffers non-permanent injury in a fight and is entitled to damages for his loss of work and medical costs (Exod 21:18–19), which is also found in CH 206 and HL 10. From the Deuteronomic laws, the rape of a maiden who is betrothed but not married (Deut 22:23–27) is also found in CE 26 and CH 130, while the woman who seizes a man's genitals in a fight (Deut 25:11–12) is dealt with in MAL A 8. Even some of the instances in the Priestly source have parallels: the case of the daughter who inherits where there are no sons and must marry a male relative (Num 27:1–11; 36:5–9) has a parallel in the Gortyn Code (VII 15–IX 24). We are therefore justified in seeing in the clusters of everyday law in the Torah law codes of the same type as their Near Eastern and Mediterranean counterparts, notwithstanding their intermingling with sacral laws and ethical rules or the addition of moral exhortation.

The Nature of the Codes

When first discovered, Codex Hammurabi was assumed to have been royal legislation, a codification or reform. It was subsequently noted, however, that neither it nor the other codes was ever cited in court or referred to as a source of law. A new theory was formulated, principally by Fritz Kraus[4] and Jean Bottéro,[5] that CH was an academic document, a product of the scribal school, not intended for citation in court. The cuneiform scribes of Mesopotamia tried to classify the world around them by means of lists–of flora, fauna, grammatical forms, gods, offices, precious stones. A more sophisticated form of list recorded conditions and consequences: medical symptoms and their diagnoses, omens and their meanings, actions and their legal redresses. The latter type of list was cast into the form of objective, hypothetical cases: "If a woman gives birth, and the left foot (of the child) is withered—that house will prosper."

The "laws" of CH present just such a list, albeit in another context. They are bracketed by a prologue and epilogue and inscribed on a monument. In the epilogue Hammurabi tells us himself what the foregoing list represents: "These are the just judgments that I decided. . . ." The judgments in question, however, if such they were, have been subjected to a process of editing. They have been stripped of all unnecessary details and turned into hypothetical cases that could serve as a rule for the future.

As Jacob Finkelstein demonstrates, the stone monument with its list of just judgments, set up in temples around his kingdom towards the end of his long reign, served as royal propaganda to show that Hammurabi had been a just king.[6] Some of the other law codes also had a monumental form, but still others were found in archives or scribal schools, so that we do not know for what purpose they had been created. In whatever context they are found, the codes' original composition relied on that same proto-scientific tradition, the Mesopotamian "science of lists."

In the biblical narrative, the laws of the Torah were legislation given by God and supposed to be applied in ancient Israel, although the kings of Israel and Judah were often neglectful of them. In post-biblical times, they were certainly applied in Jewish courts as normative law.

While modern scholarship questioned the historicity of the biblical account of law-giving, it did not at first doubt that in historical times, at least during the monarchy, the laws written in the Torah were the laws of the land. Scholars soon noted, however, as in the case of CH, that the laws were never mentioned in any historical context after the settlement. Citation only appears after the Babylonian exile, under Ezra the scribe. Here, then, is another characteristic shared by biblical and Mesopotamian law.

The biblical laws are located not in a law book or monument, but in a religious historical narrative set in the distant past. The natural conclusion is that those everyday laws that occur at various places in the Torah were drawn from another source before being embedded in their present context. That source was likely a law code or codes, or at least arose independently through the same process that gave rise to the other law codes.

The nature of the law codes is a vital element in determining the next question: the connection between them.

The Law Code Tradition

Assyriologists have not addressed the question of the relationship between the different law codes of Mesopotamia, except to assume that their transmission followed the path of the cuneiform script, which by the second millennium had spread from Mesopotamia, where it had been invented, across most of the Near East, with the exception of Egypt. Classicists have assumed a direct borrowing by the Romans of Greek law (as Roman legend relates), but have considered the relationship between the Greek or Roman codes and the Near Eastern codes only to the extent of expending significant energy on denying its existence. It has been left to biblicists to inquire into the connection between the law codes. On the one hand, they have focused on how the Mesopotamian format got into the biblical codes, and on the other they have examined the relationship, chronological and literary, between the biblical codes themselves. As biblical codes, they identify the Covenant Code (including the Mishpatim), the Deuteronomic Code, and the Priestly source (including a special section called the Holiness Code). In recent years, several different schools of thought have emerged. Most current scholars subscribe to one of two models: the evolutionary or the literary.

The Evolutionary Model

The main protagonists of this school today are Eckhardt Otto (in many publications from the 1980s to the present) and Bernard Jackson.[7] They rely heavily on a form-critical approach, which finds in the current form of a law evidence of its original setting. Their starting point is an influential theory developed by Albrecht Alt. Alt divided the biblical laws by form into two types: casuistic, as we have just described, and apodictic, or direct commands (e.g., "Thou shalt not kill"). He took apodictic laws to be a native Israelite product, while casuistic laws were copied from Canaanite law codes, which in turn were copied from Mesopotamian law codes. The Covenant Code (and thus the Mishpatim), being mostly casuistic but with a smattering of apodictic commands, dated from the early Israelite settlement in Canaan.[8]

Otto has modified this theory, proposing a different milieu for the two forms. Apodictic law evolved from within the family or clan, where the paterfamilias dictated rules and enforced them. Casuistic law evolved from precedents in disputes between families, which were settled by arbitration at the town gate. The two were fused together in the early monarchy to form the Covenant Code, which continued to undergo a complex process of editing as the society and its laws developed. Later in the monarchy, the Deuteronomic code was an adaptation and development of the earlier code. As for the connection with the cuneiform codes, Otto explains that they went through a parallel but separate developmental process as biblical casuistic law, from local precedents. The similarity of form derives from the fact that the Israelites adopted cuneiform drafting techniques they encountered in the Canaanite towns.

Jackson also attributes apodictic rules to a family setting, but his main distinction is between oral and written law. Following the theories of the anthropologist Jack Goody,[9] he considers that law changes entirely in character when written down. Early written texts, however, may retain features of primitive oral law—an "oral residue." The Mishpatim are early, primitive laws that retain many traces of their origins in pre-institutional dispute resolution. They are wisdom rather than binding law. The paradox of their close literary connection with the cuneiform law codes is to be explained by an oral tradition that preceded scribal formulation of these laws and had elements in common with the orally transmitted custom of the region. The Deuteronomic laws are more developed, but all biblical laws retain the character of wisdom literature until the time of Ezra, when they begin to be cited in court like modern law.

The Literary Model

Most of the protagonists of the literary model rely on the work of Meir Malul. Malul casts doubt on any connection through common legal practice. Since the law codes are a literary product, their appearance in the Bible is a result of contact through scribal practice. Malul takes as his example the laws of the goring ox, where there is a remarkable affinity between the versions found in CE, CH, and Mishpatim. Indeed, the law of an ox goring an ox in Mishpatim (Exod 21:35) is almost identical to that in CE (53). Malul therefore suggests that the biblical author or editor knew firsthand the Mesopotamian laws and that he may even have had a copy (or copies?) of them in front of him when he composed or edited his biblical version.[10]

Anne Fitzpatrick-McKinley adopts the same model of a scribal tradition, in a more extreme form. She takes up a theory of Alan Watson that relates to the spread of Roman law in much later times. Watson argues that law is structurally autonomous. It develops under its own momentum, to the point where there can be a marked divergence between the law and the needs of society or its rulers.[11] Fitzpatrick-McKinley applies this theory to the much earlier law of the Ancient Near East by means of Goody's distinction between the oral and the written. Like Jackson, she considers that with the introduction of writing in the Ancient Near East the flexibility of the oral law, allowing gradual adjustments without apparent alteration, was lost. Writing has two effects. First, it severs rules from their original context, making the text of the law multipurpose. Some oral rules were incorporated into the text, but once incorporated, they would eventually cease to reflect social practice. Second, it creates a class of specialized scribes. The law codes are the work of such scribes: they were not legislation but wisdom-moral teachings propagated by scribes. The biblical laws were based on this literary tradition, shared with Israel's neighbors, that was developed by literary elites.[12]

John Van Seters adopts the image projected by Malul of a scribe or scholar sitting in a library surrounded by texts. The writer plagiarizes those texts, or rather emulates them, writing material of his own creation that imitates the sources before him. The author of the Covenant Code borrowed material from other law codes at his disposal, which included the Deuteronomic and Priestly Codes but also the Babylonian codes, in the form of CH or its successor.[13] David Wright likewise considers that the author of the Mishpatim knew the Akkadian text of CH and drew directly from it, together with other cuneiform sources.[14]

Cutting across the question of which model applies to the biblical codes has been a furious debate over the dating of the codes. It has long been accepted that the book of Deuteronomy dates to the period of Assyrian hegemony over Israel in the seventh century. The Deuteronomic laws also have strong affinities to the Middle Assyrian Laws, both in style and in content. There is a broad consensus that the Priestly source dates to the Babylonian exile (after 587 B.C.E.) or the post-exilic period. The problem is the Covenant Code. Alt considered it to be a very old, pre-monarchic source, and although many would now place it in the monarchy, most scholars still agree that it predated Deuteronomy. This chronology has been challenged by Van Seters, who places the Covenant Code in the Babylonian Exile of the sixth century.

The issue at stake is the relationship between the Deuteronomic and Covenant Codes. Most scholars consider that the author of Deuteronomy knew the Covenant Code and introduced reforms to its long-standing provisions. Van Seters considers that it was the author of the Covenant Code who knew the Deuteronomic Code and adapted some of its laws. I have no wish to enter into this debate. There is no external evidence by which we could date the Covenant Code, and attempts to do so on the basis of its style or of the state of development of its laws are an exercise in futile speculation. My concern is rather with the mode of transmission of the laws that end up in the biblical codes.

Critique of the Current Models

Neither of the two current models furnishes an entirely satisfactory explanation of the origins of the biblical laws. The evolutionary model relies on a series of unwarranted assumptions.

(1) It assumes that the present form reflects the circumstances in which the law was created: in a family setting, in inter-clan arbitration, from a foreign source, *et cetera*. There is not a shred of evidence to support this assumption. Legislation, such as there is in the Ancient Near East, takes all sorts of forms.[15] It is true that the casuistic form is characteristic of Mesopotamian "scientific" style, but the law codes were not purely scientific documents like the omen or medical lists. They served other purposes, and some of them contain other forms when it suits them.

(2) It imagines a world for which we have no evidence and which may never have existed. The model has its roots in nineteenth-century ethnology and the equation of ancient civilizations with contemporary primitive tribes. Already the earliest codes, however, come from long-standing urban civilizations, and the law code tradition had existed for more than a millennium before the advent of the biblical codes.

(3) The weakest point of this model is that it suits a self-contained society, isolated from its neighbors, and is embarrassed by the biblical codes' close affinity with foreign law codes. Attempts to distinguish between local form and foreign content founder on the close correlation in content, while the projection of the connection back into a primitive pre-writing phase faces a chronological chasm of several thousand years between the Mesopotamian and Israelite experiences of such a phase.

At first sight, the literary model seems a simpler and more satisfying explanation. It is particularly suited to the reception of foreign sources. However, like all simple solutions, it would only work well if reality were as simple.

(1) It assumes that each biblical code had a different document to copy from: MAL for Deuteronomy and CH for the Mishpatim. MAL are not complete, so it is impossible to say whether or not they contain all the laws found in the Deuteronomic Code. CH, on the other hand, is virtually complete, so it is strange that the Mishpatim contain laws found in other cuneiform codes but not in CH.

Wright's answer is to say that almost all the laws in the Mishpatim are in fact derived from or inspired by CH, even though the relationship may not be obvious at first sight. He can only achieve this result by special pleading, forcing the laws into categories that make them a match or seizing upon the most tangential resemblances as evidence of influence. Even then, there remain a hard core of laws that resist "Hammurabification," such as the case of the ox goring an ox (Exod 21:35), which is only found in CE (53), or the burning of a neighbor's field (Exod 22:5), which is found only in HL (106).

Van Seters's answer is inconsistent. On the one hand, he wants to see CH as the Mesopotamian text the Covenant Code (Mishpatim) used, and tries to show that it was the model not only in content but also in structure and ideology, with Moses being portrayed as the Jewish Hammurabi. He speaks of a Babylonian legal tradition for the Covenant Code, whereas the earlier Deuteronomic Code came from an Assyrian source.[16] On the other hand, he refers to other literary codes at the disposal of the Covenant Code's author, and at times to the Mesopotamian legal tradition or the cuneiform legal tradition.[17] Yet again, he accounts for the existence of material in the Covenant Code that is not in CH by referring to a single text, namely CH's "literary descendant."[18]

(2) For this model, it is important to know exactly when and how the biblical authors had the opportunity to read the Mesopotamian codes.

Alt's idea of Canaanite law codes has been criticized, given the failure to discover any law code among the abundant legal material from Late Bronze Age sites in Syria and Canaan, such as Emar, Alalakh, and Ugarit. Malul assumes a cuneiform library that the Davidic monarchy inherited with the conquest of the Canaanite cities, but as has been pointed out, cuneiform died out in the region at the end of the Bronze Age. Wright therefore places both the Covenant and Deuteronomic Codes in the period of Assyrian hegemony, when there was access to Mesopotamian learning. Van Seters agrees as regards the Deuteronomic Code, but puts the author of the Covenant Code in Babylonia during the exile, where he would have come in direct contact with the local culture.

Both of the latter scholars rely on a complete cultural discontinuity in the countries of the Eastern Mediterranean between the Late Bronze Age and the Iron Age, leading to total loss of knowledge of cuneiform law. Thus each biblical author came to the text that was his model in a pristine state. In a sense, it is the same technique of encapsulation that is employed by the evolutionary school to preserve the purity of their developmental model, and it is equally misleading, as we shall see.

(3) The literary model divorces the text from any relationship with the law in force. This is of great advantage to biblical scholars, who are trained in literary criticism and not in jurisprudence. Not all literature is alike, however, and legal literature is simply not the same as scientific literature or myth or historiography. Even if it is not legislation, or not binding in any way, legal literature cannot so easily escape consciousness of the living law of the society that produced it.[19] The codes themselves occasionally make conscious reference to the creation of rules they contain: CE 58 and HL 55 both explain that the rule in question had its origin in a royal decree. The Hittite Laws go further and consciously update the text in response to changes in the practice of law: "formerly the punishment was x, now it is y."

The biblical codes likewise were the product of the law in practice and not just of other codes. A clear example is the case in Deut 21:1–9 of the corpse found murdered in a field. The law places responsibility upon the members of the local authority, who must undergo an exculpatory ceremony and take an exculpatory oath:

> If a corpse is found in the land which the LORD your God gives you to possess, lying in the open fields and it is not known who killed him: your elders and magistrates shall go out and measure the distance of the towns around

the corpse. The elders of the town nearest to the corpse shall take an un-worked heifer not yet put to the yoke. The elders of that town shall bring the heifer down into a wadi with a constant stream, in which no plowing or sowing has been done and they shall break the heifer's neck in that wadi. . . . And all the elders of that town near the corpse shall wash their hands over the heifer whose neck was broken in the wadi. And they shall say: "Our hands have not shed this blood and our eyes have not seen."

Exactly the same oath in the same situation is attested in practice in correspondence from the Canaanite city of Ugarit in the thirteenth century:[20]

And concerning the case of the woman whose husband was killed in Arzi-gana along with the son of Hutiya, about which you wrote to me. Now let the men of Arzigana swear in the town of Arruwa as follows: "We did not kill the woman's husband, brother of Abdi-Anatu in the town, nor do we know who killed him."

From the same city come international treaties regulating the liability of the local authorities for the unresolved homicide of foreign mer-chants.[21] Moreover, the principle of collective responsibility of the local community for unsolved homicides is found in HL IV and in CH 22–24.[22] There is thus an interplay between the codes and practice that continues over centuries.

The above example has equally important implications for the question of the biblical authors' access to sources. It completely destroys the argu-ment that the demise of cuneiform script at the end of the Bronze Age consigned to oblivion all the law and learning that had been written in that medium. However influenced Deuteronomy may have been by Assyr-ian culture, it did not rely on the Assyrian law code as its sole source.

New Perspectives

The perspectives the two models share may also be called into question. In this regard, it is necessary to reconsider two fundamental relationships.

(1) Biblicists have concentrated on the relationship between the biblical and cuneiform codes and between the biblical codes themselves. Neither can be understood, it seems to me, without taking into account all the

known codes, not only from the Near East but also from the Mediterranean basin.

The cuneiform codes are part of a long-standing scribal tradition, but their transmission is far from simple. Codex Hammurabi continued to be copied in Mesopotamia and perhaps elsewhere well into the Neo-Babylonian period (sixth century). The reason was not legal; it had become a classic work of literature in the scribal curriculum. The Hittite Laws and the Middle Assyrian Laws were not only copied but also developed for several centuries within those societies; MAL is also found in copies from Neo-Assyrian sources (seventh century), apparently as part of the Assyrian scribal tradition. The Sumerian codes were copied in Old Babylonian scribal schools (twentieth to sixteenth centuries), but not, apparently, in later times. CE and HL disappeared in the second millennium with the demise of their respective kingdoms, but provisions from them reappear in later times. Doubtless there were many more law codes than have survived, but such breaks in continuity make it more likely that an earlier law code was not the only medium through which laws could enter a later law code.

The Roman Twelve Tables is traditionally dated to around 450 B.C.E., in the early Republic, but only on the basis of later legends. It could be later or much earlier, from the time of the monarchy. The text exists only in fragmentary quotations from much later authors. With the discovery of CH, attempts were made to link the Twelve Tables with the Near Eastern Codes, but such efforts have met with resistance. The prevailing approach among Romanists is still to emphasize self-contained evolutionary development. This is in spite of close correlations in the law of injury, theft, and accidental homicide.

The Greek Gortyn Code is dated to the sixth century B.C.E., mostly on the basis of its language and writing, and is one of many legal inscriptions from Crete of that period. Surprisingly, Hellenists have been much more receptive to the idea of Near Eastern influence on early Greek law. The Code provides spectacular confirmation. It is headed, as are many similar Greek legal inscriptions, with a single word: Gods! Robert Pounder has traced the origins of this enigmatic heading through earlier Greek inscriptions back into the Ancient Near East, into the curses and blessings that are common at the end of inscriptions such as CH.[23]

Accordingly, our perspective needs to widen to account for the transmission of laws to these latter codes, beyond the bounds of imperial conquest.

(2) Scholars from both schools have relied on the dichotomy between orality and writing as formulated by Goody. That dichotomy is not applicable to the transmission of law.

According to Goody, oral tradition is a poor vehicle for transmitting legal texts, because of its inaccuracy over time. Biblical scholars have concluded from this that the written codes were the sole mode of transmitting theoretical statements of the law. Legal rules, however, do not need to be formulated in precisely the same language every time, unless they are the words of a statute, which, as we have seen, the law codes were not. In fact, there exists an immense body of evidence for the efficacy of oral legal tradition. It is called the Talmud. Committed to writing only in the fifth century C.E., it is a record of the "oral law"—cases and rulings transmitted orally by generations of rabbis over hundreds of years. Nor is the Talmud unique: the early Roman jurists had a similar source of law in "ancestral custom" (*mos maiorum*), despite reliance on written sources such as the Twelve Tables.

If anything, it would appear that in both these cases written sources and oral traditions reinforced each other as mnemonic devices. Rabbinic oral traditions had already been partially committed to writing before the Talmud, in the much smaller collection of the Mishnah from the second century C.E. The written Mishnah and the much larger oral traditions not included in it then continued side by side for several centuries until the latter were included in the Talmud. Moreover, although drawn from the post-biblical period, this model of intellectual coexistence between the written and the oral had deep roots in the Ancient Near East. In a letter to king Esarhaddon from the seventh century B.C.E., his chief scribe and astrologer warns the king: "If Mars, retrograding, enters Scorpius, do not neglect your guard! The king should not go outdoors on an evil day. This omen is not from the Series [i.e., the written canonical series *Enuma Anu Enlil*]; it is from the oral tradition of the masters."[24]

Notwithstanding the strong scribal tradition in the Ancient Near East, in legal matters writing remained secondary. Contracts were oral transactions and although some types were usually recorded in writing, a document was not essential to their validity and could be rejected in favor of oral testimony. Even in the recording of judgments writing played a surprisingly minor role. The *di-til-la* documents of the Neo-Sumerian period (twenty-first century B.C.E.) are official records of court cases, presumably kept in a public archive. Nevertheless, when the court needed to hear evidence of a previous judgment, it relied not on the written record but on the testimony of a court officer (*maškim*), who had to be present at every case.

Affinities

The origin of the biblical law codes is thus only part of a wider question: why do the different legal systems of the ancient Near East and (to a lesser extent) of the ancient Mediterranean region show such close connections and continuity over a period of several thousand years? Seen in this light, there are elements in both models of biblical transmission that can contribute to the answer, which is complex and multi-layered. Three levels of affinity may be discerned.

First, there is some evidence for Jackson's idea of an orally transmitted custom of the region. There appears to be a deep structure of legal institutions. A prime example is inheritance, which displays the same underlying pattern in every legal system attested: universal inheritance by the legitimate heirs with a period of joint ownership until they divide by mutual consent. It is impossible to say when this pattern originated, but archaeological evidence suggests that it may date to prehistoric times, as far back as the eighth millennium B.C.E.[25] Any hypothesis as to its transmission would be highly speculative, facing the same barriers as attempts to trace the spread of prehistoric languages. But its widespread occurrence would not have been possible without long continuity as law in practice.

Second, there is the patent affinity of form and content between the law codes. Since the earliest known examples are from Mesopotamia and are closely associated with the protoscientific traditions of cuneiform literature, it is reasonable to posit a diffusion from that area into the rest of the Near East and even the Mediterranean basin. As Van Seters rightly observes, an obvious mode of transmission would have been copying and emulation, but it cannot provide the whole explanation. It would require the creation either of a "super-code" to cram in all the information scattered over the extant codes or of a law library for every budding author of a new code. Nor would it explain how a later code could be aware of the context of the words in an earlier text, especially one translated from a foreign language.

There is, I suggest, a third, intermediate level of affinity that derives from the intellectual activity through which law codes were created. The institution of inheritance provides a starting point. Its period of joint ownership gave rise to a myriad of problems that made the topic a favorite of the law codes, perhaps because of the intellectual challenge they presented. CE, MAL, Deuteronomy, Gortyn, and the Twelve Tables all tackle different problems arising from joint ownership by co-heirs, with little overlap between them.

Codex Eshnunna

16. A loan of fungibles shall not be given to an undivided son or to a slave.

Middle Assyrian Laws

B2. If one of undivided brothers kills a person, they shall give him to the person's avenger. If he chooses, the avenger may kill him, or if he chooses he may accept composition and take his inheritance-share.

B3. If one of undivided brothers utters treason or is a fugitive, the king may do as he pleases in respect of his inheritance-share.

Deuteronomy

25:5. If brothers dwell together and one of them dies and he has no son, the deceased's wife shall not marry outside to a stranger. Her brother-in-law shall come in unto her and take her as his wife and perform the levirate. The first-born that she shall bear will rise up upon the name of his deceased brother and his name will not be erased from Israel.

Gaius—Institutes (Roman)

III 154a–b. But there is another kind of partnership special to Roman citizens. For at one time, when a father died, between his legitimate heirs there was a certain partnership at the same time of positive and natural law, which was called *ercto non cito,* meaning undivided ownership. . . . Now in this kind of partnership there was this peculiarity, that even one of its members by freeing a slave held in common made him free . . . and also one member by selling a thing held in common made it the property of the person receiving it.

Justinian's Digest (Roman)

10.2. THE ACTION FOR DIVIDING AN INHERITANCE (*familia*)

1. (Gaius, Provincial Edict, book 7): This action is derived from the Law of the Twelve Tables; for when co-heirs wished to dissolve their common ownership it seemed necessary to establish some action by which the inherited property could be distributed among them.

Gortyn Code
V 28–34. If some of the heirs wish to divide the inheritance while others do not, the judge shall order that all the property shall be in the possession of those who wish to divide until they divide.

Furthermore, these provisions were not just an intellectual game: as testaments from Emar and Egypt attest, testators tried to create ingenious solutions to some of the difficulties arising from joint ownership and management:

TBR 71 (Emar on the Euphrates, fourteenth century)
Dagan-bel, son of Itur-Dagan spoke as follows: I have made my wife Ba'alat-ummi father and mother over my house. I have given my house and all my property to my wife Ba'alat-ummi. I have five sons: Ilanu, Baba, Amzahi, Himashi-Dagan, and Ibni-Dagan. My five sons shall honor [= support] Ba'alat-ummi, their mother and father. If they honor her, they may divide my house and all my property after her death. If any of my five sons, while Ba'alat-ummi their mother is still alive, says: "(I claim) my share," he shall have no rights in my house and property. He shall place his garment on a stool and go where he pleases. . . .

Lawsuit of Mose (Egypt, thirteenth century)
Testimony of Ramesses-Meiamun: I was the child of Huy, son of Urnero, daughter of Neshi. A share was allocated for Urnero together with her brothers and sisters in the great court in the time of king Haremhab. . . . Allocation was made for me together with my brothers and sisters. My mother, the citizeness Urnero, was made administrator (of the undivided estate) for her brothers and sisters. . . .

Here then is a case where many law codes were focused on the same legal institution, were applying the same intellectual effort to analogous problems (in tandem with devices being applied in practice), but were not dependent on each other.

A second point of reference is the Talmud. Much of its discussion focuses on specific legal problems, derived either from a law in the Torah or from an actual case or possibly a fictitious case created for the sake of argument. The method is to ask, what if? What if we change the facts slightly —do we reach the same result, or should we change the legal consequence, on the basis of reasoning by analogy or because the new circumstances bring into play another rule? It is a method of reasoning that is universally used in legal education to this very day. Looking backwards, it is also the method that lies behind the ancient law codes. For example, CH has the following sequence:

229. If a builder builds a house for a man and does not make his work strong and the house that he built collapses and causes the death of the householder, the builder shall be killed.

230. If it causes the death of the householder's son, they shall kill the builder's son.

231. If it causes the death of the householder's slave, he shall give slave for slave to the householder.

The sequence man, son, slave (or analogous degrees of status) frequently recurs in the law codes, giving the impression that it was a regular device used to expand the discussion of a case in a scholarly manner. I suggest that among the sources that made up a law code, alongside material taken directly from other law codes or directly from actual cases were scholarly problems that were familiar objects of discussion. Since a law code cannot include all aspects of the discussion, different excerpts of the same problem would appear in different codes, with perhaps a different emphasis or with an extension of the discussion in a different direction. Consider the problem of the rape or seduction of a girl who is betrothed but not married, as discussed in the following law codes:

Deuteronomy 22

23–24. If there is a maiden betrothed to a husband and a man finds her in town and lies with her, you shall take them both out to the gate of that town and stone them to death—the girl because she did not cry out in town and the man because he forced his neighbor's wife, and you shall purge the evil from your midst.

25–27. And if the man finds the betrothed girl in the country and seizes her and lies with her, the man who lay with her shall die and only he. To the girl you shall do nothing, she has no sin meriting death . . . for he found her in the country—the betrothed girl cried out but there was none to save her.

28–29. If a man finds a girl, a virgin who is not betrothed, and seizes her and lies with her and they are found, the man who lay with her shall give fifty of silver to the girl's father and she shall be his wife. Because he forced her, he may not divorce her all his days.

Codex Eshnunna

26. If a man brings the betrothal payment for a man's daughter but another seizes her and deflowers her without asking her father and mother, it is a case of life: he shall die.

Codex Hammurabi

130. If a man binds and lies in the lap of the wife of a man who has not known a man and is (still) dwelling in her father's house and they seize him, that man shall be killed; that woman shall be freed.

Codex Ur-Namma

6. If a man uses force with the virgin wife of a man and rapes her, he shall kill that man.

Exodus 22

15–16. If a man seduces a virgin who is not betrothed and lies with her, he shall make her his wife with a betrothal payment. If her father refuses to give her to him, he shall pay silver like the betrothal payment of virgins.

Middle Assyrian Laws

A 55. If a man seizes with force and rapes a virgin, a man's daughter who is living in her father's house . . . whose . . . has not been opened, who is not married and there is no claim against her father's house—whether in the city or in the country or at night or in the square or in a granary or at a town festival—the virgin's father shall take the wife of the man who had intercourse with his daughter and give her to be raped. He shall not return her to her husband; he shall take her. The father shall give his deflowered daughter in marriage to the man who slept with her. If he has no wife, the man who lay with her shall pay her father three times(?) the silver of the value of a virgin and he shall marry her. He shall not . . . her. If the father does not wish, he shall receive the silver, three-fold(?) that of a virgin, and give his daughter to whomever he wishes.

56. If the virgin gave herself to the man, the man shall swear and his wife shall not be touched. He shall give three times(?) the silver of the value of a virgin. The father shall deal with his daughter as he chooses.

Hittite Laws

197. If a man seizes a woman in the hills, it is the man's sin: he shall die. If he seizes her in a house, it is the woman's sin: she shall die. If the husband finds them and kills them, there is no liability upon him.

Deut 22:23–27 extends the discussion to include the rape of an unbetrothed girl. CE 26 and CH 130 discuss only the rape of a betrothed girl, while Mishpatim (Ex. 22:15–16) consider only the seduction of an unbetrothed girl. MAL A 55 considers both rape and seduction, but only of an unbetrothed girl, and has a curious discussion of the site of the offense, the purpose of which is apparently to show that it is of no legal consequence. The rationale becomes clear from the Deuteronomic law, which contains an evidentiary test of the betrothed girl's complicity based on whether the offense took place in the town or in the country. That same test is found in HL 197, but in a very terse form with regard to the adultery of a married woman. Rather than assume that Deuteronomy had access to yet another law code that happened to spell out the distinction more explicitly, it is reasonable to suppose that Deuteronomy, MAL, and HL all were aware of the whole scholarly problem and were content to allude to it in their written versions.

Consequently, there existed behind the text of the law codes a penumbra of legal discussion to which the authors of the codes had access. This "oral law" (better regarded as a canon of traditional scholarly problems) informed the written text of codes but also existed as an independent source of law, or rather of wisdom about law.

Conclusions

The genre of text we call the law codes drew in varying measure upon three resources: an oral scholarly tradition, a written scribal tradition, and an inter-reaction with the law in practice. The first two stretched for thousands of years across the Near East and the Mediterranean, with no respect for borders or rulers.

The two clusters of everyday law in the Torah that we call law codes should be seen in this light. They are now embedded in a literary-historical account set during Israel's wanderings in the desert before the settlement of the promised land. They appear to have originated, however, in an intellectual tradition that biblical Israel shared with its neighbors to the east and west alike and that can be traced back more a thousand years earlier.

Scholars may continue to debate the date of the literary sources in which these biblical codes are embedded. But given the complex interaction of legal traditions behind law codes in general, it would be rash indeed to "date" the origins of the biblical codes, whether by suggesting that their contents could only have developed when certain social conditions prevailed within Israelite society or that they could only have been acquired when certain foreign texts became available.

NOTES

1. All the cuneiform codes are translated in Martha Roth, *Law Collections from Mesopotamia and Asia Minor* (Writings from the Ancient World 6; Atlanta, Ga.: Scholars Press, 1995), but there is a more recent translation of the Hittite Laws by Harry A. Hoffner, *The Laws of the Hittites: A Critical Edition* (Leiden: Brill, 1997).

2. Drakon's law is translated by Ronald S. Stroud, *Drakon's Law on Homicide* (Berkeley: University of California Press, 1979), and the Gortyn Code by Ronald F. Willetts, *The Law Code of Gortyn* (Berlin: De Gruyter, 1967).

3. Translated in Michael H. Crawford, ed., *Roman Statutes* (Bulletin of the Institute of Classical Studies 64; London: Institute of Classical Studies, 1996), vol. II, pp. 555–72.

4. Fritz R. Kraus, "Ein zentrales Problem des altmesopotamischen Rechtes: Was ist der Codex Hammu-rabi?" *Genava* n.s. 8 (1960): 283–96.

5. Jean Bottéro, "The 'Code' of Hammurabi," in *Mesopotamia: Writing, Reasoning and the Gods* (Paris, 1987; Chicago: University of Chicago Press, 1992), 156–84.

6. Jacob J. Finkelstein, "Ammisaduqa's Edict and the Babylonian 'Law Codes,'" *Journal of Cuneiform Studies* 15 (1961): 103.

7. E.g., Bernard S. Jackson, *Studies in the Semiotics of Biblical Law* (JSOTSupp 314; Sheffield: Sheffield Academic Press, 2000).

8. Albrecht Alt, "The Origins of Israelite Law," in *Essays in Old Testament History and Religion* (Garden City, N.Y.: Doubleday, 1966), 79–132. Translation of *Die Ursprünge des israelitischen Rechts* (Leipzig, 1934) = *Kleine Schriften zur Geschichte des Volkes Israel*, vol. 1 (Munich, 1959), 278–332.

9. E.g., Jack Goody, *The Logic of Writing and the Organization of Society* (Cambridge: Cambridge University Press, 1986).

10. Meir Malul, *The Comparative Method in Ancient Near Eastern and Biblical Legal Studies* (AOAT 227; Kevelaer: Butzon & Bercker, 1990).

11. Alan Watson, *The Evolution of Law* (Oxford: Blackwell, 1985).

12. Anne Fitzpatrick-McKinley, *The Transformation of Torah from Scribal Advice to Law* (JSOTSupp. 287; Sheffield: Sheffield Academic Press, 1999).

13. John Van Seters, *A Law Book for the Diaspora* (Oxford: Oxford University Press, 2003).

14. David P. Wright, "The Laws of Hammurabi as a Source for the Covenant Collection (Exodus 20:23–23:19)," *Maarav* 10 (2003): 11–87.

15. A decree of the Babylonian king Ammi-Saduqa (from the dynasty of Hammurabi), for example, contains a mix of different styles:
§1. The arrears of feudal tenants, shepherds, knackers, seasonal herders and palace fee-payers—in order to give them support and deal equitably with them—are released. The debt-collector shall not dun the family of a fee-payer.
§17. A taverness who has lent beer or barley shall not collect what she lent.
§20. If a free man of Numhia, etc. has been bound by a debt and has sold or pledged himself, his wife, or his children; because the king has established equity for the land, he is released, his freedom is established.

16. John Van Seters, *Law Book for the Diaspora* (Oxford: Oxford University Press, 2003), 43–45, 56–57.

17. John Van Seters, *Law Book for the Diaspora*, 123–24

18. John Van Seters, *Law Book for the Diaspora*, 98.

19. The fact that later legal systems sometimes develop rules in disregard of social reality (Fitzpatrick-McKinley, following Watson) is irrelevant. In later systems such as Roman law those rules still had normative force; they impacted society even if they were anachronistic or unrealistic.

20. RS 20.22. Edited in Ugaritica V 94–97.

21. RS 17.146 & 18.115. Edited in Palais Royal d'Ugarit (PRU) IV 154–60.

22. HL IV: If a man is (found) killed in another's field, if he is a free man, he (the owner) shall give field, house and 60 shekels of silver. . . . If it is not a field but uncultivated land, (they shall measure) 3 danna hither and 3 danna thither, and whichever town is reckoned within, he shall take those very persons. . . .

CH 22–24: 22-24. If a man commits robbery and is caught, that man shall be killed. If the robber is not caught, the person robbed shall declare his losses before the god and the city and mayor in whose district the robbery was committed shall compensate him for his lost property. If it is life (i.e., murder), the city and mayor shall pay his family one mina of silver.

23. Robert Pounder, "The Origin of θεοι as Inscription-Heading," in *Studies Presented to Sterling Dow on His Eightieth Birthday*, ed. A. Boegehold et al. (Durham, N.C.: Duke University Press, 1984), 243–50.

24. SAA X 8:24–r.2.

25. Norman Yoffee, "Aspects of Mesopotamian Land Sales," *American Anthropologist* 90 (1988): 119–30.

Chapter 6

The Study of Ritual in the Hebrew Bible

David P. Wright

The past forty years have seen significant developments in the study of ritual in the Bible. Several factors are responsible for this. First of all, anthropologists, sociologists, scholars of religion, and even philosophers have expanded the methods and perspectives with which we approach the topic. The development of interdisciplinary ritual studies has naturally led biblical as well as nonbiblical scholars to bring insights from this general field to bear on biblical data. A second factor is the comparative literary evidence that has come to light over the last century and a half from the ancient Near East, including Hittite, Ugaritic, Sumerian, and Akkadian ritual texts. Third, the growth of biblical studies itself has led to increasing specialization, with several scholars devoting much of their careers to questions of ritual. And fourth, there has been continued questioning about the development of the Torah and especially its priestly source, which contains more information about ritual matters than any other single corpus in the Bible. Understanding this literature has thrown light on the development of both the Torah and the religious history of ancient Israel.

Ritual

As the particulars of the study of biblical ritual have advanced, so has the definition of ritual among non-biblical scholars. Earlier definitions, which still hold some sway, tried to provide a list of criteria for identifying an act as ritual. For example, the anthropologist Victor Turner defined ritual as "prescribed formal behavior for occasions not given over to technological routine, having reference to beliefs in mystical beings or power."[1] Other definitions have focused on the function of ritual behavior, specifically as a mode of communication in the spirit of Edmund Leach's pithy summary statement: "We engage in rituals in order to transmit collective messages to ourselves."[2]

Sally Moore and Barbara Myerhoff combined the elements of form and function in their discussion of ritual.[3] The basic formal properties include: repetition, acting (which involves doing and not just thinking or speaking), special behavior or stylization, order, evocative presentation style or staging, and a collective or social dimension. Ritual is thereby a "traditionalizing instrument" that makes what is expressed acceptable and common by hiding the novelty and even the radical nature of new ideas, while allowing people from diverse social groups to participate together and feel commonality and solidarity. In addition to any direct teaching it may include, ritual communicates latently about morality, authority, the legitimacy of the social order, and the nature of social reality. And at the same time that it reflects these social aspects, it also transforms society by its performance.

One of the strengths of these definitions is their avoidance of a strict dichotomy between ritual and non-ritual activity.[4] As Robert Wuthnow noted, "Ritual is not a type of social activity that can be set off from the rest of the world for special investigation. It is a dimension of all social activity."[5]

The problem for these definitions, all of which involve expressiveness, is that ritual does not really function like a language. True, it often involves symbols (objects and actions), but it does not consist solely of these. Moreover, what ritual does communicate is often described as happening latently or implicitly, to the point that only analysts, and not the performers, are consciously able to recognize the message. Frits Staal has cast this problem in the starkest terms by arguing that in some cases ritual does not mean anything to those who perform it.[6] Another way of looking at this is that ritual apparently works despite the fact that participants may hold different views about its meaning; what it does lies beyond or below the symbolism that is attached to it. The recognition of symbols in a rite and the determination of their meaning is something that occurs as part of secondary reflection outside the ritual context. This does not mean that ritual has no expressive capability; rather, it suggests that meaning may not be its primary defining feature.

Catherine Bell objects to defining ritual as expressive behavior on philosophical grounds. She warns that distinguishing ritual action, which is supposedly expressive or symbolic, over against non-ritual action, which is supposedly instrumental or practical, can turn into a contrast between irrationality and rationality or between emotion and logic.[7] Moreover, viewing ritual as expressive presupposes that ritual's content or meaning can be separated from the action itself, a dichotomy she rejects. For Bell, ritual does not symbolize, communicate, or reflect as much as create relationships between the individuals involved.[8] As such, ritual is not separate from other behavior, but an extension of it.

How rituals are distinguishable from other activities can be seen by comparing mundane and ritualized versions of the same basic phenomenon. Meals provide a good example.[9] Ritualized meals can be recognized as such by their happening less frequently or more frequently than regular meals, by the involvement of participants who do not normally participate in regular meals (e.g., priests, the community), or by formal seating arrangements, unusual amounts of food (too little or too much), unusual clothing, special preparations, or connection with other ritualized activities (e.g., prayers and sacrifice).

Because all activities lie on a continuum from those that contain little or no ritualization to those that are highly ritualized, they cannot be understood without reference to the related activities on that continuum. For example, to understand the highly ritualized activity of sacrifice, one must look at the larger context of both gift-giving and meals in the culture in which the sacrifice takes place.

The Priestly Torah versus the Holiness School

As we turn to the particulars, it is natural to focus on the extensive priestly writings of the Torah, where ritual matters are densely attested. Modern scholarship has long recognized that the Torah is composed of various sources or traditions that developed after the time of Moses, roughly in the middle centuries of the first millennium B.C.E.

While there is dispute about their absolute and relative chronology, their exact content, and how they came to be joined and edited together, most scholars recognize the existence of four basic bodies of literature, which have come to be designated as J (Jahwist = Yahwist), E (Elohist), P (Priestly), and D (Deuteronomic). The D material is mainly the book of Deuteronomy. P includes the entire book of Leviticus, the chapters in Exodus and Numbers about the wilderness sanctuary and its institutions, plus several chapters in Genesis. The J and E sources (which some scholars group together under the rubric JE because of the difficulty of sorting them out) cover the remaining material in Genesis, Exodus, and Numbers. Each of these sources contains information about ritual activities, though P is the one most concerned about these matters, with chapter after chapter of laws on sanctuary-building, sacrifice, priesthood, purity, and so forth. The D material stands second in the amount of information it contains about ritual.

These sources reflect religious customs and perspectives that differ significantly from each other. For example, D allows slaughter of animals outside a temple context and not as a sacrifice (Deuteronomy 12) while P requires all animal slaughter to be performed as a sacrifice at the sanctuary (Leviticus 17). D allows the worshipper to use and benefit from the tithe (Deut 14:22–29) while P has it given as a donation to the priests (Numbers 18). JE places the wilderness sanctuary outside the camp (Exodus 33) while P places it at the center of a symmetrically arranged camp (Numbers 2). Identifying and explaining these differences are the beginnings of a historian's work in reconstructing biblical and Israelite religion.

Scholarship becomes more speculative when it attempts to identify subdivisions within these basic sources. Nonetheless, there are strong indications that these main sources or traditions, especially P and D, are not simple unities. One subdivision, the understanding of which has been clarified in recent decades, is in the priestly writings. Scholars have long recognized that Leviticus 17–26 stand out from the rest of the priestly writings in their general idiom and in their concern for holiness. Because of this concern, these chapters are designated the Holiness Code. Until recently it had been thought that the Holiness Code predated the codification of the rest of the priestly writings, which took up, edited, and incorporated the Holiness Code into P. In the mid-1980s, Israel Knohl argued that the Holiness Code is actually later than the larger priestly writings, which it in part supplements.[10] He also showed that material related to the Holiness Code is found in other places hitherto ascribed to the priestly writings, including significant parts of Numbers and a few parts of Exodus. As an expansion of the priestly writings, the Holiness Code tended to "democratize" ritual perspectives. For example, it was particularly interested in defining the people's holiness, especially as a reflection of divine holiness (cf. Lev 19:2; 20:26). This went beyond the priestly writings, whose interest was more limited to priestly holiness (compare Leviticus 8). While the exact scope and the conceptual relationship of these components can be disputed (for example, Baruch Schwartz differs with Knohl and Jacob Milgrom in seeing the Holiness Code material as complementary to the priestly Torah rather than at ideological odds with it),[11] the conclusions of these scholars are the starting place for future discussion.

The chronological relationship of the various sources is disputed. Most see JE as the earliest. Scholars such as Jacob Milgrom, Israel Knohl, and Baruch Schwartz see the priestly Torah and Holiness Code as earlier than D. Most scholars, however, see them as later than D. Deuteronomy provides the fixed point for dating for the majority of scholars. Its laws appear to be the law book found during the time of Josiah (c. 620 B.C.E.; 2 Kings 22), and they reflect his religious reforms (2 Kings 23). JE is therefore earlier than the time of Josiah by one or two centuries, and the Priestly Torah and Holiness Code are later, by a few decades or more.

Sacrifice

Sacrifice stands out as a point of primary concern throughout the priestly corpus. For understanding the priestly system of thought, Jacob Milgrom's work has been foundational.[12] He has focused on the sacrifices that are essentially unique to the priestly writings (and to associated or dependent literature, like Ezekiel and Chronicles) and which are offered to rectify wrongs: the "purgation/purification offering" (ḥaṭṭā't, translated by some as "sin offering") and the "reparation offering" ('āšām, sometimes translated as "guilt/trespass offering"). These stand over against other sacrifices that are brought for positive circumstances, such as the fulfillment of vows and giving a freewill offering, which include the burnt offering ('ōlâ; in some instance this can be brought to atone for sins; cf. Lev 1:4), the "well-being offering" (zebaḥ šelamîm), and its subtype, the "thanksgiving offering" (tôdâ).[13] Another implicit positive motivation is to ensure future blessing; this would be found particularly in offerings made at the annual agricultural festivals (cf. Numbers 28–29).

Most theories of sacrifice focus on the killing of the animal as the primary act. One such theory sees the animal as a substitute for the person offering it.[14] There are two main versions of this theory. One is that sin or guilt is transferred to the animal, which is then killed as a punishment. According to this perspective, the animal's identity remains distinct from that of the person offering it. The other version looks at the animal as representing the person who offers it, becoming symbolically or mystically equivalent to the offerer.

A primary evidence for the first of these substitution theories is the gesture of placing the hand on the head of a sacrificial animal before it is slaughtered (e.g., Lev 1:4; 3:2, 8, 13; 4:4, 24, 29, 33). This has been interpreted as transferring sin to the animal, much as Leviticus 16:21 describes hand placement as a means for transferring sins to the head of the scapegoat. But the scapegoat is not a sacrifice: it is not killed, but simply driven into the wilderness, to the demon Azazel which is imagined to live there. Moreover, its ritual is performed with two hands, whereas sacrifice proper uses only one hand. Furthermore, the one-handed gesture is also used for the well-being offering (*zebah šelamîm;* Lev 3:2, 8, 13), which is brought for positive occasions (thanksgiving, praise, requesting blessing) where it has nothing to do with sin. The one-handed gesture is more likely a way of showing that the animal *belongs* to the offerer, signifying that "this is mine" rather than "this is me," especially since other personnel (priests and their assistants) are involved thereafter in making the offering. Indeed, a similar gesture was used by the Hittites, who lived in ancient Turkey from about 1600 to 1200 B.C.E. In that practice, an individual held his or her hand at a slight distance over an animal or prepared foods before other officiants presented the offering to the gods.[15] The purpose of this gesture was to symbolize who was actually providing the offering.

In a classic study, Henri Hubert and Marcel Mauss argued that sacrifice connects the profane and sacred spheres.[16] This is true to some extent. As we will see, sacrifice is a means of communicating with a god, a gift that lubricates the wheels of divine-human interaction. It also allows the offerer to stand in the divine presence (cf. Exod 23:17; 34:23; Deut 16:16). On the human level, sacrifice brings people together to define their relationship to each other. But *killing* the animal is not what creates that link. The Bible does not even require that the offerer or the priest kill the animal; that could be done by others who are physically able and expert. Ezekiel 44:11 specifically says that the Levites, not the lay offerers, kill the animals (cf. 40:38–43). Therefore the act of slaughtering cannot be seen as achieving this supposed goal for the offerer personally. Nor does the Bible prescribe the method of killing. That the animal's neck blood vessels were cut can only be deduced from the requirements that its blood be gathered (in bowls) for the rites that follow. The text thus seems uninterested in slaughter itself as a means of establishing communion with God.

Another type of substitution theory is René Girard's idea that sacrifice is a representation of original human-against-human violence.[17] Animal sacrifice reduced and controlled this society-damaging aggression. Thus rather than being a proxy for the offerer, the animal victim is a surrogate for the person against whom the sacrificer's anger may be directed.

The story of Isaac's near sacrifice in Genesis 22 can support Girard's theory, since it seems to encapsulate the idea that original animal sacrifice evolved from human sacrifice, with God providing a ram instead of requiring the butchery of Abraham's son. Other passages also look on human sacrifice negatively.[18] In contrast, Leviticus 27:29 views killing humans in dedication to Israel's God more positively, listing it among other legitimate dedications, such as vows, firstborn animals, and tithes. This law requires the death of a "proscribed" human (one under *ḥerem*), likely someone who is to be destroyed in war (cf. Deut 20:15–18; 1 Sam 15:7–9, 13–33, esp. vv. 18, 33). That person cannot be redeemed nor can a substitute take her or his place. Putting humans under proscription in war may be said to reflect a middle stage in Girard's theory, a stage in which the ritualized killing of humans was still allowed.

However, it is doubtful that we can draw an evolutionary line from human sacrifice (or "ritual killing") to animal sacrifice. The biblical evidence speaks primarily of child sacrifice, not adult human sacrifice. It seems better to conceive of child sacrifice as having developed out of animal sacrifice. One shows extreme devotion by offering what is closest or most prized (note especially Judges 11:30–40 and 2 Kings 3:22–27 in addition to Genesis 22). Hence the practice evolved in the opposite direction from that which Girard proposed. Furthermore, the method of killing humans in war is not the same as sacrifice. Even the ritualized killing of Agag, whom Samuel "hacked up (*šisēp*) before YHWH" in Gilgal (1 Sam 15:33) is quite distinct from sacrifice. Finally, for sacrifice to quell violent tendencies, the act of killing would have to be performed in a way that releases emotions, but the Bible gives no indication that slaughtering involved rage or frenzy.

Ithamar Gruenwald has recently proposed that sacrifice is a symbolic enactment of a crisis.[19] His theory rests primarily on the relationship between the story of the death of Aaron's sons for bringing illicit coals or incense (Leviticus 10) and the consequent Day of Atonement sacrifices (Leviticus 16; note the connection to chapter 10 in 16:1). Gruenwald sees the purification offerings of the Day of Atonement (16:6–20) as a reaction to the priests' sin. His theory is similar to other substitution theories in his belief that sacrifice replaced injurious calamity with symbolic and controlled killing. But it is unique in that the animal's killing takes the place of an expected misfortune rather than of the offerer. The rest of the ritual procedure—distributing the sacrificial pieces and eating the sacrifice—is part of a process of restoration to wholeness and vitality.

Though his theoretical analysis is insightful, Gruenwald's specific interpretation of sacrifice is ultimately difficult. Leviticus 16 describes slaughtering animals only in passing (cf. 16:11, 15, 24), as is the case elsewhere in the priestly corpus (and throughout the Bible, for that matter). If this were the controlled enactment of a catastrophe, one would expect it to receive elaborate attention. The brief mention of slaughter here and in the rest of the Bible makes it appear to be a secondary and subordinate act, and instead presents the blood rites as the focus of the purification offerings (vv. 11–20). Their purpose is to purify the sanctuary areas and furniture where the blood is sprinkled or placed from sins and impurity (vv. 16, 19, 20). Furthermore, the logic of how the blood of an animal, which is perceived as an object of punishment, can also be used to remove impurity in the holy sanctuary and to provide God with pleasing fat pieces (16:25; cf. 4:31) is not clear. This objection also applies to the other substitution theories.

Another interpretation that focuses on killing is Walter Burkert's view that sacrifice is a ritual reenactment of the hunt.[20] As human economy and subsistence moved from hunting and gathering to raising domestic animals and settled agriculture, the practice of sacrifice preserved a memory of the earlier or alternate mode of existence. This interpretation is not purely historical. Societies subsisting mainly on domesticated animals continue to engage in hunting. Hence sacrifice can be seen as a ritual performance of that alternate way of killing animals.

Jonathan Z. Smith would change the focus. In his view, sacrifice is "the artificial (i.e., ritualized) killing of an artificial (i.e., domesticated) animal."[21] Thus, he says, "The starting point for a theory of sacrifice, that which looms largest in a redescription of sacrifice, ought no longer to be the verb 'to kill,' or the noun 'animal,' but the adjective 'domesticated.'"[22]

Deuteronomy and P's rules about hunting may seem to confirm these theories, particularly Burkert's. Because Deuteronomy limited cultic worship to a single centralized sanctuary, it allowed non-religious slaughter of animals whenever one was hungry for meat (Deut 12:15–16, 20–25). The blood of these animals was to be treated like the blood of hunted animals by being poured onto the ground. P addresses the treatment of the blood of hunted animals in the larger context of its requirement that all domestic animals that can be sacrificed (i.e., those that are pure and unblemished) be offered as sacrifice and their blood placed on the altar (Leviticus 17). The blood of game animals is also to be treated with respect; however, since these cannot be offered as sacrifice, their blood is simply to be poured out and covered with dirt (17:13), thereby exonerating hunters from blood guilt for having killed the animal (cf. v. 4 and vv. 11–14).[23]

These explanations view sacrifice as a modification of hunting, but in fact sacrifice is a radically different phenomenon. Hunting is not undertaken with any special deference to a god, but simply to obtain meat for the human diet, whereas sacrifice seeks to engage a supernatural force for one's benefit. Sacrificial animals are slaughtered primarily to provide a meal for the god, not for humans. Lay people receive flesh from only one type of sacrifice, the well-being offering (cf. Leviticus 3, 7), as a special dispensation. The flesh of purification and guilt offerings goes only to priests (Leviticus 4–5; 6:17–23). No human eats any of the burnt offering (Leviticus 1; 6:2–6). This restricted distribution of meat makes no sense if sacrifice is a way for humans to obtain food from domestic animals.

Theories that focus on killing as primary seem misguided. The main problem is that this approach cannot explain the multiple types of offerings, the disposition of animal parts on the altar, the various uses of blood, and especially the non-animal sacrifices (i.e., cereal/grain offerings and wine libations), all of which are included in biblical descriptions of sacrifice. Nor does a theory that focuses on killing fit with the larger ancient Near Eastern context, where killing seems relatively unimportant and is often not even mentioned.

Theories that focus on the act of presentation rather than on the death of a victim are more helpful. These see the presentation of offerings as a metaphorical act based upon the presentation of gifts, food gifts in particular, to human superiors. In this approach, the animal, the grain offerings brought in place of animals, and other accompaniments are given to the deity in order to elicit a positive response.

Theological constructs often arise out of metaphorical and specifically "anthropo-metaphorical" contexts. For example, the descriptions of God as redeemer, savior, father, and king all stem from human institutions— the economy, the military, the family, and the monarchy. Moreover, as analysts such as S. Tambiah have shown, metaphor—or analogy, as I prefer to call it—though certainly not unique to ritual, is one of its basic components.[24]

Hittite rituals include instructive examples of explicit verbal analogy that clarify the goal of a particular rite. For example, a ritual performed in the fourteenth century B.C.E., which seeks to relieve or purify the king and queen from the effects of palace intrigue, sickness, and other misfortunes, includes the following analogical incantation:

> As a door turns on its socket, so may evil day, short year, the anger of the gods, and the tongue of the many turn back from their course.[25]

This refers to an unrelated phenomenon (the door turning) in order to describe the result that is sought in the ritual context (turning back the gods' anger). Such analogies may be to events from everyday life, as in the example above, or to ritual actions, like burning a wax figurine.

Analogies such as these illustrate a hoped-for wish and make it concrete. The incantation, or any accompanying rite, does not mechanically achieve the goal, although the performer may think and expect this. Analogy's primary function is to make the situation tangible and manageable by defining indescribable suffering or blessing. It is broadly similar to the way science and technology use metaphor, speaking of "wave" theories and computer "viruses" in order to describe something unknown or newly discovered in terms of something already known. Analogy makes it possible to conceive of, discuss, and develop hitherto unexpressed ideas. Analogy's power to advance conceptualization is one of the reasons rituals are performed. They give participants some control—at least psychological control—over something that is threatening or elusive. This alone may be sufficient reason to perform a rite, even if the desired outcome does not have a history or likelihood of being fulfilled.

Analogy is found in abbreviated forms as simile or metaphor. A Ugaritic ritual for impotence is an example of simile:

> You (the debilitating evil) shall depart at the voice of
> the *t'y*-priest like smoke through a hatch hole, like a
> snake from a wall, like mountain goats to the summit, like
> lions to the lair.[26]

The analogical phenomenon here is not a complete sentence with subject and predicate, but simply a prepositional phrase of comparison.

An example of metaphor is found in the Akkadian *utukki lemnūti* ritual. One incantation that seeks to remove demonic sickness says:

> May he (the ritual patient) not be confined! May his bond be loosed![27]

Each of these statements contains a metaphorical description of the goal ("not be confined"; "bond be loosed"). For analytical purposes, we may expand these to full analogies:

Just as a person is not confined in prison, so may the patient be free of demonic trouble. Just as a person is loosed from bonds, so may the patient be freed from demonic trouble.

Biblical sacrifice involves an implied analogy, which may be expressed in full form as follows:

Just as a human lord is honored, praised, entreated, or appeased through feasts and food gifts, so the divine Lord is honored, praised, entreated, or appeased through feasts and food gifts in sacrifice.

Near Eastern custom supports this interpretation of biblical offerings as meals. A. L. Oppenheim summarized the offering practices in the southern Mesopotamian city of Uruk just after the time of Alexander the Great.[28] Though late, this custom reflects in general the nature of the practice for earlier eras. There, the gods' images were served two meals each day. Offerings of liquid and semi-liquid foods, the main dish of meats, and also fruits were placed on a table before the images. The food was then given to the king to eat (which shows that there was no notion that the gods physically consumed the food, contrary, for example, to the polemic of the tale of Bel and the Dragon found as a supplement [often as chapter 14] to the book of Daniel in the Apocrypha). In a more recent study, W. G. Lambert deliberately avoids calling Mesopotamian offerings "sacrifices," since the texts describing this practice do not focus on killing the animal.[29] The emphasis is on the foods—meat, breads, drinks, and so forth—presented to the gods as a meal.

The Hittite "Instructions for Temple Officials" also makes it clear that offerings were considered the gods' food.[30] The beginning of the text compares the offerings made to the gods to meals given human masters:

Are the minds of men and of the gods generally different? No! With regard to the matter with which we are dealing? No! Their minds are exactly alike. When a servant is to stand before his master, he is bathed and clothed in clean garments; he either gives him his food, or he gives him his beverage. And because he, his master, eats and drinks, he is relaxed in spirit and feels one with him.[31]

Note that the analogy is expanded to include reference to the proper grooming of one waiting on a master. This helps explain the rationale for the purity rules in P (Leviticus 11–15; Numbers 19) and other biblical texts. They are part of the larger metaphor of waiting on God in His "palace" (the sanctuary). Before entering the divine complex, one has to be cleansed of ritual dirt that is incompatible with the divine king. Biblical impurities in particular derive from phenomena not associated with and presumably incompatible with the character of God: sexual emissions, death (of humans and certain animals), and visible "surface" disease (i.e., *ṣāraʿat*, which refers to various human skin diseases, including psoriasis, though not to leprosy = Hansen's Disease; the Hebrew term also refers to certain fungal growth in fabrics and on walls). The Hittite text also sheds light on why officiating priests and offering animals must be unblemished (Lev 21:16–23; 22:17–25).

The first chapter of Malachi, an anonymous prophetic work, perhaps dating to the mid-fifth century B.C.E., makes this analogy explicit. The full context is worth citing, since it develops the notion that sacrifice is a meal for God:

A son honors his father, and a servant, his master. But if I am a father, where is the honor due Me? If I am a master, where is the fear due me? So says YHWH of hosts to you priests who despise My name. But you say, "How have we despised Your name?" By offering contemptible food on my altar. But you say, "How have we made You (variant: it) contemptible?" When you say, "The table of YHWH is despicable." When you bring up a blind animal for slaughter, is there nothing wrong with that? When you bring up a lame and sick animal, is there nothing wrong with that? Just try offering such to your civil governor—will he accept you or grant you respect? So says YHWH of hosts. Entreat the presence of God so that he may show us mercy. This is from your doing—will He grant you respect? So says YHWH of hosts. Would that one of you would just shut the (temple) doors, so that you no longer light My altar to no purpose! I have no pleasure in you. So says YHWH of hosts. I will not accept your offering from you! Indeed, from the rising of the sun to its setting My name is revered among the nations. In every place incense is offered to My name, as well as a pure offering, because My name is revered among the nations. So says YHWH of hosts. But you profane it when you say, "The table of the Lord is contemptible and His food is despicable." (Mal 1:6–12)

According to this passage, offerings are divine food and the altar is the divine table. The presentation of offerings is specifically compared to presenting a feast to the civil leader. Even the motivation is similar. The use of the metaphor of God as father and master underscores the analogical interpretation of sacrifice as a feast. YHWH is a superior, deserving of proper respect.

Descriptions of sacrifice as food for God and of the altar as God's table are not unique to Malachi. Consistent with the analogy suggested here, the offerings made at the altar consist of food items. The animals used for sacrifice include bulls and cows, sheep and goats, and birds of the pigeon family. These are parts of every Israelite's permitted diet. Offerings may also consist of grain and wine as well as animal flesh. Numbers 15:1–16 (part of P) lists the cereal and wine offerings that accompany burnt and well-being sacrifices. Leviticus 2 gives various recipes for cereal offerings, raw and cooked. The cooked versions (vv. 4–10) in particular are prepared as if they are meal items. In cases of poverty, the cereal offering may have been offered as a substitute for a burnt-offering animal, inasmuch as the prescriptions in Leviticus 2 follow directly upon the prescriptions for the burnt offering in chapter 1. The cereal offering often contains oil as an ingredient (Leviticus 2); this element is omitted when the cereal is brought as a purification offering (Lev 5:11; Num 5:15). Salt was also used on cereal and other offerings (Lev 2:13). Sacrifice thus contains a full menu of food items: meat, bread, wine, oil, and salt.[32]

It is not clear whether animal blood should be considered a food item. As we saw above, the book of Ezekiel defines the divine food as consisting of "fat and blood" (Ezek 44:7). In Psalm 50, God asks, "Do I drink the blood of goats?" (v. 13), indirectly reflecting at least a popular notion that blood in sacrifice is a food.[33] Since blood was prohibited from Israel's diet —and, according to P, from the diet of all humans (Gen 9:4; Lev 7:26–27; 17:11–14)—one might expect it to be excluded from God's diet as well, at least in the minds of the most systematic thinkers. Different schools of thought no doubt existed in biblical antiquity. P might have implicitly rejected the notion that the blood is divine food in its discussion of the proper disposition of sacrificial blood (and game animal blood) in Leviticus 17. The blood is placed on the altar to ransom the offerers' lives for killing the animal (pouring blood on the ground and then covering it has a parallel function for hunted animals). This does not fit its having been understood as divine food. Moreover, sacrificial blood is not placed on top of the altar and burned in the way other sacrificial portions are. Treating blood differently may have allowed it to be viewed as distinct from food portions.

In any event, within P, sacrifices provide a "sweet aroma to God" (e.g., Lev 1:9; 2:2; 3:5). This is further evidence that they were understood as meals. The sanctuary or temple is set up as the divine abode and the open-air altar called God's "table" (Ezek 44:16; Mal 1:7, 12). P's legislation says that priests must remain holy and must not profane God's name because "they offer the offerings of YHWH, the food (*leḥem*) of their God" (Lev 21:6; similarly v. 8). The offerings on the holy days are called "My (i.e., YHWH's) food" (*laḥmī*; Num 28:2, 24). The fat parts of the well-being offering that are burned on the altar are called "food" (*leḥem*; Lev 3:11, 16). A blemished priest is not to offer "the food (*leḥem*) of his God" (Lev 21:6, 17, 21, 22), referring to portions of sacrifices that are given to the priests to eat. One is not to offer "the food of your God" (*leḥem 'elōhêkem*, i.e., sacrifices) "from the hand of a foreigner" (Lev 22:25). The book of Ezekiel, which is related to P-legislation, also makes reference to "My [i.e., YHWH's] food," which is defined as sacrificial "fat and blood" (44:7).

In the J strand of the flood story, Noah builds an altar and makes a burnt offering from the pure land animals and birds on the ark. YHWH smells the offering. This pacifies God and leads to the promise not to curse the ground and destroy life again (Gen 8:20–22). The story about Cain and Abel's sacrifice (J) also appears to employ the motif of sacrifice-as-divine-food. YHWH favors Abel's animal offering over Cain's vegetarian fare (Gen 4:3–7)—barbeque is preferred over the salad bar. Other stories describe offerings as hospitality meals for divine messengers. These are then consumed by divine fire (Gideon: Judg 6:18–24; Samson's parents: Judg 13:15–23; cf. Genesis 18) in much the same way that offerings are consumed by divine fire in the priestly source (Lev 9:24). This act of divine acceptance stands out as the pinnacle of the sacrificial act.

Understanding that sacrifices are God's food explains an aspect of the dietary laws in P. Israel's diet approximates that of its God. The only latitude given beyond the sacrifices is permission to eat pure game animals (e.g., antelope) and fish (with fins and scales), whereas God is limited to domesticated quadrupeds and birds of the pigeon family.[34] Israel's limited choice of meats reflects its election out of the rest of humanity (Lev 20:24–26; cf. 11:41–45). Its dietary restrictions reflect the holiness of its God.

One feature which at first glance raises problems for this interpretation of sacrifice is that God is generally given portions that humans would consider unpalatable: the visceral fat, the kidneys, and a lobe of the liver for the well-being offering, the purification offering, and the guilt offering (Lev 3:3–5, 9–11, 14–16; 4:8–10, 19–20, 26, 31, 33; 7:3–4). The only sacrifice in which the deity receives appealing muscular meat is the burnt offering, whose flesh is entirely burned on the altar (cf. Leviticus 1). This problem has a practical solution. Theoretically, the entirety of every sacrificial animal is considered God's. Portions eaten by humans are transferred to them as a gift or allowance (cf. Num 18:8–20); humans are given the portions that they find most palatable as part of this concession. The fact that humans eat portions of the sacrifices further demonstrates that these are to be considered food for the deity. God is sharing the meal with servants and worshippers.

Conclusion

Any ritual act may be interpreted in a variety of ways, and sacrifice is no exception. The situation was and is similar to the interpretation of literature, art, or music. While an author, artist, or composer may intend one thing, the beholder is free to imagine something quite different. The vitality of ritual actually depends on its ability to bear multiple interpretations. Following Catherine Bell's observation that ritual is a means of creating and articulating interpersonal power relationships, one's position in the power structure may well determine the meaning one gives to ritual symbols. This means that different participants may have different interpretations of the same performance. In addition, the experiences of individuals and communities over time lead to a redefinition of the meaning of ritual symbols, much like the modern Passover Seder, which takes on new meanings and even forms from year to year and from generation to generation (especially, for example, as articulated over against events in the state of Israel or as feminist concerns come to the fore). Hence it is likely that the biblical peoples gave sacrifice a variety of interpretations. Nevertheless, the various voices in the Hebrew biblical text tend to agree that at base sacrifice was a feast presented to God; other nuances build on this basic notion.

NOTES

1. V. Turner, *Forest of Symbols* (Ithaca, N.Y.: Cornell University Press, 1967), 19; also *The Drums of Affliction* (Ithaca, N.Y.: Cornell University Press, 1968), 15. Similarly, the relatively recent *Encyclopedia of Religion* defined ritual as "those conscious and voluntary, repetitious and stylized symbolic bodily actions that are cen-

tered on cosmic structure and/or sacred presences" (Evan M. Zuesse, "Ritual," *Encyclopedia of Religion* 12 [1987]: 405).

2. Cf. E. Leach, *Culture and Communication* (Cambridge: Cambridge University Press, 1976), 45.

3. S. F. Moore and B. G. Myerhoff, "Secular Ritual: Forms and Meanings," in *Secular Ritual,* ed. S. F. Moore and B. G. Myerhoff (Assen/Amsterdam: Van Gorcum, 1977), 3–24.

4. For a similar view of ritual, cf. B. Lincoln, *Discourse and the Construction of Society: Comparative Studies of Myth, Ritual, and Classification* (New York: Oxford University Press, 1989), 53.

5. Robert Wuthnow, *Meaning and Moral Order: Explorations in Cultural Analysis* (Berkeley: University of California Press, 1987), 101.

6. See F. Staal, *Rules Without Meaning: Ritual, Mantras and the Human Sciences* (New York: Peter Lang, 1989), 115–140. A work in biblical studies highly influenced by Staal's approach is that of Milgrom's student Roy E. Gane, "Ritual Dynamic Structure: Systems Theory and Ritual Syntax Applied to Selected Ancient Israelite, Babylonian and Hittite Festival Days" (Ph.D. dissertation, University of California, Berkeley, 1992). Gane, however, recognizes that meaning or purpose is important to identifying and analyzing ritual; it cannot be viewed as pure activity. He also sees ritual as effecting an interaction with an "inaccessible entity" (abstract or invisible impurity, holiness, a supernatural being, etc.). Ithamar Gruenwald's *Rituals and Ritual Theory in Ancient Israel* (BRLJ Judaism 10; Leiden: Brill, 2003) similarly stresses the incommensurate relationship between ritual and meaning (see pp. 1–39).

7. C. Bell, *Ritual Theory, Ritual Practice* (New York: Oxford University Press, 1992), 71.

8. C. Bell, *Ritual Theory,* 69–93. This "productive" (as opposed to "reflective") character of ritual is emphasized in Saul Olyan's study, *Rites and Rank: Hierarchy in Biblical Representations of Cult* (Princeton, N.J.: Princeton University Press, 2000).

9. C. Bell, *Ritual Theory,* 90–91.

10. Israel Knohl, *The Sanctuary of Silence: The Priestly Torah and the Holiness School* (Minneapolis, Minn.: Fortress Press, 1995). See pp. 104–106 for a summary listing of Holiness versus Priestly materials.

11. Baruch J. Schwartz, *The Holiness Legislation: Studies in the Priestly Code* (Jerusalem: Magnes Press, 1999) [Hebrew].

12. For a brief overview, see his articles: "Atonement, Day of," "First-born," "First-fruits," "Sacrifices and Offerings, OT," *Interpreter's Dictionary of the Bible, Supplement Volume* (1976): 82–83, 336–338, 763–771. These articles, especially the last, are the primary starting place for study. For another summary article, see Gary Anderson, "Sacrifice and Sacrificial Offerings (OT)," *Anchor Bible Dictionary* 5 (1992): 870–886. For books in English on the topic, see Jonathan Klawans, *Purity,*

Sacrifice, and the Temple: Symbolism and Supersessionism in the Study of Ancient Judaism (Oxford: Oxford University Press, 2005); David Janzen, *The Social Meanings of Sacrifice in the Hebrew Bible: A Study of Four Writings* (BZAW 344; Berlin: de Gruyter, 2004); Gary A. Anderson, *Sacrifices and Offerings in Ancient Israel: Studies in their Social and Political Importance* (Harvard Semitic Monographs 41; Atlanta, Ga.: Scholars Press, 1987); Jacob Milgrom, *Cult and Conscience: The Asham and the Priestly Doctrine of Repentance* (Studies in Judaism in Late Antiquity 18; Leiden: Brill, 1976); Baruch A. Levine, *In the Presence of the Lord* (Studies in Judaism in Late Antiquity 5; Leiden: Brill, 1974).

13. The cereal offering (*minḥâ*) substitutes for or supplements another type of offering; it is not a separate category.

14. I will not review here various theories that interpret sacrifice from a sociological point of view. I agree with Catherine Bell that ritual, including sacrifice, does not symbolize, communicate, or reflect as much as it does what it does, i.e., creates relationships between the individuals involved (*Ritual Theory*, throughout). On a human sociological level, sacrifice enacts and sustains relationships of power between different classes (priests, lay persons, family members, offerer versus invited guests, etc.). Nancy Jay theorizes that sacrifice is a means of establishing and sustaining descent through males; this is not a fact of nature and so must be ritually created (*Throughout Your Generations Forever: Sacrifice, Religion and Paternity* [Chicago: University of Chicago Press, 1992]). It should be noted that, while Jay speaks more broadly about the consumption of sacrificial flesh and not just killing, the killing of the animal is an integral part of her theory (cf. pp. 71, 149, 150). While biblical society is clearly patriarchal, it is difficult to verify Jay's argument as applied to biblical sacrifice. On gender interpretation of sacrifice, see also Ivan Strenski, "Between Theory and Speciality: Sacrifice in the 90s," *Religious Studies Review* 22, no. 1 (January 1996): 10–20); Susan Sered, "Towards a Gendered Typology of Sacrifice: Women & Feasting, Men & Death in an Okinawan Village," in *Sacrifice in Religious Experience*, ed. Albert I. Baumgarten (Numen Book Series: Studies in the History of Religion 93; Leiden: Brill, 2002), 13–38.

15. For a comprehensive study, see David P. Wright, "The Gesture of Hand Placement in the Hebrew Bible and in Hittite Literature," *Journal of the American Oriental Society* 106 (1986): 433–446.

16. H. Hubert and M. Mauss, *Sacrifice: Its Nature and Function* (Chicago: University of Chicago Press, 1964). T. P. van Baaren ("Theoretical Speculations on Sacrifice," *Numen* 11 [1964]: 9) notes that in sacrifice killing the animal may be "little more than a technical requirement" and thus not symbolically or conceptually significant to the rite.

17. René Girard, *Violence and the Sacred* (Baltimore, Md.: Johns Hopkins University Press, 1977); cf. Burton Mack, "Introduction: Religion and Ritual," in *Violent Origins: Walter Burkert, René Girard, and Jonathan Z. Smith on Ritual Killing*

and Cultural Formation, ed. Robert G. Hamerton-Kelly (Stanford, Calif.: Stanford University Press, 1987), 6–22.

18. The Bible otherwise attests to the practice of child sacrifice, especially to the god Molech, a practice that may be indirectly associated with (later) Punic child sacrifice (Lev 18:21; 20:2–6; Deut 12:31; 18:10; 1 Kings 11:7; 2 Kings 3:22–27; 16:3; 17:17, 31; 21:6; 23:10, 13; Jer 7:31; 19:5; 32:35; Ezek 16:21; 20:26, 31; 23:37–39; Ps 106:37–38; 2 Chron 33:6).

19. Ithamar Gruenwald, *Rituals and Ritual Theory*, esp. 180–230.

20. Walter Burkert, *Homo Necans: The Anthropology of Ancient Greek Sacrificial Ritual and Myth* (Berkeley: University of California Press, 1983); cf. Mack, "Introduction," 22–32.

21. J. Z. Smith, "The Domestication of Sacrifice," in *Violent Origins: Walter Burkert, René Girard, and Jonathan Z. Smith on Ritual Killing and Cultural Formation*, ed. R. G. Hamerton-Kelly (Stanford, Calif.: Stanford University Press, 1987), 201, and cf. 196–202.

22. J. Smith, "The Domestication," 199.

23. One could flesh this theory out by saying that domestication creates a more extensive "social" tie with the animal that, to be broken, requires a more ritualized form of slaughter.

24. S. J. Tambiah, "The Magical Power of Words," *Man* 3 (1968): 175–208; "Form and Meaning of Magical Acts: A Point of View," in *Modes of Thought: Essays on Thinking in Western and Non-Western Societies*, ed. R. Horton and R. Finnegan (London: Faber and Faber, 1973), 199–229. For a full discussion of theoretical aspects of analogy in ritual and a list of the literature, see David P. Wright, "Analogy in Biblical and Hittite Ritual," in *Internationales Symposion: Religionsgeschichtliche Beziehungen zwischen Kleinasien, Nord-syrien und dem Alten Testament im 2. und 1. vorchristlichen Jahrtausend*, ed. Klaus Koch, Bernd Janowski, and Gernot Wilhelm (Orbis Biblicus et Orientalis 129; Freiburg/Göttingen: Vandenhoeck & Ruprecht, 1993), 473–506; "Ritual Analogy in Psalm 109," *Journal of Biblical Literature* 113 (1994): 385–404; "Blown Away Like a Bramble: The Dynamics of Analogy in Psalm 58," *Revue Biblique* 102 (1996): 213–236.

25. *KBo* 21.6 vs. 4–5; Manfred Hutter, *Behexung, Entsühnung und Heilung: Das Ritual der Tunnawiya für ein Königspaar au mittelhethitischer Zeit* (Orbis Biblicus et Orientalis 82; Freiburg: Universitätsverlag; Göttingen: Vandenhoeck & Ruprecht, 1988), 44–45, 52. The translation has been simplified.

26. *KTU/CAT* 169:3–5; D. Fleming, "The Voice of the Ugaritic Incantation Priest (RIH 78/20)," *Ugarit-Forschungen* 23 (1991): 141–154.

27. *CT* 16.3:126.

28. A. Leo Oppenheim and Erica Reiner, *Ancient Mesopotamia: Portrait of a Dead Civilization* (Chicago: University of Chicago Press, 1977), 183–198.

29. W. G. Lambert, "Donations of Food and Drink to the Gods in Ancient

Mesopotamia," in *Ritual and Sacrifice in the Ancient Near East,* ed. J. Quaegebeur (Orientalia Lovaniensia Analecta 55; Leuven: Uitgeverij Peeters en Departement Oriëntalistiek, 1993), 191–201. See also the recent essay by Tzvi Abusch, "Sacrifice in Mesopotamia," in *Sacrifice in Religious Experience,* ed. Albert I. Baumgarten (Leiden: E. J. Brill, 2002), 39–48. He notes that "The act of killing the animal is almost hidden behind the construct of feeding the god, a construct which emerges out of a combination of the earlier offering and storage and the later image of feeding a divine king in his palace." He sees the interest in blood in west Semitic sacrifice as a function of tribal-kinship relations and perhaps a livelihood based on the flesh and blood of animals. See also his "Blood in Israel and Mesopotamia," in *Emanuel: Studies in Hebrew Bible, Septuagint, and Dead Sea Scrolls in Honor of Emanuel Tov,* ed. Shalom Paul et al. (Leiden: Brill, 2003), 675–84.

30. See Oliver Gurney, *Some Aspects of Hittite Religion* (Oxford: Oxford University for the British Academy, 1977), 28–34. There are some other practices that use the blood of animals in a ritual way or where the death of the victim is of importance (see D. Wright, *The Disposal of Impurity* [Atlanta, Ga.: Scholars Press, 1987], 36 note 67). This is not to be confused with the regular system of offerings. Ugaritic practice also presents sacrifice as food given to the gods (David P. Wright, *Ritual in Narrative: The Dynamics of Feasting, Mourning, and Retaliation Rites in the Ugaritic Tale of Aqhat* [Winona Lake, Ind.: Eisenbrauns, 2001], 21–22, 32–36, 81–82, 89–90).

31. *KUB* 13.4 i 21–26; J. Pritchard, *Ancient Near Eastern Texts Relating to the Old Testament* (Princeton, N.J.: Princeton University Press, 1964), 207. Translation simplified.

32. The incense placed on cereal offerings (cf. Lev 2) is clearly not a food item. However, it does fit the larger context of feasting where pleasing smell plays a role alongside taste. Incense was also regularly offered on the small altar inside the tent shrine (Exod 30:1–10). A special bread offering of twelve loaves was set out on a table in the outer room of the tent of the wilderness tabernacle according to the P legislation (Lev 24:5–9; cf. Exod 25:23–30).

33. Although denying that sacrifices are literally divine food (a similar denial that camel sacrifice, particularly that made on pilgrimage to Mecca, is God's food can be found in the Qur'an 22:37), the psalm does not supply another interpretation, nor does it ever deny that this is in fact the meaning that underlies sacrifice.

34. In P, Israelites are technically allowed to eat the flesh of pure animals that have died on their own (*nebēlâ*) or that have been killed by other animals (*ṭerēpâ;* see the implications of Lev 11:39–40 and 17:15–16, which do not *prohibit* ingestion). They must make sure, though, that they purify afterwards; and priests are not allowed to eat this type of meat (Lev 22:8). Deuteronomy, however (14:21), following the Covenant Code (Exod 22:30), does not allow Israelites to eat this type of meat.

Part IV

Judaism and the Bible

Chapter 7

By the Letter?/Word for Word?

Scripture in the Jewish Tradition

Leonard Greenspoon

Introduction

For those interested in reading or consulting the Hebrew Bible, the modern world offers unprecedented opportunities. Modern-language versions are readily available in print or on line, along with editions in the original languages and an array of commentaries on all matters theological and philological.[1]

At the same time, and paradoxically, this ease of access serves to make abundantly clear that choices have to be made—and probably have been for centuries, if not millennia. How is it possible for so many translations, ranging from interlinear to paraphrase, to exist—all claiming to be a (if not the) true representation of the Word of God? With many of the Dead Sea Scrolls presenting ancient evidence of a Hebrew text at variance with the Masoretic Text (the traditional consonantal text of the Hebrew Bible; in its fullest form, it also includes vowel points, accents, and other notations), is it possible to know the original wording of any biblical passage? And with heightened awareness that certain books appear to have been accepted as authoritative by some Jews but not by others, how can we be certain that the contents (to say nothing of the ordering) of today's Hebrew Bible accurately mirror the circumstances in earlier Jewish communities?

These are among the questions we raise and attempt to answer in this chapter. As is often the case with our most important concerns, we ought to start by defining—or better, describing or delineating—key terms.

Canon Defined and Described

We begin, in reverse order, with the word "canon." In a succinct manner, Eugene Ulrich defines "canon" as "the definitive list of inspired, authoritative books which constitute the recognized and accepted body of sacred scripture of a major religious group, that definite list being the result of inclusive and exclusive decisions after serious deliberation."[2] Ulrich clearly understands that each element or phrase of this definition is essential. In so doing, he tacitly or explicitly rejects a number of possibilities.

What is canonized is a "body of sacred scripture," that is, a collection of books, but not necessarily a specific text for each of the books in this collection.[3] So, for example, it would be possible to speak of the Book of Jeremiah as "canonical," in the Jewish canon and in the canon of Orthodox Christianity, even though the latter is one-seventh shorter than the former and the two "Jeremiahs" exhibit many other differences in ordering of chapters and verses.[4]

Second, this is a "definitive" or "definite" list—in other words, a closed canon. Although Ulrich, in line with almost all other scholars, envisions a period, perhaps a protracted one, of "serious deliberation," this process is completed, at least for a particular "religious group," by canonization. To be sure, the canon remains open for this group in its interpretive richness; for another group, this canon may serve as a building block for the construction of its own canon. But for the religious group under consideration, the fixing of the "canon" brings to an end the possibility of adding or deleting any books (even when the text of the "canonical" books is still fluid).[5]

That this literature is "inspired," "authoritative," "recognized," and "accepted" is crucial. We don't have to get bogged down over definitions of inspiration, nor is it essential that these books be the only (or even the major) authority within a community.[6] Nonetheless, some level of inspiration and authority must be recognized (which I would understand as requiring a formal sort of acknowledgment) and accepted (which I see as referring to the practical consequences of acknowledgment).

Ulrich then speaks of "a major religious group." I hesitate to limit canon in this way to "major" groups, since this is surely a subjective, evaluative term that seems extraneous to what "canon" is all about. Thus, we may debate (as many have debated) whether there was a biblical canon at Qumran (where the Dead Sea Scrolls were found). I think such debate is fruitful whether or not Qumran would have been viewed as "major" in its own era.

Although Ulrich says nothing about how this recognition takes place and how acceptance moves from potentiality to reality, I believe we have to acknowledge a structure or organization equipped or empowered both to make such momentous decisions and to carry them out (or at least to attempt to carry them out). It is certainly far-fetched to imagine referenda or large-scale polling to determine the contents of a canon.

From some perspectives, but not Ulrich's, it would be possible to leave out the second part of his definition/description, especially "inclusive and exclusive decisions after serious deliberation." For Ulrich, it is this process of canonization and the reflective judgment—even the give-and-take of acceptance and rejection—accompanying it that is at the heart of our study.[7] With, for example, so many potential "candidates for canonization" known in Jewish circles of the last three centuries B.C.E. and the first century C.E., why these books "made it" while others didn't is a perplexing, fascinating, and ultimately unanswerable question.

But from another perspective, a conservative confessional one (as I would term it), no serious deliberation was needed, nor did it take place, at least as envisioned by Ulrich. For these individuals, the canon represents those books (or authors) that God uniquely inspired. There was never a question of the identity, extent, or—for that matter—wording of Scripture. All humans did, and had to do, was to recognize as canonical that which was in fact canonical.[8] Since the present study is an academic one, informed by but not based on faith (in general or in particular), we reject such confessional statements as witnesses to the historical process, while at the same time accepting them as witnesses to what people at a particular time believed.

Books ultimately accepted into (or not rejected from) a canon may receive special "treatment" in any or all of the following ways. (1) During the period of transmission (that is, when the Hebrew Bible was copied in its original Semitic languages), such a book may have been copied using special materials, written with greatest care, and/or with a unique script, orthography, and vocabulary.[9] (2) Such books may have been thought of as uniquely worthy of extended or extensive commentaries. (3) These works could well have been cited in later literature (including liturgy) more often than literature outside the canon, and with special introductory phrases such as "It was written. . . ."[10] (4) Canonical literature may have been selected as the first to be translated when the original languages were forgotten or had fallen out of usage.

As ultimately understood in Judaism and in the various forms of Christianity, the Bible is the book that contains their "sacred scripture." Our task is to seek out the origins of the canon preserved in the Hebrew Bible (also known as Tanakh, Mikra, and Old Testament, among other designations).[11] Two further, briefer explorations are required to prepare for an examination of the ancient evidence itself.

Origins of the Term "Canon"

The word "canon" comes from the Greek *kanon*, which is derived from a Semitic word meaning "measuring rod/stick" or, in Egyptian, a reed used to mark measurements. Although Greeks and others in antiquity could use the term concretely, they quickly adapted it to refer to a standard or norm by which other items or phenomena would be judged; this could apply to physical shape and size or, more broadly, to aesthetic or moral attributes. Its application to a collection of exemplars, in artistic or written form, flows from these earlier usages. We are consistently, and with good reason, cautioned against the facile identification of an expression's meaning with its etymology (or origins); in this instance, however, knowing that the term encompassed both a norm or "rule" and a collection expressive of those norms or "rules" helps us to comprehend "canon" in the fullness of its applications.[12]

Of course, the concept of "canon" may well have preceded the use of this term or may have been known in some other way in a preceding period. As early as the end of the first century C.E., Clement of Rome spoke of the "glorious and venerable rule [*kanona*] of our tradition"; in the next century similar expressions appear in the writings of Irenaeus and Clement of Alexandria. The fourth-century Church historian Eusebius did on occasion use the term *kanon* with reference to sacred literature, but it not certain that he intended its reference to extend beyond the Gospels.

Only in the middle of the fourth century, with Athanasius, does a form of *kanon* clearly apply to an extensive collection of scriptures, in this instance, of course, binding on Christians (therefore, including both testaments). Surprisingly, it was not until another 1400 years later, in 1768, that "canon," as a specific reference to a collection of scripture books, appeared in any language (in David Ruhnken, *Historia critica oratorum graecorum*).

We reserve the discussion of terminology within the Jewish tradition to a later point.

In comparison with the extended discussion of the term "canon," the concept of "text" seems admirably straightforward. In some ways, this is indeed so, inasmuch as text refers to written material, in this case written in the Hebrew language. But, as is well known, almost all examples of written Hebrew before the tenth century C.E. lacked explicit indications of vowels, with the exception of the so-called *matres lectionis* (whereby certain letters, most commonly the *yod* and the *waw*, could, as "mothers of reading," indicate the desired sound).[13]

Text Defined and Described

Therefore, we might have to content ourselves with limiting "text" to Hebrew consonants (along with the occasional semi-vowel noted just above). However, we need not always limit ourselves in this way. This is especially the case with those proper names (both of people and of places) for which we have ancient Greek transcriptions.[14] Moreover, there is little appeal, at least for this author, to the view that the Masoretes of the tenth century, to whom are attributed the first vocalized texts of the Hebrew Bible (see especially the Aleppo Codex and the St. Petersburg Codex), simply guessed at or made up the vowels they inserted. Without tying myself to some sort of "Masoretic fundamentalism," through which we might equate the vowels of the tenth century C.E. with a reputed ancestor a thousand years earlier, I do not dismiss out of hand the evidence of these Masoretes, who were themselves the heirs of old(er) traditions.[15]

Canonization: Within the Hebrew Bible

Does the Hebrew Bible itself bear any witness to the process of canonization? On this, as on so many other issues, there is considerable difference of opinion (often creating a chasm) between more traditional interpreters and those who make use of the array of critical approaches available to modern scholars.[16] We will look at a few of what I would term the key biblical passages that ought at least to be mentioned.

We begin, as it were, at the end, with the books of Ezra and Nehemiah. At Ezra 7:14, the reigning Persian monarch, Artaxerxes "king of kings," commissions Ezra "to regulate Judah and Jerusalem according to the law [*dat*] of your God, which is in your care." This implies a written code, recognized as authoritative by Persians and Judaeans alike, that Ezra is empowered to enforce and interpret, albeit primarily as the "servant" of the state.

We learn something of the extent of that "law" and of its promulgation from Nehemiah chapter 8. In verse 1, "the entire people assembled as one man in the square before [Jerusalem's] Water Gate, and they asked Ezra the scribe to bring the scroll of the Teaching of Moses [*torat Moshe*] with which the Lord had charged Moses." In verse 3, Ezra "read it from the first light until midday." As we learn in the following verses, the text, which would have been in Hebrew, was apparently translated simultaneously into the language of the people, Aramaic, so that it would be understood by all. Through repeated "Amens" and prostrations, the people gave their assent, and this was followed by intense study on the part of the leaders and ritual acts of mourning by the community (alas, none of this led the people to "sin no more"). It is certainly tempting to see in these extended ceremonies, which would have taken place around the mid-fifth century B.C.E., a formal canonization (or at least acceptance) of the Torah (that is, the Five Books of Moses) on the part of the Jerusalem community.[17] Such recognition may also be viewed at 2 Chr 23:18, 30:16; Dan 9:11; Mal 3:22, and elsewhere in writings that are widely dated to the post-exilic period.

A more conservative approach would find analogous references in earlier texts as well, even in the Torah, as for example, at Deut 31:24–26: "When Moses had put down in writing the words of this Teaching to the very end, Moses charged the Levites . . . saying: Take this book of Teaching."[18] Passages from the Former Prophets can, according to this approach, be linked to texts from the Torah itself; these would include Josh 8:31–32, 23:6;[19] 1 Kgs 2:3; 2 Kgs 14:6, 23:25.

2 Kings contains another narrative that ought to be brought into this discussion as well: namely, chapter 22, which describes the discovery of "the scroll of the Teaching" during repairs of the Temple under King Josiah. Immediately after this scroll was authenticated by the female prophet Huldah, the king summoned all the inhabitants of his kingdom, before whom he read "the entire text of [what is termed] the covenant scroll." In actions similar to those that accompanied Ezra's ceremony more than a century later, the people and their leaders acknowledged the authority of the words of this scroll. In the opinion of a number of scholars,

this scroll contained much, if not most, of the material found (later) in the book of Deuteronomy.[20]

Canonization: From the Hebrew Bible to the Dead Sea Scrolls

Within the relatively sparse, yet rich remnants of a large Jewish "post-biblical" literature from pre-Christian times,[21] we find a very interesting affirmation of the role played by Nehemiah in what we might call the canonization of sections of the Hebrew Bible: Nehemiah is said to have "founded a library and collected books about the kings and prophets, and the writings of David, and letters of kings about votive offerings."[22] This passage comes from 2 Maccabees 2:13, a book that, interestingly enough, is "canonical" for Roman Catholics and Orthodox Christians, but not for Jews or Protestants (on this see below). At this point, we may simply note that the author of 2 Maccabees seems to be referring in a general sense to the Former and Latter Prophets, and to some of the contents of the Writings. "Letters of kings about votive offerings" is not clear. The omission of the Law (or Torah) is not likely to be an oversight; it may well stem from its universally acknowledged traditional place at the center of the Jewish community long before Nehemiah's time.

But the main purpose of the reference to Nehemiah seems less an emphasis on past history than on one of the achievements of a contemporary (that is, second century B.C.E.) leader, Judah Maccabee. So, the author of 2 Maccabees continues: "In the same way, Judah also collected all the books that had been lost on account of the war which had come upon us, and they are in our possession. So if you have need of them, send people to get them for you" (2:14–15; see also 1 Macc 1:56, 2:48). Admittedly, the language here is vague as to what Judah did, the object (or contents) of his collecting, and the circumstances under which they would be consulted. Nonetheless, the parallel with some earlier activity on the part of Nehemiah (and his associate [at least in the Hebrew Bible] Ezra) is intended. Moreover, both 1 and 2 Maccabees portray Judah and his family as figures of considerable authority, at least over the troops and others whose loyalty they commanded (see, for example, 1 Macc 2:39–41, on Sabbath laws). With these thoughts in mind, I am not uncomfortable with attributing to Judah some formal action akin to what would later be called canonization.[23]

In using such language, I am in a distinct minority among modern researchers, who might ask, among other queries, "If Judah 'canonized' the
text, why is there no more formal listing of the contents on this 'canon'
and why is the issue of 'canon' still unsettled for several centuries after
him?" While not intending to push this admittedly meager and ambiguous
evidence too far, I think it is worth noting that Judah's establishment of a
"canon," while in some way binding on his group, did not necessarily meet
with assent in later generations and among other groups. Here I want to
emphasize my lack of sympathy with the view that the establishment of
"the canon" was a linear process, with one generation building on the
structure established by others (thus, for example, the Torah was canonized, then the Torah and Prophets, then the Torah and Prophets and the
Writings).[24] Given the diversity of the Jewish community in this period, it
is not in the least far-fetched to speak of "canons," any or all of them being
closed for their intended audience, but not "written in stone" (as it were)
for others.

As it turns out, we are not without further evidence as to what 2 Maccabees had in mind. Around the year 200 B.C.E. (that is, about a half a
century earlier than the Maccabees), Ben Sirach wrote a work that is often
called Ecclesiasticus, which, like 1 and 2 Maccabees, is found in the Old
Testament of Roman Catholics and Orthodox Christians. Chapters 44–49
of this fascinating work are often referred to with the subtitle, "In Praise
of Famous Men"; Ben Sirach structures his "praise" of these men in the
order they appear in today's Hebrew Bible—and presumably in his text
(however he understood it in terms of "sacredness"). Thus we find Enoch,
Noah, Abraham, Isaac, Jacob, Moses, Aaron, Phineas [from the Torah];
Joshua, Caleb, Samuel, Nathan, David, Solomon, Rehoboam, Jeroboam,
Elijah, Elisha, Hezekiah, Isaiah, Josiah [Former Prophets]; Jeremiah, Ezekiel, the Twelve [Latter Prophets]; Zerubbabel, Joshua, the high priest Nehemiah [possibly from the Writings].

When Ben Sirach's grandson translated his grandfather's Hebrew book
into Greek, sometime after 132 B.C.E., he prefaced his work with a short
explanatory prologue. In this foreword the grandson comments on his ancestor's reasons for writing:

Many great teachings have been given to us through the law and the prophets and the others that followed them, and for these we should praise Israel
for instruction and wisdom. Now, those who read the scriptures must not
only themselves understand them, but must also as lovers of learning be

able through the spoken and written word to help the outsiders. So my grandfather Jesus, who had devoted himself especially to the reading of the law and the prophets and the other books of our ancestors, and had acquired considerable proficiency in them, was himself also led to write something pertaining to instruction and wisdom, so that by becoming familiar also with his book those who love learning might make even greater progress in living according to the law.[25]

He then adds an always apt caution about the limitations of any translation, including his own:

You are invited therefore to read it with good will and attention, and to be indulgent in cases where, despite our diligent labor in translating, we may seem to have rendered some phrases imperfectly. For what was originally expressed in Hebrew does not have exactly the same sense when translated into another language. Not only this work, but even the law itself, the prophecies, and the rest of the books differ not a little when read in the original.

Twice in the first paragraph we find very similar language: "the law and the prophets and the others that followed them" and "the law and the prophets and the other books of our ancestors." It is not unreasonable to see in the phrase "the law and the prophets" an explicit recognition of a collection of works, equivalent (if not equal) to our Torah and Prophets, held as authoritative in the acquisition of "instruction and wisdom." Along with his grandfather's work (was it perceived as equally authoritative?), these books were essential for making "progress in living according to the law" (a, if not the, goal of a "practicing Jew"). In the second paragraph, the grandson expounds, if only briefly, upon the difficulties of providing in translation (in this case Greek) "the same sense" as the Hebrew of "the law itself, the prophecies, and the rest of the books."[26]

The combined witness of Ben Sirach and his grandson spans the second century B.C.E. and reflects a conscious (and perhaps also self-conscious) understanding of the unique nature of a body of literature. These statements provide a background or context for the activity attributed to Judah Maccabee. Whatever we call this "consciousness," it does, in my opinion, partake of many of the distinctive characteristics of the process by which a "canon" is produced. Be that as it may, there were still many other developments to follow.

Canonization: Within the Dead Sea Scrolls

Were time travel a reality, I would hasten to the western shores of the Dead Sea, sometime around 100 B.C.E., to ask inhabitants of Qumran, who lived in relative seclusion, whether they would be surprised to learn how central a role their settlements and documents were destined to play in twentieth- and twenty-first-century studies. Among the most remarkable of the Scrolls' finds are those that relate to issues of text and (possibly) of canon. We restrict our interest to the latter topic for the moment.

Among the last published but first produced of the Scrolls' documents is a text known as *Miqṣat Ma'aseh Torah* (MMT), whose origins may well antedate the foundation of the community itself.[27] MMT C lines 10–11 read: "We have [written] to you so that you may study (carefully) the book of Moses and the books of the Prophets and [the writings of] David [and the events of] ages past." This phrasing is quite similar to the wording discussed above and fits in well with the concept of an authoritative body of writings—to be "studied (carefully)"—consisting of the Torah, the Prophets, Psalms (with which David was especially identified as author), and some other materials. If *Miqṣat Ma'aseh Torah* reflects the thoughts, if not the *ipsissima verba*, of the Teacher of Righteousness, a (the) leader of Qumran and (possibly) its founder, it would not be inappropriate to see in this phrasing the promulgation, or at least the citation, of a canon, even if its precise contents are unclear to us.[28]

Although there are a few other fragmentary citations like this among the Scrolls, most scholarly discussion about a canon, or lack of a canon, at Qumran revolves around documents that may, or may not, have been held as authoritative there. Thus, we regularly read that all of the books of the Hebrew Bible, with the probable exception of Esther, were found at Qumran and were doubtless held in high(est) esteem.

However, this statement is not nearly as straightforward as it appears. First, it is not the case that Esther is the only probable "exception," since not all of the Minor Prophets are well represented at Qumran and there are no fragments of Nehemiah (it is assumed to be part of "the book" of Ezra-Nehemiah).[29] Beyond that, it is anachronistic, although in this case rather likely, that each book of "our" Bible was thought of in the same way at Qumran.[30] Since there are other likely "candidates" for authoritative texts among the Scrolls that are not part of "our" Bible—see especially Jubilees, some of the Ezra material, and the Temple Scroll[31]—we must at least reckon with the outside chance that parts of "our" Bible were not sacred to this community.

We earlier listed a number of ways in which canonical literature might be isolated in terms of its special "treatment." Many of them can be brought into the discussion of "the canon at Qumran," but none can be argued conclusively with the possible exception of the restriction of Pesharim (commentaries) to "biblical" books such as Psalms, Isaiah, Nahum, and Habakkuk.

It is fair to say, I think, that most contemporary scholars do not believe that a canon existed at Qumran, at least in the sense of a "closed" listing—which is, as argued above, the only sense in which I would use the term.[32] It may also be held that Qumran represents a stage along the road to canonization. Since the community's road became a dead end around 70 C.E., with the abandonment of the settlement in the face of Roman armies, we have no idea where such a road might have led.

Canonization: From Philo through the Rabbinic Sources

From a source coterminous with the latter years of Qumran comes another piece of fascinating evidence. The Jewish philosopher Philo, resident of Alexandria, Egypt, was a prolific writer on a wide variety of subjects. In discussing a Jewish sect known as the Therapeutae (in his *De Vita Contemplativa* 25), he refers to its use of "laws and oracles delivered through the mouth of prophets, and psalms and other books [or: anything else] by which knowledge and piety may be increased and perfected."[33] The Therapeutae, who apparently lived somewhere in the Egyptian desert, were similar in some respects to the Qumran community, although there is no reason to suspect a direct link between them. To the degree that Philo's statement reflects the beliefs and perhaps even the language (although Philo wrote in Greek) of the Therapeutae, this Egyptian sect acknowledged as authoritative a body of literature very close to the sacred writings at Qumran and elsewhere in Palestine prior to 70 C.E.

It is difficult to believe that any Jew or any aspect of Judaism, whether in the Land or the Diaspora, was untouched by the destruction of the Jerusalem Temple by the Romans in 70 C.E. As their physical and spiritual world collapsed, those Jews who survived began the process of adapting and rebuilding that led to the founding and eventual supremacy of rabbinic Judaism. These rabbis understood themselves as successors to the Pharisees and drew many links between themselves and their "predecessors," among whom Hillel was preeminent. A contemporary of Philo and of Jesus, Hillel is reported to have taken a special interest in the interpretation of sacred literature and may well have played a role in rounding out the structure of the third division of the Hebrew Bible, the Writings.

Such activities took on even greater importance and immediacy with the fall of the Temple, its priests, and their rituals. Much recent scholarship (primarily through the 1970s) asserted, on the basis of what now seems extraordinarily flimsy evidence, that at a council (sometimes referred to as a synod) at Jamnia, or Yavneh, the canon of the Hebrew Bible was finally and firmly fixed around 90 C.E. It was not clear exactly what action was or needed to be taken there: Was it a detailed investigation, book by book, or more of a ratification of what was by then accepted and acceptable? This Council of Yavneh, although widely supported by Christian scholars of the first half of the twentieth century, was in fact the "discovery" of Jewish researchers of the previous century.[34]

As it turns out, far too much emphasis was being placed on reputed activities that were far from well documented or well understood. It is not unexpected that certain rabbis, who took upon themselves the leadership roles that had at least in part been filled by priests earlier, would be concerned that a secure collection of authoritative writings be delineated. The process by which this took place was gradual, but it seems to have been essentially complete by the time of Bar Kochba and Rabbi Akiba, in the first third of the second century C.E. Thus we read:

All the holy writings defile the hands. The Song of Songs and Ecclesiastes defile the hands. Rabbi Judah said, "The Song of Songs defiles the hands, but Ecclesiastes was in dispute." . . . But Rabbi Akiba said, "God forbid! No one in Israel ever disputed the status of the Song of Songs saying that it does not defile the hands, for the whole world is not worth the day that Song of Songs was given to Israel; for the writings are holy, but Song of Songs is holiest of all. If there was a dispute, it was only about Ecclesiastes" (*Mishna Yadaim* 3:5).[35]

The following have no share in the world to come: he who maintains that the resurrection is not intimated in the Torah, or that the Torah was not divinely revealed, and an Epicurean. Rabbi Akiba adds: one who reads the outside books. (*Mishna Sanhedrin* 10:1).

The expression "defiles the hands" appears to be the rabbinic equivalent of "canonical"; other documents are "outside books."[36] It is not clear exactly why holy writings would "defile the hands," but it is in line with priestly thinking of the Hebrew Bible, where what is sacred to God can actually render a human impure.

In any case, Rabbi Akiba's association with the process is well documented. It is also worth noting that the books "in dispute" here, Song of Songs and Ecclesiastes, are part of the Ketuvim (Writings), the last part of the Hebrew Bible in order of appearance and apparently in order of canonization. Some have argued that Esther, another book in Ketuvim, was also disputed, but this is far from clear. Moreover, Ben Sirach continued to be cited for many centuries in contexts that included canonical works, even if its "canonical" status was never asserted by anyone with the possible exception of his grandson.[37]

There is other evidence from this period as well. Among several statements from the New Testament, the most clear is this from Luke: "the Law of Moses and the Prophets and [the] Psalms" (24:44). This is very much in keeping with pre-70 C.E. evidence from Jewish sources. It is also possible to gain a sense of the early church's understanding of authoritative writings by examining citations throughout the New Testament that are introduced by expressions such as, "As it is written. . . ." The Latter Prophets and Psalms predominate in such passages, without however yielding any decisive information about the contours or extent of what an early Christian might cite as authoritative.[38]

The Jewish historian Josephus, who had been a general in the first revolt against the Romans before becoming their ally, provides us with what may well be the earliest indication of the number of books in the canon:

> For we have not an innumerable multitude of books among us, disagreeing from and contradicting one another, [as the Greeks have,] but only twenty-two books, which contain the records of all the past times; which are justly believed to be divine; and of them five belong to Moses, which contain his laws and the traditions of the origin of mankind till his death. This interval of time was little short of three thousand years; but as to the time from the death of Moses till the reign of Artaxerxes king of Persia, who reigned after Xerxes, the prophets, who were after Moses, wrote down what was done in their times in thirteen books. The remaining four books contain hymns to God, and precepts for the conduct of human life. It is true, our history hath been written since Artaxerxes very particularly, but hath not been esteemed

of the like authority with the former by our forefathers, because there hath not been an exact succession of prophets since that time; and how firmly we have given credit to these books of our own nation is evident by what we do; for during so many ages as have already passed, no one has been so bold as either to add any thing to them, to take any thing from them, or to make any change in them; but it is become natural to all Jews immediately, and from their very birth, to esteem these books to contain Divine doctrines, and to persist in them, and, if occasion be willingly to die for them. (*Contra Apionem* 1:37ff)

This fascinating passage offers up much for discussion, but we limit ourselves here to three points: The number of books Josephus gives, 22, is at variance with what became the traditional number, 24 (see just below). Either he has counted differently or his "canon" was shorter than that affirmed by the rabbis. Second, he ends the "age of prophetic authority" with the Persian king Artaxerxes. While signaling that much of value was written thereafter, this means that none of it was considered to contain "Divine doctrines." Third, Josephus contends that the acknowledgment and application of this "canon" is nothing new; it had been this way for "so many ages."[39]

The first reference to a 24-book Jewish canon is found in 2 Esdras 14:45–46, which was probably written in the first half of the second century C.E.: "Make public the twenty-four books that you wrote first, and let the worthy and the unworthy read them; but keep the seventy that were written last, in order to give them to the wise among your people."[40] If this enumeration goes back to the previous century, Josephus appears to be unaware of it, or perhaps he simply differed.

All evidence indicates that anything we might call a canon list was not codified until considerably later. For this we turn to the Talmud:

> Our Rabbis taught: The order of the Prophets is, Joshua, Judges, Samuel, Kings, Jeremiah, Ezekiel, Isaiah, and the Twelve Minor Prophets. Let us examine this. Hosea came first, as it is written, God spake first to Hosea. But did God speak first to Hosea? Were there not many prophets between Moses and Hosea? R. Johanan, however, has explained that [what it means is that] he was the first of the four prophets who prophesied at that period, namely, Hosea, Isaiah, Amos and Micah. Should not then Hosea come first?—Since his prophecy is written along with those of Haggai, Zechariah and Malachi, and Haggai, Zechariah and Malachi came at the end of the prophets, he is

reckoned with them. But why should he not be written separately and placed first?—Since his book is so small, it might be lost [if copied separately]. Let us see again. Isaiah was prior to Jeremiah and Ezekiel. Then why should not Isaiah be placed first?—Because the Book of Kings ends with a record of destruction and Jeremiah speaks throughout of destruction and Ezekiel commences with destruction and ends with consolation and Isaiah is full of consolation; therefore we put destruction next to destruction and consolation next to consolation.

The order of the Hagiographa is Ruth, the Book of Psalms, Job, Prophets, Ecclesiastes, Song of Songs, Lamentations, Daniel and the Scroll of Esther, Ezra and Chronicles. Now on the view that Job lived in the days of Moses, should not the book of Job come first?—We do not begin with a record of suffering. But Ruth also is a record of suffering?—It is a suffering with a sequel [of happiness], as R. Johanan said: Why was her name called Ruth?—Because there issued from her David who replenished the Holy One, blessed be He, with hymns and praises.[41] (*Baba Batra* 14b)

Baba Batra passes over in silence the Torah, a phenomenon we remarked on in earlier Jewish sources as well; its place of prominence and the ordering of its contents were too well known to require explicit notice. But even this listing was not the last word. For example, we are used to the order Isaiah, Jeremiah, and Ezekiel, rather than the one given here. And *Baba Batra*'s ordering of the books of Ketuvim is quite different from what is now accepted. Moreover, even the placement championed by this passage did not go unchallenged: Chronicles appeared as first, rather than last, among the Ketuvim in the great Tiberian codices of the tenth century C.E.[42] Final acceptance of a "table of contents," which may or may not be part of canonization, is then a very late development within Judaism.

Canonization: The Septuagint and the New Testament

We have not referred to a possibly parallel line of "canonization" that began with the translation of the Hebrew Bible into Greek in the first half of the third century B.C.E. This process culminated, perhaps in the first century B.C.E., with a collection that included Greek texts of the twenty-four books of the Hebrew Bible, with considerable additions to two (Daniel and Esther), along with translations of books not part of the Hebrew

Bible, and original Greek compositions. Together, these disparate materials came to be known as the Septuagint. Although its origins are thoroughly Jewish, its development into an "Old Testament canon" is part of the history of early Christianity.[43] The Septuagint is more relevant for our purposes in the discussion that follows on text.

It was known, if only imperfectly, for many centuries that in pre-Christian times and at least through the first century C.E., sacred books circulated in more than one textual form in terms of order of chapters and verses (both of which, as formal elements, are medieval in origin), contents, and wording. Thus, for example, a comparison of the Greek text of the Septuagint with the traditional Hebrew (or Masoretic Text) shows literally thousands of differences throughout the canon of the Hebrew Bible. However, it was—and, to an extent, continues to be—difficult to know how to assess such differences. First, it is important to distinguish divergences between the Masoretic Text and the Hebrew that lay in front of the Septuagint translators from changes made by the translators on their own volition. This is obviously a huge task, one that must be resolved (to the extent it can) on an almost case-by-case basis. Moreover, we cannot be certain, even now, how much of the Masoretic Text is ancient (and this in spite of my optimistic comments in this regard above). Nonetheless, and with all scholarly safeguards and caveats in place, there can be no doubt that the Septuagint does witness to an ancient Hebrew text that differs from the Masoretic Text in many respects and in many passages.[44]

Another ancient source is the New Testament, where "Scripture" is frequently cited (more so in some of its parts than in others). It used to be commonplace to identify such citations with the Septuagint; after all, they are both in Greek. More refined studies over the past few decades have yielded a more varied pattern: Some of the New Testament "scriptural" citations are from the Septuagint, others from revisions of that older Greek. Still others have been consciously adapted to their context by a New Testament author, whose memory (as fallible as any human's) might also be responsible for some of the wording. Moreover, we cannot discount the probability that at least certain New Testament writers translated the Hebrew on their own. Again, there is no one answer to explain this phenomenon in the New Testament, but it is clear that its authors did have access to a variety of texts from a number of different sources.[45]

The major "Bible" of the Samaritans has also long been known. It encompasses (only) the Torah. Throughout these five books, there are thousands of differences from the MT, some large, others small.[46] Was this simply a sectarian, aberrant phenomenon?

The Text of the Hebrew Bible: Before the First Jewish Revolt

As in several other areas of scholarly inquiry, the discovery, analysis, and publication of the Dead Sea Scrolls, begun in the latter half of the twentieth century and still going full steam in our day, has helped to clarify many issues relating to text. As noted above, among the hundreds of manuscripts uncovered are many containing "biblical" material.

As it turns out, much of this biblical material is very close to the Masoretic Text (of course, at Qumran the vowels were not written in, nor were the accents). There are other manuscripts exhibiting a text very close to what the Septuagint translators had before them. For the Five Books of Moses, a "Samaritan" tradition has been identified—although the Qumran community itself had nothing to do with the Samaritans. Moreover, there are many biblical manuscripts from Qumran that are unique in comparison with what was known before their discovery.

In and of itself, this is interesting; the true significance of these different text types (as they are often termed) at Qumran provides more than a little additional interest. First, it is clear that different texts of the same book, for example Jeremiah and Samuel-Kings, circulated at Qumran at the same time, presumably among the same people. If we accept the existence of a canon at Qumran, one that would surely have included the Prophets (as well as the Torah), then we are led to reflect positively on the validity of a point made earlier: namely, that it is a body of literature and not a specific text that is canonized. Moreover, there is little if any evidence that one of these text types—say, for example, the Masoretic Text—was dominant or preferred over the others, which might then be considered inferior. The absence of any extended marginal or interlinear corrections demonstrates quite conclusively that all of the versions, say of Jeremiah, were equally valid.[47]

The Text of the Hebrew Bible in the Early Rabbinic Period

From other sources we can learn that such textual fluidity was not uncommon prior to the First Jewish Revolt.[48] Thereafter, in tandem with the gradual (but discernible) process that led to the delineating of the Writings, we can observe developments that led rather quickly (all things considered) to the primacy of the Masoretic Text (or rather, its unvocalized predecessor). It is not known whether the rabbis made conscious, deliberate choices between available texts for each book or section of their canon or simply adopted what was at hand. Given the uneven quality of what they included (for example, the text of the Torah is evaluated very highly; for Samuel-Kings, on the other hand, a Hebrew text more like the one available to the Septuagint translators would have been preferable), the latter alternative is more likely.

It undoubtedly served the interests of the rabbinic leadership to suppress all non-authoritative texts, and they seem to have done a fairly thorough job. Nonetheless, the Masoretic tradition actually enshrines divergent readings on many occasions through marginal notations known as *qere-ketiv*. Through this mechanism, the preservers (that is, Masoretes) signaled that what was listed in the margin should be read (*qere*) instead of what was written (*ketiv*) in the text. Much scholarly debate has centered on the origin(s) of these divergent readings; there is no consensus. But they are at the least indicative of the rabbis' recognition that "canonized" text, while it must always be reproduced, was subject to interpretation at many levels.

Conclusion: A Continuing Process

Through our discussion and analysis we have located the late first century and early second century C.E. as the time when a widespread acknowledgment of a biblical canon, along with a general acceptance of a biblical text, came about. In so doing, we have traced many significant developments leading up to this undoubtedly momentous series of events. There is one further observation, at which we have thus far only hinted: rabbinic decisions in the early centuries of the common era were in some ways the end of the process, or, better, they ended some processes. But exegetical engagement with the biblical text was hardly brought to a halt; rather, we are brought to a new stage in the interpreting and application of Sacred Writ.[49] And that stage led to others, not just in the past but continuing to this day and (I hope) far into the future. For it is my firmest conviction that having an authoritative body of sacred literature, with a fixed text, frees us to use our individual and collective talents to the fullest. This "liberation" is a gift to, and a responsibility of, all who are part of the Jewish community. We must never allow it to be taken from us or misapplied for narrow, partisan reasons.[50]

NOTES

1. For an up-to-date discussion of the wide array of English-language Bibles available, see Leonard Greenspoon, "The Holy Bible: A Buyer's Guide," *Bible Review* 21, no. 4 (2005): 37–44. Of course, this is only part of a far larger phenomenon.

2. Eugene Ulrich, "The Notion and Definition of Canon," in Lee Martin Mc-Donald and James A. Sanders, eds., *The Canon Debate* (Peabody, Mass.: Hendrickson, 2002), 29; a slightly expanded definition appears in Eugene Ulrich, "Qumran and the Canon of the Old Testament," in J.-M. Auwers and H. J. de Jonge, *The Biblical Canons* (Leuven: University Press, 2003), 58. In my opinion, the more succinct formulation, on which I base the discussion that follows, is cleaner and clearer.

3. So also Lawrence H. Schiffman, *Reclaiming the Dead Sea Scrolls: The History of Judaism, the Background of Christianity, the Lost Library of Qumran* (Philadelphia: Jewish Publication Society, 1994), 161: "Once the accepted body of divinely inspired books 'the biblical canon' is defined, the authoritative, standardized text of the Bible must be established."

4. For a discussion of the text(s) of Jeremiah, along with a full bibliography, see Emanuel Tov, *Textual Criticism of the Hebrew Bible* (second revised edition; Minneapolis: Fortress Press, 2001), 319–327.

5. For a somewhat different point of view on the issues raised in this paragraph, see the "Introduction" in Christine Helmer and Christof Landsmesser, eds., *One Scripture or Many? Canon from Biblical, Theological and Philosophical Perspectives* (Oxford: Oxford University Press, 2004).

6. Traditionally, the Bible has held a more central position of authority for Protestants than for Jews or Roman Catholics.

7. Many other scholars would agree. Among them are James A. Sanders, "The Issue of Closure in the Canonical Process," in Lee Martin McDonald and James A. Sanders, eds., *The Canon Debate* (Peabody, Mass.: Hendrickson, 2002), 252–263.

8. See, for example, this statement from the website of Bible.org ("Trustworthy Bible Study Resources"): "It is important to note that religious councils at no time had any power to cause books to be inspired, rather they simply recognized that which God had inspired at the exact moment the books were written."

9. On the possibility that there were distinctive scribal practices for "biblical" manuscripts at Qumran, see Tov, *Textual Criticism*, 107–111.

10. On criteria (2) and (3) and their relevance to the discussion of a "canon" at Qumran, see James C. VanderKam, *The Dead Sea Scrolls Today* (Grand Rapids, Mich.: Eerdmans, 1994), 150–157.

11. For a succinct discussion of these names and their significance, see Marc Zvi Brettler, *How To Read the Bible* (Philadelphia: Jewish Publication Society, 2005), 7–9.

12. On this and the following two paragraphs, see Lee Martin McDonald and James A. Sanders, "Introduction," in Lee Martin McDonald and James A. Sanders, eds., *The Canon Debate* (Peabody, Mass.: Hendrickson, 2002), 11-13.

13. For an excellent introduction to topics mentioned in this paragraph, see Angel Sáenz-Badillos, *A History of the Hebrew Language* (Cambridge: Cambridge University Press, 1996).

14. For important examples from the Book of Joshua, see Leonard Green-spoon, *Textual Studies in the Book of Joshua* (Harvard Semitic Monographs 28; Chico, Calif.: Scholars Press, 1983).

15. On the textual history of the Hebrew Bible and its transmission, see Page H. Kelley et al., *The Masorah of Biblia Hebraica Stuttgartensia: Introduction and Annotated Glossary* (Grand Rapids, Mich.: Eerdmans, 1998); and the articles in the second part of Sid Z. Leiman, ed., *The Canon and Masorah of the Hebrew Bible: An Introductory Reader* (New York: Ktav, 1974).

16. For a brief, insightful overview, see Philip Stern, "Torah," in Bruce M. Metzger and Michael D. Coogan, eds., *The Oxford Companion to the Bible* (New York: Oxford University Press, 1993), 747–748.

17. For a succinct discussion and evaluation of scholarly opinions on this Teaching of Moses, see Ralph Klein, *ABD*, vol. 2, 737–738.

18. On these verses in particular, see Jeffrey H. Tigay, *Deuteronomy* (The JPS Torah Commentary; Philadelphia: Jewish Publication Society, 1996), 296–297. More broadly, see his Excursus 28, "The Writing and Reading of the Teaching," and his comments at Deut 1:5 and other passages that refer to "Teaching."

19. For the range of understandings in traditional Judaism for Joshua, especially the verses in chapter 8, see R. Drucker, *Yehoshua: The Book of Joshua* (Art-scroll: Tanach Series; Brooklyn: Mesorah, 1982), 224–225 and 444.

20. For Josiah and this scroll of Teaching from the perspective of mainstream critical biblical scholarship, see the *HarperCollins Bible Commentary*, ed. James L. Mays (revised ed.; San Francisco: HarperCollins, 2000), 308–309.

21. For a masterful and up-to-date survey, see George W. E. Nickelsburg, *Jewish Literature between the Bible and the Mishnah* (2d ed.; Minneapolis: Fortress Press, 2005).

22. On this and related passages in the books of 1 and 2 Maccabees, see Julio C. Trebolle Barrera, "Origins of a Tripartite Old Testament Canon," in Lee Martin McDonald and James A. Sanders, eds., *The Canon Debate* (Peabody, Mass.: Hendrickson, 2002), 129–130.

23. On this possibility, see Van Der Kooij, "Canonization of Ancient Hebrew Books and Hasmonaean Politics," in J.-M. Auwers and H. J. de Jonge, eds., *The Biblical Canons* (Leuven: University Press, 2003), 36–38.

24. This view is in line with the sentiments expressed by Jack N. Lightstone, "The Rabbis' Bible: The Canon of the Hebrew Bible and the Early Rabbinic Guild," in Lee Martin McDonald and James A. Sanders, eds., *The Canon Debate* (Peabody, Mass.: Hendrickson, 2002), 166: "Scholars wrongly presume that the tripartite Jewish canon (Torah, Prophets, and Hagiographa) developed in linear fashion, with each part being, for the most part irrevocably, 'closed' in succession. Such historical 'mono-linearity' is highly unlikely."

25. On this passage, see Van Der Kooij, "Canonization," 29–32. He contrasts this with the sentiments expressed by the grandfather himself in 39:1–3 (35–36).

26. The translation of Ben Sirach is taken from VanderKam, *Dead Sea Scrolls Today,* 143. See also his accompanying remarks.

27. For a full discussion of this document, also known as the Halakhic Letter, see Schiffman, *Reclaiming the Dead Sea Scrolls,* 83–95.

28. In Schiffman's view, "The 'Words [or, writings] of David' are probably the Psalms and 'the chronicles [or, events]' probably refers to the Books of Chronicles, perhaps to Ezra and Nehemiah as well. So here again we encounter the Writings, although we do not yet have a fixed named for them. Nor can we be certain that this third part of the canon has been finally closed" (Schiffman, *Reclaiming the Dead Sea Scrolls,* 166).

29. For an up-to-date catalogue of "biblical" materials and their translation into English, see Martin Abegg Jr. et al., *The Dead Sea Scrolls Bible* (New York: HarperCollins, 1999).

30. So also Schiffman (*Reclaiming the Dead Sea Scrolls,* 164): "We cannot assume simply because the same books considered canonical in later rabbinic tradition are present in the Qumran caves that these books were considered authoritative by members of the sect or by other Second Temple period Jews."

31. On this text, as well as the "Reworked Pentateuch," see James C. VanderKam, "Questions of Canon Viewed through the Dead Sea Scrolls," in Lee Martin McDonald and James A. Sanders, eds., *The Canon Debate* (Peabody, Mass.: Hendrickson, 2002), 91–109.

32. For Schiffman's understanding of the biblical canon at Qumran, see his *Reclaiming the Dead Sea Scrolls,* 162–169.

33. On this passage, see Alfred C. Sundberg Jr., "The Septuagint: The Bible of Hellenistic Judaism," in Lee Martin McDonald and James A. Sanders, eds., *The Canon Debate* (Peabody, Mass.: Hendrickson, 2002), 81–82.

34. On this issue, see especially Jack P. Lewis, "What Do We Mean by Jabneh?" *JBR* 32 (April 1964): 125–132; and "Jamnia Revisited," in Lee Martin McDonald and James A. Sanders, eds., *The Canon Debate* (Peabody, Mass.: Hendrickson, 2002), 146–162.

35. For this translation, see Sid Z. Leiman, *The Canonization of Hebrew Scripture: The Talmudic and Midrashic Evidence* (Hamden: Connecticut Academy of Arts and Sciences, 1976), 121 and accompanying discussion.

36. For a full discussion of this term, its possible origins and applications, see Leiman, *Canonization*, 103–120.

37. See Leiman, *Canonization*, 92–102.

38. Among the best discussions of this evidence is Craig A. Evans, "The Scriptures of Jesus and His Earliest Followers," in Lee Martin McDonald and James A. Sanders, eds., *The Canon Debate* (Peabody, Mass.: Hendrickson, 2002), 185–195.

39. For an extensive discussion of this and related passages in Josephus, see Steve Mason, "Josephus and His Twenty-Two-Book Canon," in Lee Martin McDonald and James A. Sanders, eds., *The Canon Debate* (Peabody, Mass.: Hendrickson, 2002), 110–127.

40. On 2 Esdras, see Nickelsburg, *Jewish Literature*, 270–277.

41. On this and related passages in the rabbinic corpus, see Lightstone, "The Rabbis' Bible," 178–182. See also Leiman, *Canonization*, 51–53 and annotations.

42. As noted by Sanders, "Closure," 254; see also Lightstone, "The Rabbis' Bible," 170–172.

43. The literature on this topic is large. Almost all contemporary discussions are indebted to Alfred C. Sundberg Jr., *The Old Testament of the Early Church* (HTS 20; Cambridge: Harvard University Press, 1964). In addition to his own later works, including " 'The Old Testament of the Early Church' Revisited," in Thomas J. Sienkewicz and James E. Betts, eds., *Festschrift in Honor of Charles Speel* (Monmouth, Ill.: Monmouth College, 1997), 88–110, and "The Septuagint," 68–90, attention may be called to M. Müller, *The First Bible of the Church: A Plea for the Septuagint* (JSOTSup 206; Copenhagen International Seminar 1; Sheffield: Sheffield Academic Press, 1996); John Lust, "Septuagint and Canon," in J.-M. Auwers and H. J. de Jonge, *The Biblical Canons* (Leuven: University Press, 2003), 39–55; and Martin Hengel, *The Septuagint as Christian Scripture: Its Prehistory and the Problem of Its Canon*, introduction by Robert Hanhart (Grand Rapids, Mich.: Baker, 2004).

44. On the possibilities as well as difficulties of retroversion from Greek to Hebrew, see Emanuel Tov, *The Text-Critical Use of the Septuagint in Biblical Research* (2nd edition, revised and enlarged; Jerusalem: Simor, 1997).

45. Leonard Greenspoon, "Hebrew into Greek: Interpretation In, By, and Of the Septuagint," in *History of Biblical Interpretation*, vol. 1, ed. Alan Hauser and Duane F. Watson (Grand Rapids, Mich.: Eerdmans, 2003), 102–105 and bibliography cited there.

46. On "pre-Samaritan texts and the Samaritan Pentateuch," see Tov, *Textual Criticism*, 80–100.

47. For the "Biblical texts found in Qumran," see Tov, *Textual Criticism*, 117. See also a number of the articles in Frank Moore Cross and Shemaryahu Talmon, eds., *Qumran and the History of the Biblical Text* (Cambridge: Harvard University Press, 1975). Also very important is the work of Eugene Ulrich, including articles in his *Dead Sea Scrolls and the Origins of the Bible* (Grand Rapids, Mich.: Eerd-

mans, 1999) and his "The Dead Sea Scrolls and the Biblical Text," in Peter W. Flint and James C. VanderKam, eds., *The Dead Sea Scrolls after Fifty Years: A Comprehensive Assessment* (Leiden: E. J. Brill, 1998), vol. 1, 79–100.

48. See, for example, Johann Cook, "Textual Diversity and Canonical Uniformity," in J.-M. Auwers and H. J. de Jonge, *The Biblical Canons* (Leuven: University Press, 2003), 135–152.

49. On this, see Shaye Cohen, "The Significance of Yavneh: Pharisees, Rabbis, and the End of Jewish Sectarianism," *HUCA* 55 (1984): 27–53.

50. For contemporary examples of such narrowness and of efforts to read this restrictiveness "into" the historical record, see B. Barry Levy, *Fixing God's Torah: The Accuracy of the Hebrew Bible Text in Jewish Law* (Oxford: Oxford University Press, 2001).

Chapter 8

From Judaism to Biblical Religion and Back Again

Ziony Zevit

Although a pseudo-historical, rabbinic tradition maintains that Judaism evolved from the biblical religion of ancient Israel and that the rabbis who lived after the destruction of the Second Temple guided this evolution through oral teachings originating at Sinai, critical historians think otherwise. A contemporary understanding of the relationship between the religion of ancient Israel and Judaism tends to see rabbinic Judaism as the end-product of a radical reformation by closely knit circles of like-minded, passionately religious men over a period of some 300 years, from about 100 B.C.E. to 200 C.E. These remarkable individuals revamped totally whatever ancient Israelite religion had become by the second Hellenistic century, reforming it in accordance with the sensibilities of their particular form of Judaeo-Hellenistic culture, transforming it into a new religion.

Although new in fact, their Judaism fiercely maintained the authority of the Bible as a divinely ordained constitutional document, the divine origin of the Torah, and the dogma of monotheism. In order to accommodate biblical texts to newly emerged social, political, economic, and intellectual circumstances, the rabbis also accepted that the older texts had to be interpreted and assumed the authority to do so. The assumption of such authority would have been meaningless had they not had supporters and followers. The institution they created as a place of gathering for study, teaching, adjudicating, and even praying was the study house.

Rabbinic Judaism differed from Israelite religion in that its leaders were not charismatic prophets and not teachers descended from priestly families passing on traditional lore. During the First Temple period and part of the Second, the office of prophet was considered the source of divine communication through oracles, and that of priest the source of instruction based on tradition (see Jer 18:18 and Ezek 7:26). However, the rabbis had achieved authority by dint of their mastery over a particular collection of texts and a body of oral learning esteemed by large groups of Jews.[1] Their Judaism also differed from the older Israelite religion in another significant way. After 70 C.E., the religion promoted in rabbinic circles preferred mourning for the destroyed Temple and longing for the reestablishment of sacrifice to promoting an activist program intended to restore sacrifice and rebuild the Temple. This reorientation was a corollary to their belief that the biblical period of temples and priests and prophets was absolutely over until some vague time in a distant future when redemption would occur.[2] Those challenging the rabbis' position were quieted in 135 C.E. after Roman legions crushed the Bar Kosiba revolt, butchered large numbers of his followers, devastated the Temple area, and banished Jews from Jerusalem.[3] This was the tipping point after which rabbinic notions and authority became widely disseminated beyond Palestine.

These circumstances give rise to the following questions: Did either the religion prescribed in the Bible or the religion actually practiced ca. 1200–586 B.C.E. persist into the late Hellenistic period when proto-Judaism emerged among Pharisaic and other groups? And, if so, did it continue in some noticeable way into rabbinic Judaism?

The differences between the pseudo-historical tradition and that proposed by contemporary historians are stark. The former emphasizes continuity while allowing for religious change from early through late antiquity. Adherents of this view do not distinguish between "Israelite religion" and "Judaism," the former simply being Early Judaism. In contrast, critical historians understand the terms "Israelite religion" and "Judaism" as referring to quite different, barely related entities. Israelite religion lacked a standardized home liturgy, ritual blessings, and a system of *halakhah* that was widely accepted, at least on the community level. Judaism lacked blood expiation, sacrifices, priestly authority, and pilgrimages.

In this chapter, I revisit the question of discontinuities and continuities through a comparative exploration of the morning service as described in the Bible and as practiced in rabbinic Judaism in order to evaluate again the imprint of Israelite and biblical religion on rabbinic Judaism.[4] I approach this through the liturgical structure of the service and the nature of its performance, by a consideration of prayer postures, prayer texts, places of prayer, and religious groups during the First Temple period. My objective is to suggest from where in the biblical milieu the movement that eventually evolved into rabbinic Judaism may have originated.

The Morning Tamid Sacrifice

Numbers 28:1–8 contains the prescription for the regular daily sacrifices Israel was commanded to prepare scrupulously and to present punctiliously as "offerings by fire of pleasing odor to Me." Each day, every day, regularly (*tamid*), two yearling lambs without blemish were to be presented, "one lamb in the morning and the other lamb you shall offer at twilight" (Num 28:3). The prescription also includes particulars about the flour offering and the libation accompanying the sacrificial lambs.

Leviticus 1:10–13 prescribes the ritual for the burnt offering. The priests, Aaron's sons, are to slaughter the animal, dash a measure of its blood against the altar's sides, skin and butcher the carcass, and then wash its entrails and legs, bring the carcass, entrails, and suet up onto the altar, and burn it, turning it into smoke, "an offering by fire, of pleasing odor to the LORD." Other details about the meal offering with its frankincense are provided in Lev 2:2 and 6:1–11.

The biblical injunctions are perfunctory. They do not provide a description of the actual ritual: who did what, where, and when. The ritual, frequently repeated with a minimum of fanfare, was rather simple and not particularly interesting. Its constant repetition and simplicity make it highly likely, on a theoretical level, that it was stable, performed routinely with little or no variation, and easily remembered.[5] Consequently, it is likely that the Mishnah's description of the *tamid* ritual as practiced in the last decades of the Second Temple (ca. 30–70 C.E.) reflects the biblical ritual as practiced in the First Temple, destroyed in 586 B.C.E.[6] This allows that knowledge of essential, basic rituals continued (with some disruptions) from the First into the Second Temple, transmitted by priests who continued altar rituals in Jerusalem even after most First Temple buildings had been destroyed. Jeremiah 41:5 refers to eighty men, ca. 582 B.C.E., transporting meal and frankincense, items used in the preparation of the meal offerings that accompanied a number of sacrifices, to the "house of YHWH" after it had been destroyed. Obviously, some rudimentary program of sacrifice requiring supplies continued to operate in Jerusalem. Ezra 3:2–3 addresses the reconstruction of the external altar and offering of sacrifices there ca. 536 B.C.E. "though the foundation of the temple of YHWH had not been set" (Ezr 3:6).[7]

After the destruction of the Second Temple by the Romans in 70 C.E., the *tamid* offerings could no longer be made. Accordingly, the rabbis are said to have instituted the morning and afternoon prayer services to replace them. This notion is preserved in a meditation recited before the beginning of the formal morning prayers:

> Master of the world, you commanded us to sacrifice the *tamid* at its appointed time . . . but now, through our sins, the Temple is destroyed and the tamid discontinued. . . . But you said, "We will pay bulls by (the offerings of) our lips" (Hos 14:3). Therefore, may it be your will Lord our God and God of our fathers that the expression of our lips be worthy and acceptable and pleasing before you, as if we sacrificed the *tamid* sacrifice at its appointed time. . . .

Rabbinic preachers provided Jews with alternative stories linked to the patriarchs that told how the prayer services came into existence. Abraham, believed to have observed almost all *halakhic* prescriptions as taught by the rabbis even before the Sinai revelation, instituted the morning service, Isaac the afternoon service, and Jacob the evening service.[8] This type of anachronistic teaching fostered and reinforced the belief that what the rabbis taught was not of their invention, but that it was old and predated even the greatest of biblical figures: the totality of what is found in rabbinic halakhic literature was revealed to Moses at Sinai and preserved as an esoteric oral tradition throughout the history of the Jewish people until eventually recorded (*m. Avot* 1:1); God revealed the order of the prayers to Moses (b. *Rosh Hash.* 17b); King David himself had studied oral law (*b. Sotah* 21a; *b. Shabb.* 30a,b). In the rabbinic hourglass where sand flows upward, it became possible to believe that the morning prayer service was antecedent even to the morning sacrifice, which, according to the Torah, had been commanded only at Sinai.

The Contemporary, Traditional Morning Prayer Service[9]

The traditional Jewish morning service may be divided into three parts.[10] (1) The first is intended to focus individuals before reaching the core of the service. It consists of blessings concerned with the physical awakening of the human body, mental alertness, and human consciousness. These are followed by meditations emphasizing the createdness of humanity and selections from rabbinic literature bearing on sacrifice followed by selected psalms. (2) The second part, the central core of the service, contains two major sections. (a) It begins with the *barechu* (call to prayer), followed by two blessings introducing the Shema, the Shema (Deut 6:4) with three accompanying paragraphs (Deut 6:5–9 and 11:13–21, and Num 15:37–41), and a multi-paragraph prayer concluding the Shema unit of the core. (b) The second section, immediately following, contains the Amidah (i.e., standing) prayer. Since it figures prominently in the following discussion, it is necessary to characterize the structure of the Amidah, the most important of all non-biblical Jewish prayers. Its nineteen blessings involve the following themes presented in the following order, established under the aegis of Rabban Gamliel II, leader of the most prestigious group of sages at Yavneh, ca. 125–35 C.E.[11]: (1) God's relationship to the patriarchs: creator of all remembers the gracious acts of (or on behalf of) the patriarchs, brings a redeemer for their descendents for the sake of His name; (2) God, resurrector of the dead and bringer of salvation; (3) God's holiness and the holiness of His name; (4) petition for wisdom, insight, and discernment; (5) petition for repentance; (6) petition for pardon; (7) petition for redemption for the sake of God's name—God is "redeemer of Israel" (see benediction #1); (8) petition for healing; (9) petition for agricultural sustenance; (10) petition for the ingathering of exiles; (11) petition for the restoration of judges and counselors as in aforetimes, for God to rule with grace and mercy and to declare Israel righteous; (12) petition that slanderers and evildoers be destroyed;[12] (13) petition that the righteous, elders, and converts benefit from divine mercy and that all who trust in God receive their just recompense; (14) petition that Jerusalem be rebuilt and the Davidic throne be established within it; (15) petition that the Davidic line be restored; (16) petition that prayers be heard; (17) petition that God be pleased with the people Israel and their prayers and that God restore the temple ritual and his divine presence to Zion; (18) thanks to God whose name is "the good"; 19) petition that God establish peace on His people Israel.[13]

Benedictions 4–16 are not recited on the Sabbath and holidays. On these days, liturgical statements relevant to the particular day are inserted. Leopold Zunz, a nineteenth-century scholar, suggested on the basis of this practice in Jewish liturgy that benedictions 1–3 and 17–19, or some earlier version of them, were the first part of the Amidah to become fixed and that subsequently other benedictions were incorporated.[14]

(3) The third part of the services includes a series of liturgical texts, poems, and psalms expressing contrition for sins and petitioning for salvation followed by concluding prayers.

Throughout the first and third parts of the services, and even during most of the second part, worshippers read silently or aloud, or sing liturgical poems. Sometimes they stand, but mostly they sit. What is deemed appropriate is simply a matter of conventional custom. They must, however, stand for the Amidah prayer. Additionally, they must bow at four points: before and after the first blessing recalling God's relationship with the patriarchs, and before and after the penultimate prayer thanking God for granting life and being present and compassionate.[15] The choreography of the ritual is ancient; the words, when not ancient, are at least rather old. The first and third parts of the morning service possess their own complex history, part of which is ancient.[16] In addition to being accruals to the core, they also contain accruals composed during the medieval and later periods that were accepted gradually throughout the Jewish world, especially after they were printed in prayer books.[17]

Prayer before Prayer Books

The oldest prayerbook known is that of Rav Amram Gaon, from the great yeshiva of Sura in Babylon, dated ca. 870 C.E. The second oldest is that of Rav Saadya Gaon, also from Sura, written about fifty years later, ca. 930 C.E. Although scholars are certain that a few written prayerbooks were composed prior to that of Rav Amram, they have not come down to us. On the basis of available manuscripts, it appears that prayerbooks became popular in the eleventh or twelfth century, paralleling the rise in popularity of poets and scholars who composed liturgical texts that others wished to preserve. Before this move to expand the collection of texts, Judaism operated with a rather slim set of prayers that, according to scholarly consensus, started to evolve in the second half of the Second Temple Period, ca. 200 B.C.E., and slowly became fixed, at least in rabbinic circles, by 200 C.E. One reason the prayers remained slim is that originally they were composed, taught, learned, and recited from memory. Some individual prayers, however, may have been set down in writing, as an aid to memory, before the rise of Islam in the seventh century, at the same time that

Jews were preserving the "oral law" as a written text.[18] The practice itself most likely started earlier, but raised the hackles of Jewish authorities. This is inferred from a statement in the (originally oral) Babylonian Talmud, edited in written form ca. 500–550 C.E., directed against the practice: "Those who write prayers are likened to those who burn Torah" (*kotvey berakot kesorfey torah, b. Shabbat,* 115b). This sensibility retreated over the centuries in the face of popular practice and changing attitudes toward writing.

As mentioned above, *m. Tamid* describes how the biblical prescriptions of Numbers 28:1–8 were realized some time during the first century C.E. in Herod's temple. It describes procedures from the time that the guards and sleeping priests were awakened to immerse themselves and dry off shortly before sunrise until the sacrifice was completed. Just before the butchered animal parts were taken to the altar, they were placed on the ramp leading up to the altar, and salted. Then all participating priests

> went down and came to the Chamber of Hewn Stone to recite the Shema. The overseer said to them, "Recite one blessing,"and they recited. And (then) they pronounced the Ten Commandments (Exod 20:2–14; Deut 5:6–18), *shema* (i.e., Hear O Israel [Deut 6:4–9]), and *wehayah 'im shamoa'* (i.e., And it shall come to pass if you listen [Deut 11:13–21]), and *wayyo'mer* (i.e., And the Lord spoke [Num 15:37–41]). They blessed the people with three blessings: *'emet weyatsiv* (i.e., true and established), *'avoda* (i.e., *retsey . . . 'avodat 'ameka,* accept, Lord God, the offering of your people Israel), and the blessing of priests. (Num 6:24–26) (*m. Tamid,* 4:3 [last eight words] and 5:1)

This, the earliest known prayer service, is recognizable because it is partially preserved in the core of the traditional morning service. The contemporary service has two expanded blessings before the Shema, so the mishnah—i.e., an individual teaching in the Mishnah—could be referring either to the first, expressing the theme of God as creator of everything, or to the second, introducing the theme of God's love for Israel. Thematically, the first blessing seems a more appropriate introduction to the Ten Commandments than the second, which links well to the "love" theme in the paragraph after the Shema.[19] Whichever benediction was intended by whoever formulated the mishnah, it was not the benediction in its extant form. Nowadays, the first contains a medieval acrostic poem along with other expansions reflecting kabbalistic doctrines of the divine light at creation, while the second contains a preamble on the theme of divine love and a series of poetic petitions for divine instruction, enlightenment, and the ingathering of exiles so that Israel can proclaim God's Oneness with love.

The Ten Commandments, recited by priests in the Temple, were removed by rabbis from their prayer liturgy, possibly because of sectarian disputes over their interpretation (*b. Ber.* 12a) or possibly because their public recitation was linked closely to priests and the temple service.[20] The sections of scripture recited after the Shema by the priests are recited in the same order immediately after the Shema today also. The priestly recitation of *'emet veyatsiv* as a form of blessing directed to the people reflects the contemporary liturgy in that these are the first words of the first paragraph (of the longish blessing) recited after the Shema. A rewritten version of the priestly *'avoda* recitation appears in the Amidah as part of the seventeenth benediction, along with a phrase requesting the restoration of sacrificial rituals to the Temple.[21]

This mishnah indicates that about 40 percent of what now constitutes the central part of the contemporary, three-part morning service—about 16 percent of the whole—had evolved by the latter part of the Second Temple period. Three points about this temple prayer service are worthy of attention:

1. Most of the priestly prayer service consisted of biblical verses out of context and rearranged. Unlike these, the short first benediction and the final *'avoda* petition were newly composed texts in post-biblical Hebrew. They date linguistically at the earliest to the second century B.C.E. and reflect the infiltration of new compositions into what was otherwise a Bible-based liturgy.
2. The service as a whole, inserted before the actual presentation of the sacrifice on the altar, was a private one culminating with a prayer that the sacrifice about to be presented on the altar be accepted.
3. Since nothing in the wording of the non-biblical sections betrays any particular rabbinic theology and the use of the Ten Commandments was discontinued by them, the original prayer service may reflect the influence of Pharisaic authorities over the Temple priests.

Following this prayer service, priests were assigned various duties in the continuation of the sacrifice at the altar and the ritual was completed. At its conclusion, the priests raised their hands toward the people and recited the benediction of priests a second time in the presence of whoever was watching (*m. Tamid* 7:2).

With regard to the biblical sacrificial ritual, prescribed in Numbers and still performed at the end of the Second Temple period, the rabbinic prayer ritual is absolutely discontinuous; with regard to the text of the prayer used by priests engaged in the sacrifice at the end of the Second Temple period, it is partially continuous (via Pharisaic traditions).

The Posture of Rabbinic Prayer: Standing

Although their particular prayer service may have been conducted when all were standing, a consequence of their being between and betwixt parts of the sacrificial ritual, the priests may have been sitting except when raising their hands to bless the people. The text ignores the question of priestly posture completely.

In Judaism, the only prayer requiring that people stand is the Amidah, the petitionary prayer *par excellence*. In and of itself, the requirement that people stand during the petitionary prayer is unique. It is atypical of prayer postures in the Persian and Hellenistic periods and most likely does not continue any Israelite tradition from the biblical period.[22] The qualifying reservation "most likely" addresses a line in Jeremiah, dated conventionally to 600–586 BCE: "Remember my standing before you (*'omdiy lepaneyka*) to speak good about them to turn your anger from them" (Jer 18:20b).

Two other verses may be cited also in support of the idea that standing in petitionary prayer is rooted in biblical tradition, but neither withstands close scrutiny.[23] Psalm 106, a petitionary psalm composed in the exilic period, ca. 586–538 B.C.E., asks God to forgive Israel, as He had done in the past, and to gather exiles from among the nations so that they might praise him.[24] Verses 30–31 refer to one such occurrence: "and Phinehas stood (*wayya'amod*) and intervened (*wayyepallel*) and the plague ceased." Although sometimes taken as indicating that Phinehas stood in prayer, the verb used is not *wayyitpallel*, the hitapael form of the root *p-l-l*, but a piel form. The former regularly refers to prayer, the latter to some other form of activity. The psalm alludes to the narrative of Num 25:6–9 that describes a sexually obscene act performed in a public setting (though not to public view) and Phinehas's zealous reaction: "and he saw . . . and he stood . . . and took a spear in his hand and he entered after the Israelite man into the chamber and stabbed both of them . . . and the plague ceased" (verses 7–8). Comprehending the psalm through the complete narrative indicates clearly that *wayya'amod* in the psalm signals the beginning of a series of actions–compressed into the word "intervened"—and should be understood along the lines of "he got up/arose to do X/he initiated action and did X."[25]

The post-exilic book of Nehemiah, ca. 400 B.C.E., describes a large, public ritual involving penitential confession: "The seed of Israel separated themselves from all foreigners, and they stood (*wayya'amdu*), and they confessed their sins and the iniquities of their fathers. And they arose in their places and read in the scroll of the teachings of the LORD their God one-quarter of the day, and one-quarter (of the day) they confessed and prostrated themselves to the LORD their God" (Neh 9:2–3). Verse 3, beginning, "And they arose," provides a fuller description of the ritual summarized compactly in verse 2. From verse 3, it is clear that the erect posture accompanied listening to the scroll while prostration accompanied the ritual of confession.

Thus, the passage from Jeremiah remains the only source for arguing that standing in prayer is rooted in ancient tradition. Whether or not it refers to actual standing may also be challenged on the basis of how the expression "to stand before (*la'amod lipney*) X" is used in Biblical Hebrew. This particular collocation of verb + preposition describes the posture of attendants before someone of higher authority as in Num 16:9; 1 Kings 10:8; 2 Kings 5:16; Dan 2:2; and 2 Chr 18:18, and has the sense of "to attend/ serve"—and see Deut 10:8 and 1 Sam 16:22 where *'amad* is used figuratively "to attend, be in the presence of."[26] Reading Jer 18:20b in the context of Jer 18:19–23 with this in mind suggests the following interpretation: "Remember my serving You to speak good about them to turn Your anger from them."

In context, this line is part of a prayer in which Jeremiah petitions God not to forgive his (Jeremiah's) enemies, but to punish them, to mow them down and to let everybody close to them suffer. It is a very human cry for revenge against those Israelites who persecuted him (cf. Jer 18:18, the line immediately before this petition). In the context of this prayer, Jeremiah asks God to remember how he served God—not as priest before the altar, but as a prophet, part of whose task is to intercede on behalf of Israel— but now, because Israel paid back his prophetic service with evil, he asks for their punishment.[27]

If correct, this interpretation indicates that the Bible contains no unambiguous datum indicating that an erect posture was required, or even
recognized as appropriate, for petitionary prayer.

Biblical texts indicate that standing erect was the appropriate posture
when praising God (Ps 134:1–2; 135:1–2; Neh 9:5) or people (Deut 27:12;
1 Kings 8:55) or judging (Isa 3:13) or being judged (Deut 19:17). People described themselves as standing before God as his faithful servants (1 Kings
17:1; 18:15; 2 Kings 3:14; 5:16). In one exceptional text, 2 Sam 7:18, David sits
while inveigling and petitioning God. But then, that was David.

Postures for Petitionary Prayer: Bowing, Genuflecting, Prostrating

The standard posture for petitionary prayer, indicated by the common
verb *hishtachaweh*—which scholarly lexicons derive from a root *shin-chet-
waw/hey*, "to be low, sink down"—seems to have required individuals to
lower their body. While this is commonly understood as involving prostration, either flat out on the ground or on bent knees, Mayer Gruber advances an alternate derivation of the verb from *chet-waw-yod*, "to curl up,"
implying that its basic meaning is "to bend/arch/curl over at the waist," to
bow. There is no questioning that the verb is regularly employed to describe a posturing in contexts unmistakably connected with worship.[28] In
these particular passages, all in the context of worship, the verb tolerates
translation into English, depending on how the passage is imbedded in the
narrative, by a range of equivalents: bow, bend, or curl (over), when a literal translation is desired; or by worship, pray, or entreat, when a translation reflecting the communicative intention of the posture or the activity
of which it was part is preferred. That is, these passages do not specify exactly what bowing or bending over as a physical act entailed. (It is possible
that 2 Kings 5:18 refers to bending over a bit from the waist to help support
a nonambulatory individual.) Gruber's general definition helps clarify this
gap in our understanding by considering contexts in which the verb is
used along with other verbs referring to posing the body.

I understand the term as referring to a range of body lowering and
bending activities: tilting the head and bowing slightly from the waist
while standing; tilting the head while bowing so that one's head is below
that of the person opposite; kneeling; kneeling and bowing from the waist;
kneeling and bowing at the waist and pressing the nose or face to the
ground; extending the whole body to the ground; extending the whole
body and pressing the nose or face to the ground; throwing oneself to the

ground; throwing oneself to the ground and groveling. These postures are described by other words alone or in combination with *yishtachaweh* and are mentioned not only in a variety of narrative prose contexts, but in poetic texts as well. The words are *npl* (to fall),[29] *kr'* (to bend the knee, hip, or leg),[30] and *qdd* (a verb derived from *qodqod*, "head, skull," that means to tilt, bend, nod the head).[31]

The interpretation of what such postures communicated, even without words, was self-evident, as 2 Sam 12:16–23 indicates. David's son by Bathsheba was born ill. David entreated God on behalf of the child; fasted, slept and "lay on the ground." This he did for seven days. In verses 22–23 he explains to his courtiers that his behavior was intended to evoke YHWH's pity: "I thought 'Who knows? The Lord may have pity on me, and the child may live.'" The posture itself, maintained over a long period of time, constituted a choreographed moment equal to a prayer expressing repentance and supplication.

The Three Postures for Petitionary Prayer and Their Theological Significance

As a consideration of the broader contexts within which passages cited in the preceding two sections of my discussion occur demonstrates, the various body-lowering postures they describe were assumed not only before God, but also before people. They were most likely conventional because convention determined which was appropriate for greeting, entreating, grieving, and groveling. Many of them are illustrated in wall reliefs and paintings from the ancient Near East, but we cannot read meaning from there into the biblical expressions.

The first unambiguous indication of a semi-erect body posture for prayer is the description of Daniel's behavior: "he went to his house—it had windows in its upper chamber facing Jerusalem—and three times a day he kneeled on his knees and prayed and made confession before his god because that is what he had always done" (Dan 6:11, and see Ps 55:17–18). This definite change in body posture can be dated loosely to between the times that the event purportedly occurred, ca. 550–400 B.C.E., and the time that Daniel was written, 200–150 B.C.E.[32] I guess that it was closer to the latter than to the former. Ezra 9:5, which may be dated to the fifth century B.C.E., is therefore relevant: "I bent my knees and spread my palms to YHWH my God."

The description of Daniel's body posture enables me to posit a three-phase development in petionary prayer-postures: body-lowering ones during the period of the First Temple; semi-erect, i.e., kneeling but with the upper body held erect, from after the First Temple period until the second half of the Second Temple period; and finally standing.

The three postures may correspond to three distinct notions about the relationship between God and Israel. (1) The oldest bowing and prostrating poses reflect obeisance to God, who is held to be awesome, feared, all-powerful, often threatening. It comes from a period in which the cosmos was imagined as structured with YHWH on high and distant; far below him were divine messengers who could do his bidding, bland figures, and still below them, humans.[33] (2) The kneeling erect pose in Daniel reflects a transition phase, indicating on the one hand the sense that God, though distant, was approachable. God could be addressed deferentially in words uttered when the body was properly posed and oriented in space. The posture of deference no longer had to express self-effacement. (3) The standing pose of the Amidah reflects polite respect to a powerful familiar addressed as if in intimate conversation.

The earliest posture reflects a period in which the primary form of communicating to God was through conventional sacrifices; the middle posture dates to a period in which both oral prayer and sacrifice were used. Standing, however, is characteristic mainly of a period when oral prayer was the only form of worship available to Jews.[34] With regard to prayer postures, rabbinic petitionary prayer is absolutely discontinuous with biblical prayer.

The Texts of Prayer: Formal Compositions

Oral prayer existed in the biblical period itself.[35] Most psalms were written during the First Temple period and present formal, poetic prayers that were most likely chanted in the Temple on various occasions: praising God (Psalms 8, 19, 33, 145–50); thanksgiving (Psalms 18, 30, 32, 34, 107); trust (Psalms 11, 16, 23, 27); Zion hymns (Psalms 46, 48, 76); royal psalms (Psalms 29, 47, 93, 95–99); individual laments (Psalms 3–7, 9–10, 13); community laments (Psalms 12, 44, 58, 60, 74); liturgical poems (Psalms 2, 44, 58, 60, 74, 79, 80, 83, 85, 90, 94, 123, 126, 129, 137). This poetry, however, belonged to the high religion of the sacred site. It was formal and liturgical, chanted for and on behalf of the people, who may or may not have been present when the texts were read. Isaiah refers to the songs and the melody of a flute on the evening that a festival is hallowed (Isa 30:29); Amos refers to the songs and melodies of the lyres (Amos 5:23); and Psalms 149–150 refer to the shofar, lyre, harp, drum, flute, and different types of cymbals as well as to dance. Although both sacrifice and psalmody characterized religion in the Temple, the recitation of psalms seems to have been background and not essential. Bible narratives present various individuals reciting what are supposed to have been spontaneous prayers, but on close examination are revealed to be literally and rhetorically complex compositions: the Song at the Sea (Exod 15:1–18); the Song of Moses (Deuteronomy 32:1–43); Hannah's prayer (1 Samuel 2:1–6); Solomon's prayer (1 Kgs 8:13–66); Jonah's prayer (Jonah 2:3–10); Ezra's prayer (Ezra 9:6–15).

The Texts of Prayers: Informal Compositions

In addition to this type of prayer, there also existed prose prayer, spontaneous compositions by individuals expressing their feelings, needs, and concerns. For example, Jacob prays, "Rescue me please from the hand of my brother Esau because I fear him, that he come and strike me, mothers and children alike. And You said 'I will do good by you and make your seed like the sand of the sea that cannot be counted" (Gen 32:12–13). Numbers 12:13 contains Moses' prayer on behalf of Miriam: "God, please, heal her, please." Judges 16:28 presents Samson's prayer: "My lord, God, remember me, please, and strengthen me, please, even this time, O God, and I will avenge myself a single vengeance for my two eyes from the Philistines."

Moshe Greenberg, who drew scholarly attention to descriptions of spontaneous prose prayer, notes that the Tanakh provides the wording of 97 such prayers and that it refers to such prayers in an additional 43 passages.[36] Greenberg's analysis of these prayers in the broad context of biblical narrative reaches an important form-critical conclusion that, in turn, is the basis for a far-reaching conclusion about Israelite religion: the pattern of such prayers follows the structure of similar requests directed by one person to another; and individual Israelites could pray freely, on any occasion, spontaneously and in prose, but for the prayers to be actual communications, they had to be sincere (cf. 1 Kings 8:38; Isa 29:13; Ps 78:36–37; 145:18; Lam 2:19).[37] Since such prayer could take place anywhere, the prayer-act was not tied to the Temple ritual with its formally prescribed and choreographed sacrificial regimen conducted by priests and its schedule of psalm performances. Greenberg argues that since biblical narratives represented people addressing God anywhere and under various circumstances, that is what people actually did. Psalm 149:5 even refers to the pious who sing hymns to God when on their beds.

An examination of the 43 passages that refer to some sort of prayer reveals that in 8, the context involves sacrifice.[38] Of the 97 places where the wording of prayers is given in the biblical narrative, only 7 occur in contexts involving sacrifice, and most of these are in the Temple precinct.[39] At a general level this suggests that in the biblical period, although spontaneous prayers could be created even where formal worship occurred, it was more common away from such places. Insofar as rabbinic prayers were short and come from within a tradition of spontaneity, they may be considered a continuation of similar popular prayer originating in the biblical period and reported in the Bible.

Places of Prayer

Although the rabbis allowed that individuals could worship God wherever they were, they deemed it best that prayers be offered with a quorum of ten males. As rabbinic prayer gradually became a thrice-daily routine and spread beyond the circle of scholars to the broader populace from the second through the fifth centuries C.E., houses of study and synagogues became increasingly important. These were the two institutions where most such quorums could convene with ease. But where did informal prayer occur during the biblical period?

In ancient Israel, according to the authoritative position adopted in the Torah legislation and presupposed in canonical prophetic literature, the worship service prescribed by YHWH consisted of set sacrifices. Those sprinkling or pouring blood according to ritual and bringing the required parts of the carcass to the altar were priests acting in silence. Rituals performed competently at the designated place by the divinely appointed Aaronic priests were automatically effective. They required no accompanying words and had no prescribed libretto.[40]

That does not mean that the Temple was silent. Quite the contrary, as some of the psalms indicate, celebrations there could involve horns, harps, lyres, lutes, pipes, cymbals, timbrels, and dance (Ps 144:9; 149:3; 150:3–6), but these human expressions were irrelevant to the efficacy of the service. Simple Israelites were not required to do or say anything, even when in the Temple precincts observing the morning ritual. They did not have to be in attendance, and they were not required to say or do anything at home.

Although the Torah literature in its final edition is adamant concerning the singularity of the Jerusalem Temple (Deut 12:4–27), archaeology has revealed the presence of temples at a number of Israelite sites: Arad, an Israelite military fortress sponsored and controlled from Jerusalem; Kuntillet Ajrud, in the eastern Sinai; Beersheba; Dan; Hazor; and perhaps Megiddo.[41] In addition to these, Menahem Haran has proposed that certain rituals could only be performed before YHWH (*lipney YHWH*), i.e., at a temple. Therefore, whenever the Tanakh describes ritual acts, such as fulfillment of a vow or a communal covenant ceremony, taking place "before YHWH," a temple must have been involved. Accordingly, temples must have stood also at the following places: Shiloh (1 Sam 1:9; 3:3); Gilgal (1 Sam 15:12–21; Amos 4:4; 5:5); Mizpah (Jud 20:1–3, 8–10); Hebron (2 Sam 5:3; 15:7); Bethlehem (Jud 19:18); and Nob (1 Sam 21:1–10; 22:16–19).[42] What this suggests is that the silent service may have been performed every morning at many different places throughout the land, but at none was the presence of anybody other than the priestly officiants necessary. Furthermore, the multiplicity of temples indicates that there was no single sacred place in Israel, no best place for sacrifice. The God of Israel was ubiquitous and immanent.

In addition to temples, archaeologists have excavated sites best described as non-temple cult rooms or corners set aside for the performance of religious rituals at Ai, Beersheba, Dan, Lachish, Megiddo, Kedesh, and Tirzah, and excavated caves that were also used for religious rituals in Jerusalem and at Khirbet Beit Lei. Some of these were rooms in larger structures, some were free-standing, and some were corners of rooms in domestic structures.[43] These sites, constructed or arranged at some expense and outlay of time, imply the presence of groups that initiated, frequented, and maintained them. They attest that Israelite religious practices were more varied than is suggested by biblical texts.

The Bible indicates that like-minded people could gather for unofficial worship. Such groups could be organized around a central figure and disparate followers (Deut 13:2–3; 17:2–3) or within extended families (Deut 13:7–8), or they could comprise all residents within a settlement (Deut 13:13–16).[44] Although the laws of Deuteronomy 13:2–16 are concerned with what it considers idolatrous cults and false worship, they reflect realistically different social constellations of individuals practicing religion, from very small to large groups. Some biblical narratives presuppose the existence of such groups and refer to them casually: disciples of Isaiah (Isa 8:16), individual families of Elisha-followers (2 Kgs 5:1), communes of Elisha-followers (2 Kgs 6:1); the Yahwistic Rehabite clan of Jehonadab that abstained from wine and agriculture and lived in tents (Jer 35:6–10; 2 Kgs 10:15–16); a congregation of Baal worshippers from around the country that gathered for worship in their own temple (2 Kgs 10:18–27).

Still one other place could have been used for meetings. Prior to 586 B.C.E., such groups could have met in the gate or main entrance areas of settlements. The gate area was a place of public assembly and as such was used by prophets intent on addressing crowds (Amos 5:10) and as a place where courts convened (Isa 29:21; Jer 38:7; Deut 17:5; 21:19 [?];) and where public ceremonies took place (1 Kgs 22:10; 2 Chr 32:6; Neh 8:1). The Bible refers to areas of cultic activity at the gate (2 Kgs 23:8), and cult sites have been excavated in and around the main gates at Bethsaida and Dan. Deuteronomy commands that Moses' instructions be written (on the walls) in the gates (Deut 6:9). In fact, on the basis of these and other passages, Lee Levine of the Hebrew University argues that the origins of the synagogue are to be sought in the custom of assembling at the city gate.[45] What is more important is that such groups could have continued to meet around city gates after 586 B.C.E. both in Eretz Israel and in the communities to which they had been exiled in Babylon.

The notion that people could petition God even when distant from the Temple, and even far beyond their ancestral borders, was widespread by the sixth century B.C.E. It is found in an epistle Jeremiah sent to exiles in Babylon ca. 595 B.C.E.—before the Temple was destroyed—instructing them to settle in their exile, to pray to God for the peace of the city in which they dwell "for in its prosperity you shall prosper" (Jer 29:4–7) and to pray on their own behalf as well: "you will call Me and continually pray to Me and I will hear you" (Jer 29:12).[46] Jeremiah wrote to a community of about 20,000 people. They were the ruling and administrative class of Jerusalem and its artisans (2 Kgs 24:8–17). In addressing his remarks to them, Jeremiah assumed that they knew how to call and pray to YHWH.

Insofar as there were no rabbinic requirements that prayers be conducted in dedicated structures, it is likely that their tradition is continuous with that of self-organized groups from the biblical period who met regularly in public places for non-temple prayer services.

The Groups and Their Prayer Service

Can one, then, reconcile what is known about the early rabbinic movement with the data available in the Bible? I hypothesize about *how* groups
of Yahwistic Israelites, not necessarily gathered around a charismatic leader
like Elisha, or moved by a peculiar ideology that led to self-isolation like
the Rechabites, or engaged in another religion like the Baalists, might have
expressed their religiosity while adhering to the Deuteronomic restriction
that sacrifice be performed only in the (or a) temple. I posit that for them,
the existence of the Temple may have been significant, but not central to
their religiosity. Consequently, neither its destruction in 586 B.C.E. nor its
reconstruction and enhancement from the fifth century B.C.E. through
the first century C.E. were critical events for them.

The Bible itself provides evidence that spiritual concerns found verbal
expression. On the one hand, there are the formal compositions reflected
in psalms which individuals may have recited on their own, away from
the Temple, even as priests may have been performing the *tamid* sacrifice
at sunrise. Or the official poems may have been recited at private festive
meals after traditional sacrifices of thanksgiving or oath-fulfillment had
been conducted: cf. the psalm-prayer of Hannah at Shiloh described as
having been recited silently (1 Sam 2:1–10). Or they could have congre-
gated simply to address their thanks or needs to God. In addition to psalmody—referred to, perhaps, as *romemot 'el* (Ps 149:6)—they might have
composed informal, spontaneous "God help me" or "Thank you, God"
types of prayers as described by Moshe Greenberg. If they liked the short
pithy direct addresses, they may have reused them over and over, convert-
ing them through repetition into fixed, conventional prayers, at least for
the individual communities. Additionally, such groups may have engaged
in another type of devotional act referred to in the Bible by the verbs *h-g-h*
(to meditate) and *s-y-ch* (to converse, discuss, express orally). They are
mentioned in Ps 1:2; 19:15; 63:7; 77:13; 119:15, 23, 27, 78, 97, 99, 148; 143:5;
and 145:5. These two activities involved considering and evaluating God's
teachings, works, mighty deeds, actions, and laws. Clearly they were prem-
ised on belief in a present, just God, so much so that Eliphaz the Taiman-
ite condemns Job for voicing views that "upset fear and diminish conversing before God" (Job 15:4).[47]

What their conversing may have involved may be guessed at by translating the above-mentioned verbs, which occur only in the poetic register of
Biblical Hebrew, to their more prosaic synonym *d-b-r* (to speak). Deut 6:7

prescribes that Israelites are to impress upon their children the instructions Moses gave their ancestors before his death, and are to speak about them when they stay at home, go out on the road, lie down, and get up.

Groups organizing themselves some time in the seventh century B.C.E. may have adopted the Deuteronomic method of reinterpretation and reapplication of the older tradition. Initially, they may have adopted teachings from Deuteronomy 5–6 as basic texts: the Ten Commandments and the Shema, in that order.[48] They may also have developed an affinity for Deuteronomic "name theology," the belief that the transcendental, bodiless deity is metaphysically immanent in His name (Deut 12:11, 21, and see Amidah benedictions 1, 3, 7,18). In Psalms 5:11, 69:37; and 119:32, those who "love Your name" are singled out as deserving of the divine bounty. Authors of these psalms undoubtedly included themselves among those committed firmly to maintaining the stipulations of the divine covenant that is implied by the Hebrew verb 'ahav, when the object of the verb is a deity or king or someone of greater authority than the one who loves.

Although accepting of much in the Deuteronomic program, including its reforming legislation, these groups did not accept its Temple orientation or its penchant for the centralization of judicial and priestly authority.[49] One way in which this may have found expression is in the adoption of a standing posture when addressing the deity. This was not only the posture of faithful servants before their immanent master; it was also that of priests as they went about their work at the altar. They were counterpriests, and the places of their prayer gatherings were counter-temples.

If the core section of the rabbinic morning prayer service is deemed comparable and congruent to what is posited in the preceding paragraph, then it is clearly continuous with one particular variety of religious life and customs from the biblical period, a type independent of temple religion and the sacrificial cult.

This discussion is suggestive of one of the ways in which biblical studies at the beginning of the twenty-first century differ from what was done in the nineteenth and twentieth centuries. During the nineteenth century, the study of the Bible managed successfully to distinguish itself from traditional modes of interpretation that evolved (differently) in Judaism and Christianity from the Middle Ages and to align itself with the newly emerged discipline of History. It fled from anything traditional and ignored it. In the twentieth century, biblical studies flourished and produced historical studies of ancient Israel's social, political, and religious institutions, its linguistic development, and the evolution of its legal, historical, prophetic, wisdom, and psalmodic literature. I have tried to illustrate how biblical studies can reengage the tradition, and to indicate how this reengagement affects our understanding of the past.

Building on the insights from the twentieth century, I have critically evaluated what I labeled the "pseudo-historical" rabbinic tradition and early contemporary ideas about the continuity between the religion of ancient Israel and rabbinic Judaism. The former argued for essential continuity and the latter for discontinuity.

I concluded that both are wanting: the first because it is historically naïve and the second because it did not engage biblical data that complicate a simple description. Rabbinic petitionary prayer does not continue similar formal, biblical prayer insofar as prayer postures are concerned, but is continuous with a type of popular, spontaneous prose prayer; it is discontinuous with the highly structured types of worship centered on temples where priests performed and audiences observed, but continues a type of non-temple service conducted by self-organized groups that met in public places; it is clearly discontinuous with the sacrificial service of the temple (despite rabbinic templification) but does reflect a strand of "name theology" clearly present in Deuteronomy.

NOTES

1. Z. Zevit, "The Second-Third Century Canonization of the Hebrew Bible and Its Implications for Christian Canonizing," in A. van der Kooij and K. van der Toorn, eds., *Canonization and Decanonization* (Leiden: E. J. Brill, 1998),133–34, 149–54.

2. Apocalyptic and the Qumran sectarian literatures were produced by groups perceiving themselves as still living in the biblical age. The former produced prophetic-like texts; the latter, writings imitative of priestly instruction. Contemporaneous Pharisaic and later rabbinic groups, in contrast, seeing themselves in a new age, studied the old works but published their own teachings in new literary genres linked to the culture of their own age.

3. Solomon's temple had been attacked and despoiled a number of times in the past and was simply restored, repaired, and reconstructed (1 Kings 14:25–26; 2 Kings 12:5–17; 14:13–14; 25:9–17. Viewed this way, the Second Temple was merely another, more extensive rebuilding, and Herod's monumental refurbishing of the

Hasmonean improvements on a Persian period structure constituted an extravagant remodeling. The Romans' devastation was simply another in a series of setbacks that required reconstruction.

The rabbis, in contrast, considered its destruction the end. (Rabbi Akiva, who supported the Bar Kosiba movement, was an exception.) Thereafter, rabbis were comfortable with using "temple" metaphors in religious life and they templified emerging synagogues, a process reinforced by their loose modeling of the daily service after temple rituals. See S. Fine, *This Holy Place: On the Sanctity of the Synagogue during the Greco-Roman Period* (Notre Dame, Ind.: University of Notre Dame Press, 1998), 35–36; and R. Langer, *To Worship God Properly: Tensions between Liturgical Custom and Halakhah in Judaism* (Cincinnati: HUC Press, 1998), 5–18. Templification involved creating a valid non-sacrificial liturgy that was deemed the only acceptable way to get through to God.

4. Implicitly, my position is at odds with those who seek the origins of Jewish liturgy and non-temple prayer in the Babylonian exile. See I. Elbogen, *Jewish Liturgy: A Comprehensive History,* translated by R. P. Sheindlin based on the original 1913 German edition and the 1972 Hebrew edition (Philadelphia: JPS, 1993), 188–95.

5. R. N. McCauley and E. T. Lawson, *Bringing Ritual to Mind: Psychological Foundations of Cultural Forms* (Cambridge: Cambridge University Press, 2002), 46–55. McCauley and Lawson provide both psychological and anthropological data to support this contention.

6. *M. Tamid* 3–7 discussed below. It is clear from *m. Tamid* 7:3, which contains a petition for the immediate *restoration* of the Temple, that this second-century C.E. composition is a literary document distilling memories.

7. Hebrew *b-n-h* refers to repair, construction, and reconstruction.

8. *B. Berachot* 26b; this tradition is interesting because the editor of the Talmud also cites a contrary view that the Men of the Great Assembly, a group that allegedly functioned in the fourth century B.C.E., instituted the three services. Finally the editor cites R. Yosi b. Chanina to the effect that although the patriarchs instituted the services, the rabbis linked them with the *tamid* sacrifices making the prayers obligatory. Consequently, the three prayer services are surrogates for the three daily sacrifices (*b. Ber.* 26b).

9. The following discussion is based on the traditional Ashkenazic ritual and assumes the correctness of historians who consider it a late evolution of an original prayer service created by the rabbis in the first centuries of the Common Era. The previous sentence will be qualified significantly by details presented below.

10. This division into three parts is for heuristic purposes related to this chapter. Others divide it into five sections.

11. *T. Ber. 27b; b.Meg. 17b-18a.* The approved format was created from pre-existing short blessings, some with early roots (e.g., Ps 103:2–6 and the Hebrew additions in Ben-Sirah 51). See B. S. Jacobs, *The Weekday Siddur* (Tel Aviv: Sinai, 1978), 178–82.

12. The history of this particular benediction and its original wording has not been settled. The basic articles are L. Finkelstein, "The Development of the Amidah," *JQR* 16 (1925): 22–23, 156; and K. Kohler, "The Origin and Composition of the Eighteen Benedictions with a Translation of the Corresponding Essene Prayers in the Apostolic Constitutions," *HUCA* 1 (1924): 401–2.

13. Since the late Tannaitic period, slightly after the time that the original "Eighteen" were redacted into the extant form, when a petition against heretics, sectarians, and members of the Jesus Movement was inserted—an earlier form of the twelfth benediction used nowadays—the regular Amidah has had nineteen benedictions. On Sabbath, it consists of seven: the first and last three of the weekly prayer plus a special one in honor of the Sabbath.

14. E. J. Bickerman argues that a Palestinian version of the Amidah, consisting of five sections (labeled above #1,8,9,14,16), is first attested ca. 200 B.C.E. See "The Civic Prayer of Jerusalem," *Harvard Theological Review* 55 (1962): 176–85.

Although the extant form of the Amidah prayer was fixed in the second century C.E., about 320 years after Bickerman dates its first appearance as part of Jerusalem's civic religion, prayer leaders could insert petitions of a personal and private nature during the public repetition (*b. Ber.* 34a). One *baraita*—an early rabbinic teaching not preserved in the Mishnah but cited in the Talmud—mentions that Rabbi Akiba would abbreviate the prayer, i.e., use the basic structure, when praying with a congregation, but expand it when praying by himself (*b. Ber.* 31a). Even today, the devout may pray longer and insert personal prayers into the standard liturgy in their private devotions, but not at the expense of the public. I thank Rabbi Y. Etshalom for these references.

15. One additional bow is made in the concluding *Aleinu leshabeach* ("It is incumbent on us to praise") prayer at the words "but we bend the knee and bow before the king of the king of kings." According to some practices nowadays, whereas the bowing during the Amidah involves dipping at the knee and bowing at the waist, that of the Aleinu prayer usually involves bowing at the waist alone. This differentiates the bowing throughout the year from the actual bowing that accompanies this prayer when recited as part of the Rosh Hashana liturgy. Introduced into the Rosh Hashana liturgy after the fourth century C.E., it was incorporated into the daily services sometime during the medieval period.

16. See M. Weinfeld, *Ha-liturgiyah haYehudit hakedumah: mehasifrut hamizmorit ve'ad latefilot bimegilot Qumran [Early Jewish Liturgy from Psalms to the Prayers in Qumran and Rabbinic Literature]* (Jerusalem: Magnes Press, 2004), 151–235.

17. During the last millennium, prayers were composed and accepted into the pre-modern, traditional services and then rejected and removed. See L. A. Hoffman, *The Canonization of the Synagogue Service* (Notre Dame, Ind. and London: University of Notre Dame Press, 1979), 66–71; and in greater detail, particularly with regard to labyrinthine *piyyutim,* the relevant chapter in R. Langer, *To Worship*

God Properly: Tensions between Liturgical Custom and Halakhah in Judaism (Cincinnati: Hebrew Union College, 1998), 110–87, where the history of the rise and fall of the use and status of piyyutim from their origin through the twentieth century is traced. Prayers were still added as recently as 150 years ago. See D. Rappel, *Pitchey she'arim: 'iyyunim u-mehkarim 'al nose ha-tefilah [Gates to the Jewish Liturgy* (Hebrew)] (Tel Aviv: Yedioth Ahronot Books/Chemed Books, 2001), 94, but see 72–103; S. C. Reif, *Judaism and Hebrew Prayer: New Perspectives on Jewish Liturgical History* (Cambridge: Cambridge University Press, 1993), 207–55.

My statement ignores the drastic changes introduced into the form and content of prayers by consciously driven ideologues of the Conservative, Reconstructionist, and Reform movements. Nobody employing these twentieth-century prayer books is under the illusion that they are traditional. In these communities, it is publicly acknowledged that though the prayers (may) follow traditional patterns and wording, and though many of the prayers are traditional and ancient, editors of the modern versions have eliminated or changed ancient texts and authored new ones, justifying these changes on theological and ideological grounds. On these, see Reif's discussion of current developments, in *Judaism and Hebrew Prayer*, 294–331. My preceding statements also ignore differences between Ashkenazic and Sephardic prayer books and the internal differences between different Ashkenazic and different Sephardic rituals.

18. H. Mack, *Mavo letefilot Yisrael [Introduction to Jewish Liturgy]* (Tel Aviv: Ministry of Defense, 2001), 15–18.

19. T. Zahavy cites Mark 12:29–30, phylacteries from Qumran, and debates between the houses of Hillel and Shammai (*m. Ber.* 1:3), ca. 10–20 C.E., about the Shema as evidence that its liturgical use is early and scribal, i.e., originating in groups with no great stake in the temple—Zahavy, *Studies in Jewish Prayer* (Lanham, Md.: University Press of America, 1990), 89–93. Its use in different and antagonistic Jewish communities suggests that it is a common legacy from before the first century B.C.E. The temple ritual described in *m. Tamid* of a chorus-like recitation of the Shema differs from the rabbinic recitation in that the rabbis saw the recitation as an extremely personal matter demanding intense concentration (*m. Ber.* 1).

20. M. Weinfeld, *'Aseret hadibrot ukeriat Shema': gilgulehem shel hatsharot emunah [The Ten Commandments and the Shema: Permutations of Declarations of Faith]* (Tel Aviv: Kibbutz Meuchad, 2001), 18–32, 99–123.

21. The form of the Amidah now used clearly reflects post-destruction theology, with petitionary prayers for the ingathering of exiles, the restoration of judges, and the restoration and rebuilding of Jerusalem.

22. U. Ehrlich, *'Kol 'atzmotay to'marnah': hasafah halo' milulit shel hatefilah [The Non-Verbal Language of Jewish Prayer]* (Jerusalem: Magnes Press, 1999), 17–21.

23. M. I. Gruber, *Aspects of Nonverbal Communication in the Ancient Near East*, Studia Pohl 12/I and II (Rome: Biblical Institute Press, 1980), 150.

24. This dating of the psalm is determined by two considerations, the first of which is more important than the second: (1) verses 41–47 assume the defeat and deportation of Israelites and their presence in exile; and (2) the bulk of its language is characteristic of pre-exilic Hebrew with one exception. The word *wayya'amod* has the sense "he rose" that in pre-exilic Hebrew would have been expressed by *wayyaqom*. See A. Hurvitz, *Bein lashon le-lashon: le-toldot lashon haMiqra biymey bayit sheni [Between Language and Language: Towards a History of Biblical Hebrew in the Days of the Second Temple]* (Jerusalem: Bialik Institute, 1972), 13–63, 177–84. Thus, even though it has the word for "stand," it employs it to indicate the beginning of an activity, not to indicate a particular posture (cf. p. 173).

25. This sense of *pillel*, "to do something about some situation/intervene," is suitable to all occurrences of the word: Gen 48:11; 1 Sam 2:25; Ezek 16:52. Consequently, the noun *tefillah*, usually rendered "prayer," should be comprehended in concert with the verb as meaning something like "a request for intervention, an intervention/intercession." For another interpretation based on the root *n-p-l*, see D. R. Ap-Thomas, "Notes on Some Hebrew Terms Relating to Prayer," *VT* 6 (1956): 230–39.

The pattern of derivation proposed follows the pattern of *tehillah*, "praise" from *hillel*, and *techinnah*, "request for (unmerited) mercy or kindness" from *chinnen*. Since the English verb "pray" means to entreat earnestly and humbly, and also smacks a bit of piety and righteousness, it is an appropriate descriptor of only *some* of the man-God communications in the Tanakh.

26. Ap-Thomas, "Notes on Some Hebrew Terms Relating to Prayer," 226; Gruber, *Aspects of Nonverbal Communication*, 145–51. Gruber presents data showing how a similar collocation of verb indicating "standing" + preposition indicating "before" means "to serve" in Akkadian.

27. On the overlooked prophetic role as divinely appointed intercessor, see the insightful essay of Y. Muffs, "Who Will Stand in the Breach? A Study of Prophetic Intercession," in Y. Muffs, *Love & Joy: Law Language and Religion in Ancient Israel* (New York and Jerusalem: Jewish Theological Seminary, 1992), 9–48, and for Jeremiah in particular, pp. 27–31.

28. See Gen 22:5; Exod 24:1; 33:10; Lev 26:1; Deut 26:10; 2 Kings 5:18; 2 Kings 18:22 (= Isa 36:7); 66:23; Ezek 8:16; 46:2–3; Ps 5:8; Gruber, *Aspects of Nonverbal Communication*, 91–92. Gruber provides a cautious analysis of the verb when used literally (pp. 94–120) as well as when it is used more figuratively with the general sense of praying, worshipping (pp. 120–23), paying close attention to how the different prepositions used with the word nuance its meaning. But of course, when indicating prayer in general, the characteristic act comes to signify everything else that may have been going on through synecdoche.

29. Cf. Num 16:22; 1 Sam 20:41; 28; 20; Ezek 9:8; Ezr 10:1, etc.

30. Cf. Gen 49:9; Jud 7:6; 2 Kings 1:13; Isa 45:23, etc.

31. Cf. Gen 24:26; Num 22:31; 1 Sam 28:14; Neh 8:6, etc. Gruber denies the connection between *q-d-d* and *qodqod*, "head/skull," preferring to interpret it through Akkadian *qadā du*, "to be low," whose exact range of nuances within its own semantic field remains to be determined. See Gruber, *Aspects of Nonverbal Communication*, 126, and C. Cohen's useful article, "The Saga of a Unique Verb in Biblical Hebrew and Ugaritic: *hishtachaweh* 'to Bow Down'—Usage and Etymology," in L. H. Ehrlich et al., eds., *Textures and Meanings: Thirty Years of Judaic Studies at University of Massachussetts Amherst* (Amherst: University of Massachusetts Press, 2004), 323–42 (on-line at www.umass.edu/judaic/anniversaryvolume/). With regard to the adequacy of scholarly understanding of Akkadian, Cohen supports Gruber but does not present new data (see pp. 336–37 note 22).

32. Solomon is described as praying in a similar posture: When Solomon completed praying to the Lord . . . he rose from before the altar of the Lord from bending on his knees, his palms spread to the heavens, and he stood and blessed the whole congregation (1 Kings 8:54–55); but this contradicts what is narrated in v. 22, "and Solomon stood before the altar of the Lord before the whole congregation of Israel and spread his palms to the heavens." These passages, which critical Biblicists and historians regard as late, but not so late as Daniel, on other grounds, suggest that perhaps the transition should be dated earlier in the Second Temple period than I suggest above.

33. For a more elaborate discussions of how ancient Israelites conceived the cosmos and the place of humans within it, see Z. Zevit, *The Religions of Ancient Israel: A Synthesis of Parallactic Approaches* (London: Continuum, 2001), 664–67; and with an attempt at greater precision, M. S. Smith, *The Memoirs of God: History, Memory and the Experience of the Divine in Ancient Israel* (Minneapolis: Fortress Press, 2004), 105–23.

34. A *baraita*, a tannaitic teaching preserved in the Talmud, observes that when Rabbi Akiba (d. ca. 137 C.E.) prayed by himself, " a man would leave him in one corner and find him later in another, on account of his many genuflections and prostrations" (*b. Ber.* 31a). It is presented as a curiosity, not a behavior to be emulated.

35. J. Day, "How Many Pre-Exilic Psalms Are There?" in J. Day, ed., *In Search of Pre-Exilic Israel*, JSOTSS 406 (London and New York: T&T Clark International, 2004), 225–50. Day undertakes to assign psalms to the pre-exilic, exilic, and post-exilic periods on the bases of their theological statements, historical allusions, and intertextual connections, as well as the type of Hebrew they employ. He locates most of the pre-exilic psalms in the first one hundred psalms and most of the post-exilic ones in the last fifty. See also A. Berlin, "Psalms and the Literature of Exile," in P. W. Flint and P. D. Miller, eds., *The Book of Psalms: Composition and Reception* (Leiden and Boston: E. J. Brill, 2005), 65–66.

36. M. Greenberg, *Biblical Prose Prayer* (Berkeley, Los Angeles, and London: University of California Press, 1983), 7–8 and 59 note 3.

37. M. Greenberg, *Biblical Prose Prayer*, 36, 47–52.

38. Lev 9:24; 16:21; 1 Sam 1:10, 12–15; 7:8–9; 2 Sam 6:18; 1 Kings 18:42; Isa 56:7; 1 Chron 21:26.

39. 1 Sam 7:6; 1 Kings 8:15–21, 22–53, 55–61; 18:36–37; 1 Chron 29:10–19; 20:5–12.

40. Z. Zevit, "The Prophet Versus Priest Antagonism Hypothesis: Its History and Origin," in L. L. Grabbe and A. O. Bellis, eds., *The Priests in the Prophets: The Portrayal of Priests and Other Religious Specialists in the Latter Prophets*, JSOTS 408 (London: T&T Clark International 2004), 200–209; I. Knohl, *The Sanctuary of Silence: The Priestly Torah and the Holiness School* (Minneapolis: Fortress Press, 1995), 148–57.

41. Zevit, *The Religions*, 248–49.

42. M. Haran, *Temples and Temple Service in Ancient Israel* (Oxford: Clarendon Press, 1978), 26–37. In support of Haran's position, I have argued that it is likely that an expression in Deut 12:14, usually translated "the place that YHWH will choose in one of your tribes" and interpreted as referring to a single temple, should be translated "a place in each of your tribes" and interpreted as referring to a temple in each tribal allotment. See the data and references to important earlier research in Zevit, *The Religions*, 286–88.

43. Zevit, *The Religions*, 153–249, 405–37. Some evidence, not available when I wrote my book, for an additional Jerusalem cult corner has recently become public. Though not published, it is mentioned with an accompanying photograph in *Biblical Archaeology Review* 30, no. 6 (2004): 29.

44. These passages are discussed in greater detail in Zevit, *The Religions*, 643–44.

45. L. Levine, *The Ancient Synagogue* (New Haven and London: Yale University Press, 2000), 19–41.

46. The same idea is expressed in Deut 4:27–31; 30:1–10. Deuteronomy's threats of a future exile and tentative ingathering of exiles rests on the reality of the Assyrian deportations from the northern kingdom of Israel in the eighth century B.C.E., when communities and various skilled groups were dispersed to various sections of the empire. Some scholars see these as post-586 B.C.E. interpolations into the text. What is important, however, is that by the second century when proto-rabbinic groups existed, they had available non-temple theology in the Pentateuch.

47. One consequence of such individual meditations may have been a desire to convey religious ideas and sentiments in words that were neither the high poetry of psalms nor the simple prose of individual requests, but something which we might recognize as formal yet simple prayer. For example, the psalmist identifies Ps 19 as a *heggyon libbi*, meditation of my mind (v. 15). It begins with creation (vss. 1–7), continues with statements about YHWH's teaching, covenant, orders, commandments, and judgments (vss. 8–11), a brief confession, and prayer for protection (vss. 12–14). Ps 102 is identified as "a request for intercession (*tefillah*) for the afflicted man when he is faint and pours his conversation (*siycho*) before YHWH."

48. S. A. Kaufman has advanced a thesis that the Ten Commandments in Deuteronomy are the organizing principle on which the following laws in the Deuteronomic Code are arranged. See "The Structure of the Deuteronomic Law," *Maarav* 1, no. 2 (1979): 105–58.

49. The implication of the reforming tradition is that once the notion that reform is possible takes root, there is no end to it. A strength of the "reform" of law and narrative in Deuteronomy is that it is not presented as prophetic revelation, but rather as Moses' own preaching and teaching, a product of his own mind.

For the Deuteronomic way of reinterpreting the legal traditions, see B. M. Levinson, *Deuteronomy and the Hermeneutics of Legal Innovation* (Oxford and New York: Oxford University Press, 1997); idem, "Is the Covenant Code an Exilic Composition? A Response to John Van Seters," in J. Day, ed., *In Search of Pre-Exilic Israel*, JSOTSS 406 (London and New York: T & T Clark International, 2004), 272–325; for its way of reinterpreting the narrative traditions, see Z. Zevit, "Converging Lines of Evidence Bearing on the Date of P," *ZAW* 94 (1982): 502–10; and in general M. Fishbane, *Biblical Interpretation in Ancient Israel* (Oxford: Clarendon Press, 1985), 58–60, 175–203, 321–22, 439–40; and M. Weinfeld, *Deuteronomy 1-11* (New York: Doubleday, 1991), 19–24, 125–230.

Chapter 9

Jewish Biblical Theology

Marvin A. Sweeney

Jews and Modern Critical Biblical Scholarship

Jews have been engaged in the critical and theological study of the Bible since the days of the writing of the Bible itself. Each of the Bible's literary works is written from a particular theological viewpoint, e.g., the present form of the Torah emphasizes the role of the holy Temple, portrayed as the wilderness tabernacle, at the center of a unified nation of Israel;[1] the books of Joshua, Judges, Samuel, and Kings present a history of Israel that asserts divine righteousness by claiming that the Babylonian exile was the result of Israel's failure to abide by Torah;[2] and the prophetic book of Isaiah is based on the principle of an eternal covenant between G-d and the people of Israel.[3] Furthermore, the Bible contains many examples in which its authors cited, debated, reinterpreted, and rewrote earlier biblical literature in order to express newer ideas concerning divine revelation, historical events, social religious policy, and the like, in relation to the needs and questions of later times. Examples include Deuteronomy's revision of earlier laws in Exodus to provide greater rights for the poor and women;[4] the Chronicler's rewriting of history in Samuel and Kings to emphasize concerns with religious observance;[5] the citation of Isaiah's prophecies in Joel, Micah, and Zechariah to articulate very different visions of Israel's future;[6] and Job's debate with Proverbs concerning the question of divine righteousness.[7]

Later Jewish writers continued such critical and theological engagement with the Bible. The Greek Septuagint, the earliest known Jewish translation of the Bible, frequently rearranges and rewrites biblical literature to present more aesthetically pleasing and logically consistent narratives (e.g., 1-2 Kings),[8] to assert divine involvement on behalf of Jews in a time of threat (e.g., Esther),[9] or to emphasize the role of Jews in the larger Hellenistic world (e.g., Isaiah).[10] The Talmud critically reinterprets the legal principle of an eye for an eye so that it no longer calls for physical retribution, but calls instead for fines or other punishments appropriate to a crime.[11] The Talmud also claims that Joshua must have written the account of Moses' death in the Torah because Moses was unable to do so.[12] Medieval interpreters, such as Abraham Ibn Ezra, take the point further by identifying additional statements in the Torah that Moses would not have written. Indeed, Ibn Ezra raises questions as to whether Samuel wrote the entire books of 1-2 Samuel and whether Isaiah wrote all of his own book.[13] Maimonides argues for a principle of historical development in Judaism that begins with the Bible. He claims that much of the Bible's language cannot be taken literally, but functions metaphorically so that it might point to larger truths that will later appear in Judaism, such as the emerging role of prayer rather than animal sacrifice as a means by which humans express themselves to G-d.[14] Lurianic kabbalists explain the presence of evil in the world by redefining the concept of G-d, claiming that the very act of creation renders G-d no longer infinite.[15]

It is somewhat ironic then that Jewish interpreters are considered as relative newcomers to the modern critical and theological study of the Bible that has emerged in the western world since the early days of the Enlightenment.[16] Modern critical and theological scholarship has been primarily a Protestant Christian enterprise as Protestants employ critical methods in an effort to recover the historical character of the Bible so that it might serve as the basis for reconstructing a pristine and authentic church that reflects the will of G-d.[17] Much of the methodology and perspectives employed actually originated in earlier periods as Jews and Muslims employed philological, historical, and theological arguments to assert the historical priority and truth of their respective traditions. As Christians were drawn into these debates, the historical character of the Bible became a fundamental concern as Christians sought to reform the church. Indeed, Martin Luther's reformation was intended to return the church to its "authentic" Jewish roots by adapting only those books of the Christian Old Testament that were found in the Jewish Bible and by eliminating much of the church hierarchy and canon law that had developed over the centuries. Nevertheless, the overwhelming importance of the New Testament in Christian theology would continue to exercise great influence in biblical interpretation as Protestant theologians sought to demonstrate the historical process by which Israel violated its covenant with G-d, thereby setting the stage for the revelation of Jesus as the agent through whom the entire world would be redeemed.

Because of the predominantly Protestant character of critical scholarship from the early days of the Enlightenment through the period following World War II, Jews and others (e.g., Roman Catholics) tended to be excluded from critical scholarship as Protestants employed it to address their own theological concerns.[18] The early years of critical scholarship were marked by a great deal of anti-Jewish sentiment, as late nineteenth- and early twentieth-century scholars such as Julius Wellhausen employed critical methodology to rewrite the Bible's history of religious development, claiming that the original spiritual impulse of the prophets had been corrupted by the growing influence of the Temple, the priesthood, and its ritual laws. Thus Torah was no longer the foundational revelation of the Bible, but a gradually developing document that was ultimately subjected to the destructive influence of Jewish priests, who rewrote the Torah in order to gain power over their own people. For Wellhausen, Judaism was "a mere empty chasm over which one springs from the Old Testament to the New."[19] Such argumentation prompted Solomon Schechter, then President of the Jewish Theological Seminary, to claim that higher biblical criticism constituted nothing more than higher anti-Semitism.[20] Derogatory attitudes toward Judaism continued among many Christian biblical scholars through much of the twentieth century, as illustrated by Walter Eichrodt's claim of Judaism's "torso-like appearance" in relation to Christianity.[21]

Nevertheless, the experience of the twentieth century, including two world wars, the attempted genocides against the Jewish people and others, and the threat of nuclear destruction, has prompted a major rethinking of the sense of optimism, progress, and self-entitlement that dominated much of Protestant thinking throughout the eighteenth and nineteenth centuries. This experience has had an especially profound effect upon Christian biblical theology because of the role the Christian Bible has played, particularly with its claims of Jewish sin in rejecting Jesus and in complicity in his death, in forming anti-Jewish attitudes that were prevalent in the cultural background of the Nazi state and its promulgation of the Shoah or Holocaust.[22] As Christians have begun to rethink their theologies, Jews and other previously marginalized groups, such as women, Roman Catholic theologians, and gays and lesbians, have begun to play increasingly greater roles in critical biblical scholarship and theological discussion. Consequently, Jews have become interested in the modern study of biblical theology and its implications for developing Jewish thought and identity and for rethinking Judaism's relationship with Christianity. Indeed, a Jewish biblical theology, which systematically interprets the Jewish Tanakh in relation to Jewish tradition and concerns, is a pressing need for modern Jewish thought and interreligious dialog. A number of important topics have emerged in recent discussion, including the rationale for Jewish biblical theology, the recognition of a distinctive Jewish Bible, the Torah and Temple as holy religious centers, the role of the nation Israel, the problem of evil, and the role of post-biblical Jewish tradition.

Jewish Biblical Theology

Reasons for Jewish Biblical Theology

Although biblical theology has largely been a Christian theological discipline throughout most of its history, Judaism has much to gain by developing its own theological approaches to the critical study of the Bible.[23] The Bible is fundamentally Jewish literature, written by Jews in ancient times to express their understandings of G-d, the nation of Israel, and the world at large, that functions as the basis for all Jewish tradition. Christian biblical theology generally addresses its own concerns: the relation of the Old Testament to the New Testament, the character of G-d, the nature of human sin and the necessity of divine redemption through Christ, and the inclusion of gentiles in the divine covenant of Israel.[24] Jewish tradition has a very different set of concerns that are rarely addressed in Christian biblical theology. Judaism discourages speculation concerning the nature and character of G-d, as attempts to portray or define G-d compromise divine sanctity and promote idolatry. Although Judaism is intimately concerned with G-d, it tends to focus far more intently on the responsibilities of human beings, who are expected to act as partners with G-d to ensure the completion and sanctity of creation at large.[25] Thus, Judaism is concerned with the character and nature of the people of Israel as an ongoing reality in world history; the development of halakhah (Jewish law or practice), which defines the holy character of Jewish life; and the role of Judaism in bringing about Tikkun Olam, "the repair of the world," working to eliminate the presence of evil in the world.

Jewish theology and biblical interpretation also has much to contribute to the field of Christian biblical theology.[26] Fundamentally, it asserts that

Judaism is not simply a prelude to the advent of Christianity in world history that will ultimately be absorbed as the entire world comes to recognize Christ. Instead, it demonstrates that Judaism constitutes a distinctive, legitimate, and continuing theological reality that must be accepted and engaged as such by Christians. Indeed, the recent proposal from within the Roman Catholic Church to regard Judaism as Christianity's "older brother" represents a step in this direction.

Although Judaism and Christianity develop out of the same roots in the Bible, they are not the same. Whereas Judaism maintains its understanding of the continuity of the Jewish people and their relationship to G-d, Christianity abandoned its originally Jewish roots very early in its history as it looked to the Gentile world for continued growth and theological development. As Christianity absorbed pagan religious systems and ideas, it developed a very distinctive theological view in which human beings were fundamentally incapable of overcoming their sinful nature and required divine intervention in order to achieve salvation. Acceptance of the principle that Judaism and Christianity are not fundamentally the same, despite their common origins in biblical tradition, is essential for the continued future development of both traditions. Such recognition has the potential to bring to an end the moral problem of a long tradition of Christian oppression of Jews,[27] and it provides an opportunity for constructive dialogue and interaction between the two traditions.[28]

The Distinctive Forms of the Jewish and Christian Bibles.

An important aspect of the recognition of the distinctive characters of Judaism and Christianity begins with consideration of the form and identity of the Bible in each.[29] Because Judaism and Christianity share a biblical tradition, the Tanakh in Judaism and the Old or First Testament in Christianity, many consider the Tanakh and Old/First Testament to be one and the same document. Although the Tanakh and Protestant versions of the Old/First Testament include the same biblical books, they are arranged in very different sequences that point to the distinctive understanding of the Bible in each tradition. The theological implications of the Christian term "Old Testament" have been long recognized.[30] The term "testament" refers to a "covenant" or "agreement" between two parties, in this case between G-d and human beings. Within the Christian Bible, the Old Testament constitutes the first major portion of the Bible, which refers to the original covenant between G-d and humanity that was established with the people Israel. The "old covenant" of Israel is expressed through the revelation of divine law to Israel through Moses at Mt. Sinai, and the purpose of such revelation was that Israel serve as the means by which G-d would be revealed to the entire world. But Christianity maintains that G-d was compelled to punish Israel for failing to keep its covenant by bringing about the destruction of Israel and Judah by the ancient Assyrian and Babylonian empires. Such failure points to the need for the "new covenant" or New Testament, the second major component of the Christian Bible, which relates the revelation of Jesus as the Christ, who will bring forgiveness from sin and redemption to the entire world. Some Christian interpreters have recently adopted the term "First Testament" to eliminate implications that the Mosaic covenant has been superseded by the revelation of Jesus in the New Testament.[31]

The basic division of the Christian Bible into the Old/First Testament and the New Testament demonstrates fundamental principles of Christian theology. But such theological tenets also appear in the basic structure of each Testament. Thus, the four-part structure of the New Testament points to the Christian belief that a sinful world has not yet accepted Christ and that a second coming of Christ is necessary. It employs a chronological sequence to portray the historical process of Christian revelation. Hence, the four Gospels relate the earliest revelation of Jesus, his crucifixion, and his resurrection as the foundation of the New Testament tradition. The Acts of the Apostles then relate the subsequent early history of the nascent church as it seeks to spread from Jerusalem to Rome, the center of the ancient Greco-Roman world. The Epistles address timeless questions of Christian theology and church organization as Christianity prepares for Christ's return. Finally, the Apocalypse of John or the Book of Revelation points to the future second coming of Christ as the culmination of human history.

The structure of the Christian Old/First Testament exhibits a similar four-part chronological sequence that traces the relationship between G-d and humanity from creation to the period immediately prior to the revelation of Jesus. This basic sequence applies both to the Protestant Old Testament and to the Old Testament of the Roman Catholic and Eastern Orthodox canons, although the latter include many more books than the Protestant version. The Christian Old Testament initially contained many books that did not appear in the Jewish version of the Bible, but Martin Luther removed those books from the Old Testament and gathered them as a distinct group of Apocryphal books in his efforts to reform Christianity and return it to its purported Jewish roots.

Like the Gospels, the Pentateuch or Five Books of Moses relate the earliest history of G-d's relationship with Israel and humanity at large, from the creation of the world through the time of the Patriarchs and Matriarchs and the time of Moses' leading Israel out of bondage in Egypt and to the promised land. Of course, the primary event related in the Pentateuch is the revelation of G-d's covenant with Israel at Mt. Sinai. The Historical Books then relate the subsequent history of Israel, from the time of its entry into the promised land under Joshua through the period of the Babylonian exile and the people Israel's life either in the land of Israel or in the diaspora under Gentile rule. The Poetical and Wisdom Books take up timeless questions of the character of G-d and the means by which human beings relate to G-d and the world in which they live. Finally, the Prophetic Books point to a future beyond the punishment suffered by Israel when G-d will reestablish a new relationship with Israel and the world at large. Within the larger context of the Christian Bible, the Prophets appear immediately prior to the New Testament so that the New Testament becomes the fulfillment of the Old.

The Jewish Tanakh is organized according to a very different set of principles, which likewise demonstrate Judaism's fundamental theological world view that the Torah serves the basis for G-d's relationship with Israel and the world at large.[32] Tanakh is an acronym for the three major parts of the Jewish Bible: Torah ("Instruction"); Nevi'im ("Prophets"); and Ketuvim ("Writings"). Although Torah is often mistranslated as "law," it actually means "instruction," "guidance," or "revelation." The Torah includes the Five Books of Moses—Genesis, Exodus, Leviticus, Numbers, and Deuteronomy—and presents the foundational history of Judaism and the world from creation, through the period of the Patriarchs and Matriarchs, and finally through the time of Moses, including the Exodus from Egypt, the revelation of Torah at Mt. Sinai, and the journey through the wilderness to the promised land of Israel.

Altogether, the Torah presents an ideal view of the relationship between G-d and Israel as G-d forms Israel into a people, reveals the Torah by which they are to live, and leads them to the land of Israel. The Nevi'im or Prophets includes two subdivisions. The *Nevi'm Rishonim* or the Former Prophets include the books of Joshua, Judges, Samuel, and Kings, which relate an interpretive history of Israel from the entry into the land of Israel under Joshua to the Babylonian exile. The books attempt to demonstrate that Israel's suffering is the result of its failure to live according to the divine commandments given through Moses. The *Nevi'im Aharonim* or Latter Prophets include the books of Isaiah, Jeremiah, Ezekiel, and the Twelve Prophets, which contain the prophetic oracles and narratives about the prophets that present their understandings of the reasons for Israel's suffering and the future restoration of the people once the punishment is complete. Altogether, the Prophets point to the disruption of the ideal relationship between Israel and G-d, but they also point to its restoration by asserting that G-d never abandons the covenant with Israel. Finally, the Ketuvim or Writings include the books of Psalms, Job, Proverbs, the Five Megillot or Scrolls (Ruth, Song of Songs, Qohelet, Lamentations, Esther), Daniel, Ezra-Nehemiah, and Chronicles. These books take up the various means by which human beings understand and express themselves in relation to G-d as a prelude to the accounts of the restoration of Jewish life around the Jerusalem Temple and divine Torah. Essentially, the books of the Ketuvim are organized to point to the restoration of the ideal relationship portrayed in the Torah and disrupted in the Nevi'im. Thus, Torah stands as the foundational and eternal basis for the relationship between G-d, Israel, and the world at large in the Tanakh.

Torah as Foundation for the Jewish Bible

Because Torah stands as the basis for the relationship between G-d and Israel in the Bible, it must be considered as a foundational concept in Jewish biblical theology. The revelation of Torah to Israel through Moses at Mt. Sinai provides the basic guidance for Israel to lead a holy life, which in turn leads to the recognition of G-d by the other nations and sanctification of the world at large. Biblical tradition maintains that the initial tablets given to Moses were housed in the ark in the Jerusalem Temple, which functions as the holy center of Israel through which Torah is revealed.[33] Consequently, Jewish biblical theology must consider the Temple, its rituals, and the priesthood together with Torah.

Christian biblical theology generally understands Torah as "law," following Paul's rendition of the term as the Greek *nomos*.[34] In keeping with Paul's critique of "Law" as the foundation of the Mosaic covenant, inherently sinful human beings are incapable of fulfilling the "Law" completely and therefore require the forgiveness of sin offered through Jesus

(Romans, Galatians). In subsequent Christian thought, "Law" is frequently characterized as legalistic priestly ritual lacking in efficacy, spirituality, and rationale.

Such a conceptualization of Torah contrasts markedly with the understanding of Torah in Judaism and even in the Bible itself. Even a cursory reading of the Torah indicates that it contains not only legal material, but a great deal of narrative and poetic material that recounts the early history of the world and the people of Israel. Furthermore, the legal material addresses a whole range of religious and social issues, indicating that it is designed to provide the basis for a just and holy life in ancient Israelite society.[35] The Hebrew term Torah is a noun derived from the hiphil form of the verb *yarah*, "to guide, show, instruct." Torah therefore refers to "guidance" or "instruction," i.e., divine guidance in such areas as the history, social identity, and religious values of the nation that would form Israel into a living society in the ancient world. Torah ultimately refers to the entire body of Jewish teaching and tradition.[36]

The Jerusalem Temple

The interrelationship between Torah and Temple must also be considered. Fundamentally, the Temple priesthood is responsible for the instruction of the people in divine Torah, including ritual matters, civil and criminal law, and Israel's sacred history. Indeed, Moses was a Levitical priest who taught his people Torah. Temples are clearly the location for such instruction in ancient Israelite society. Interpreters have noted the correlation between Mt. Zion, the traditional location of the Jerusalem Temple, and Mt. Sinai in that both serve as the location from which Torah is revealed to Israel and the world.[37]

The Temple symbolizes G-d's presence in the world, functions as the center of all creation, and symbolizes many aspects of Israel's sacred history.[38] The Holy of Holies where the ark of the covenant is housed is built according to the pattern of an ancient throne room; the inner walls, doors, and columns of the Temple are decorated with symbols of the Garden of Eden, such as pomegranates, palm trees, animals, and cherubim; the molten sea, situated across from the altar outside the Temple, likely symbolizes the sea from which creation proceeds and through which Israel walks dryshod in its escape from the Egyptian chariots; the seven-branched Temple Menorah or lampstand symbolizes light at creation, the seven days of the week, and the tree in the Garden of Eden. The major Temple festivals likewise symbolize both the natural world of G-d's creation and the sacred history of Israel. Pesach or Passover begins the grain harvest, and commemorates the Exodus from Egypt; Shavuot or Weeks concludes the grain harvest, and commemorates the revelation of Torah at Sinai; and Sukkot or Booths marks the fruit harvest and the beginning of the rainy season, and commemorates the journey through the wilderness to the land of Israel. Altogether, the Temple and Torah symbolize the stability and perpetuation of creation together with the instruction and sanctification of Israel within the created world.

The Nation Israel

The central role of the nation Israel in Jewish biblical theology is self-evident.[39] Israel's origins are related to the creation of the world and the need for human beings to act as partners with G-d to complete and sanctify creation. G-d therefore chooses Abram/Abraham and Sarai/Sarah for a special covenant relationship through which their descendants will form the nation Israel. The Bible contends that Israel is constituted as a nation holy to G-d and a kingdom of priests that stands at the center of all the nations of the world.[40] The Bible is careful to specify that Israel was chosen for this role not by any special merit, but because G-d chose to keep the promises made to Israel's ancestors.[41] Israel's experiences thereby become an example to the nations concerning divine power, justice, and mercy.

Although Israel appears in the Bible as a theological construct that is tied to the order of creation and the recognition of G-d as the creator, the sociohistorical reality of Israel that stands behind the construct must also be considered. Archeological evidence confirms the emergence of the nation Israel in Canaan, beginning in the late thirteenth century B.C.E. and continuing until the Babylonian destruction of Jerusalem in 587 B.C.E.[42] The Egyptian Pharaoh Merneptah lists Israel among the various Canaanite nations he claims to have defeated in 1220 B.C.E., and the hieroglyphs employed for Israel indicate that it is a semi-nomadic group.[43] Extensive building of fortified cities in the land from the tenth century B.C.E. on points to the emergence of the Israelite and Judean kingdoms.[44] The recently discovered Tel Dan inscription makes reference to the ruling "house of David."[45]

The Davidic Monarchy

Indeed, the line of Israelite/Judean kings founded by David is a key institution of the Israelite state, since David established his capital at Jerusalem, his son Solomon built the Jerusalem Temple, and the subsequent Davidic monarchs continued to rule over Judah in Jerusalem even after the northern tribes broke away to form the northern kingdom of Israel. The Bible presents a great deal of information concerning both the theological character of the Davidic dynasty and its secular functions. Like the nation Israel, the house of David understands itself to have been chosen by G-d;[46] just as David and his successors established and maintained G-d's Temple in Jerusalem, so G-d established and protected the house of David, promising that it would rule in Jerusalem forever (Psalm 132).

The theology undergirds the king's right to exercise power over and on behalf of the people; he collects revenues from the people, i.e., one tenth of their income in grain, wine, oil, and animals from herd and flock, to support the Temple and the monarchy in the form of holy offerings presented by the people at the Temple during the major holidays, Pesach, Shavuot, and Sukkot. The king is also responsible for the defense of the nation and the administration of justice. Israelite men are required to serve in the army at times of crisis, and the king is ultimately responsible for applying G-d's Torah in carrying out the rule of the nation (Deuteronomy 17:14–20). He may serve as a judge or appoint judges from among the people and the priests. It is important therefore to note that the laws in Exodus, Leviticus, Numbers, and Deuteronomy include religious, criminal, and civil laws that are intended to guide life in ancient Israelite society. Thus, Israelite law treats all manner of situations that might arise in a living society, such as murder, manslaughter, theft, marriage, commerce, labor relations, property rights, and debt, in order to ensure a just, orderly, and viable society defined according to divine Torah.[47]

The Problem of Evil/Shoah

The divine covenant articulated in the Bible clearly envisions Israel as an eternal nation that will not come to an end (Genesis 15, 17). Nevertheless, the continuity of Israel was threatened at various historical periods when enemy nations invaded the land, destroyed its cities, and carried off large numbers of its population into foreign exile. Examples include the

Assyrian destruction of northern Israel in 722–21 B.C.E. and the Babylonian destruction of Judah and Jerusalem in 587 B.C.E. Just as the modern experience of the Shoah or Holocaust has prompted extensive theological discussion of the problem of evil,[48] so the ancient experiences of Assyrian and Babylonian destruction and exile prompted a wide variety of approaches to understanding these catastrophes.[49] Such concerns are especially prominent in the writing of history in the Bible. The books of Joshua, Judges, Samuel, and Kings present the basic history of Israel from the time of Joshua to the Babylonian exile, but they are written with the intention of attempting to explain the Assyrian and Babylonian disasters.[50] These books represent an example of theodicy, i.e., an attempt to defend the righteousness of G-d by claiming that Israel had violated the terms of its covenant by failing to abide by G-d's Torah.[51] The prophetic books take a similar stance, arguing that Israel and not G-d was to blame for the disasters that overtook the people. Although these traditions have often been understood as proof that Israel is sinful and deserved punishment, it must be recognized that such works are inherently theological in nature.[52] They are written by authors who choose not to blame G-d for evil but to take responsibility for evil themselves and to learn from past experience in order to build a new future. Consequently, the prophetic and historical writings point to the restoration of Israel as well, in which Jerusalem and the Temple will be rebuilt and the Davidic monarchy reinstated as G-d maintains the covenant with Israel.

Of course, these writings do not express the totality of the Bible's approach to the problem of evil. Other works are quite willing to raise questions concerning divine righteousness. Perhaps the best known is the book of Job, which portrays G-d's punishment of a fully righteous man for no apparent reason other than Satan's contention that Job would curse G-d if punished.[53] Job engages in extensive debate with his friends concerning the nature of G-d. When G-d appears to him at the end of the book, Job submits to G-d's power and righteousness even though it is never clear that his punishment was justified. Other books raise similar questions, such as Esther, in which G-d never appears at a time when the Jewish people faces complete annihilation,[54] or Habakkuk, who asks G-d for deliverance from the Babylonians only to learn that G-d brought them in the first place.[55] Even Moses must argue with G-d to prevent the destruction of Israel in the wilderness.[56] The Bible offers a wide range of responses to the problem of evil, pointing to both human wrongdoing and divine capriciousness as causes of evil. Nevertheless, it never advocates the rejection of

G-d, and it consistently points to the restoration of Israel following a period of punishment.

The Role of Later Jewish Tradition

Finally, the role of later Jewish tradition must be considered in relation to Jewish biblical theology. Much of modern, critical scholarship maintains that the Bible must be interpreted only in relation to the historical realities of the ancient world in which it was written, and that post-biblical tradition, whether Jewish or Christian, only distorts the Bible's original meaning.[57] There is a certain element of truth to such claims, and the study of archeology together with the languages and literatures of ancient Mesopotamia, Egypt, and Canaan has contributed much to understanding the Bible. But the Bible is not simply a historical document that chronicles the life of an ancient people; rather, it functions as the foundational text of a much larger Jewish tradition that extends from antiquity to the present.[58] Later Jewish tradition, such as the Talmuds, the medieval philosophical tradition, the kabbalah, modern Zionism, and the modern religious movements of Reform, Conservative, Reconstructionist, and Orthodox Judaism, have continued to interact with the Bible and other elements of the tradition as they have developed their distinctive understandings of Judaism.[59] Indeed, Jewish tradition embodies a process of dialogue with G-d, with itself, and with the outside world as Jews forge their ideas and identities for the future.[60]

NOTES

1. See Jon D. Levenson, *Sinai and Zion: An Entry into the Jewish Bible* (Minneapolis: Winston Press, 1985).

2. Martin Noth, *The Deuteronomistic History* (JSOTSup 15; Sheffield: JSOT Press, 1981); Marvin A. Sweeney, *King Josiah of Judah: The Lost Messiah of Israel* (Oxford and New York: Oxford University Press, 2001), 21–177.

3. See the chapter on Isaiah in Marvin A. Sweeney, *The Prophetic Literature* (Interpreting Biblical Texts; Nashville, Tenn.: Abingdon, 2005), 45–84; cf. Christopher R. Seitz, *Zion's Final Destiny: The Development of the Book of Isaiah. A Reassessment of Isaiah 36–39* (Minneapolis: Fortress Press, 1991), who emphasizes the role of Zion as the central concern of the book of Isaiah.

4. Bernard M. Levinson, *Deuteronomy and the Hermeneutics of Legal Innovation* (Oxford and New York: Oxford University Press, 1997).

5. Sara Japhet, *1 and 2 Chronicles: A Commentary* (OTL; Louisville, Ky.: Westminster John Knox, 1993).

6. Marvin A. Sweeney, "The Place and Function of Joel in the Book of the Twelve," in *Thematic Threads in the Book of the Twelve*, ed. P. Redditt and A. Schart (BZAW 325; Berlin and New York: Walter de Gruyter, 2003), 133–154; idem, "Micah's Debate with Isaiah," JSOT 93 (2001): 111–124; idem, "Zechariah's Debate with Isaiah," in *The Changing Face of Form Criticism for the Twenty-First Century*, ed. M. A. Sweeney and E. Ben Zvi (Grand Rapids, Mich. and Cambridge: Eerdmans, 2003), 335–350.

7. Carol A. Newsom, *The Book of Job: A Contest of Moral Imaginations* (Oxford and New York: Oxford University Press, 2003).

8. E.g., Percy S. F. van Keulen, *Two Versions of the Solomon Narrative: An Inquiry into the Relationship between MT 1 Kgs. 2–11 and LXX 3 Reg. 2–11* (VTSup 104; Leiden: E. J. Brill, 2005).

9. See Kristin De Troyer, *The End of the Alpha Text of Esther: Translation and Narrative Technique in MT 8:1–17, LXX 8:1–17; and AT 7:14–41* (SCS 48; Atlanta, Ga.: Society of Biblical Literature, 2000).

10. See Arie van der Kooij, *The Oracle of Tyre: The Septuagint of Isaiah 23 as Version and Vision* (VTSup 71; Leiden: E. J. Brill, 1998).

11. Exod 21.24–25; Lev 24.20; Deut 19.21; *m. Baba Kamma* 8.1; *b. Baba Kamma* 83b–84a

12. *B. Baba Batra* 15a.

13. M. Friedländer, *The Commentary of Ibn Ezra on Isaiah* (New York: Philip Feldheim, n.d.), 1:169–171.

14. *Guide for the Perplexed* 3.32.

15. For discussion of Lurianic Kabbalah and its concept of G-d, see Gershom Scholem, *Major Trends in Jewish Mysticism* (New York: Schocken, 1972), 244–286.

16. See Leon A. Jick, ed., *The Teaching of Judaica in American Universities: The Proceedings of a Colloquium* (New York: Ktav, 1970); S. David Sperling, ed., *Students of the Covenant: A History of Jewish Scholarship in North America* (Atlanta, Ga.: Scholars Press, 1992); idem, "Modern Jewish Interpretation," in *The Jewish Study Bible*, ed. A. Berlin and M. Z. Brettler (Oxford and New York: Oxford University Press, 2003), 1908–1919.

17. Emil G. Kraeling, *The Old Testament since the Reformation* (New York: Schocken, 1969); Hans-Joachim Kraus, *Geschichte der Historisch-Kritischen Erforschung des Alten Testaments von der Reformation bis zur Gegenwart* (Neukirchen Kreis Moers: Verlag der Buchhandlung des Erziehungsvereins, 1956).

18. In addition to the works cited above, see Jon D. Levenson, "Why Jews Are Not Interested in Biblical Theology," in *The Hebrew Bible, the Old Testament and Historical Criticism: Jews and Christians in Biblical Studies* (Louisville, Ky.: Westminster John Knox, 1993), 33–61, 165–170; cf. idem, *The Death and Resurrection of*

the Beloved Son: The Transformation of Child Sacrifice in Judaism and Christianity (New Haven, Conn. and London: Yale University Press, 1993).

19. Julius Wellhausen, *Prolegomenon to the History of Ancient Israel* (Gloucester, Mass.: Peter Smith, 1973/1885), 1.

20. Solomon Schechter, "Higher Criticism—Higher Anti-Semitism," in *Seminary Addresses and Other Papers* (Cincinnati, Ohio: Ark, 1915), 36–37.

21. Walter Eichrodt, *Theology of the Old Testament* (OTL; Philadelphia: Westminster, 1961–67), 1:26.

22. See Clark Williamson, *A Guest in the House of Israel* (Louisville, Ky.: Westminster John Knox, 1993); Paul van Buren, "On Reading Someone Else's Mail: The Church and Israel's Scriptures," in *Die Hebräische Bibel und ihre zweifache Nachgeschichte* (Festschrift for Rolf Rendtorff), ed. E. Blum et al. (Neukirchen-Vluyn: Neukirchener, 1990), 595–606; Rolf Rendtorff, "Toward a Common Jewish Christian Reading of the Hebrew Bible," in *Canon and Theology* (OBT; Minneapolis: Fortress Press, 1993), 31–45.

23. See my essay, "Why Jews Should Be Interested in Biblical Theology," *CCAR Journal* 44, no. 1 (winter 1997): 67–75.

24. For introductions to the field of biblical theology, see especially Gerhard Hasel, *Old Testament Theology: Basic Issues in the Current Debate*, 4th edition (Grand Rapids, Mich.: Eerdmans, 1991); John H. Hayes and Frederick Prussner, *Old Testament Theology: Its History and Development* (Atlanta, Ga.: John Knox, 1985); Leo Perdue, *The Collapse of History: Reconstructing Old Testament Theology* (OBT; Minneapolis: Fortress Press, 1994).

25. E.g., Eliezer Berkovits, *Man and God: Studies in Biblical Theology* (Detroit, Mich.: Wayne State University Press, 1969); cf. Marvin A. Sweeney, "Reconceiving the Paradigms of Old Testament Theology in the Post-Shoah Period," *Biblical Interpretation* 6 (1998): 142–161.

26. For discussion of Jewish contributions to the field of biblical theology, see Hasel, *Old Testament Theology*, 34–38; Brevard S. Childs, *Biblical Theology of the Old and New Testaments: Theological Reflection on the Christian Bible* (Minneapolis: Fortress Press, 1992), 25–26; James Barr, *The Concept of Biblical Theology: An Old Testament Perspective* (Minneapolis: Fortress Press, 1999), 286–311; Marvin A. Sweeney, "The Emerging Field of Jewish Biblical Theology," in *Academic Approaches to Teaching Jewish Studies* (Lanham, Md.: University Press of America, 2000), 83–105. For a critique of Jewish biblical theology, see Ziony Zevit, "Jewish Biblical Theology: Whence? Why? and Whither?" *HUCA* 76 (2005): 289–340.

27. In addition to Williamson, *A Guest in the House of Israel*, see Jules Isaac, *The Teaching of Contempt: Christian Roots of Anti-Semitism* (New York: Holt, Rinehart, and Winston, 1964); Rosemary Ruether, *Faith and Fratricide: The Theological Roots of Anti-Semitism* (Eugene, Ore.: Wipf and Stock, 1997); Shmuel Almog, ed., *Antisemitism through the Ages* (Oxford: Pergamon, 1988).

28. For examples of the interaction between Jewish and Christian biblical scholars, see Frederick E. Greenspahn, ed., *Scripture in the Jewish and Christian Traditions: Authority, Interpretation, Relevance* (Nashville, Tenn.: Abingdon, 1982); Roger Brooks and John J. Collins, eds., *Hebrew Bible or Old Testament: Studying the Bible in Judaism and Christianity* (Notre Dame, Ind.: University of Notre Dame Press, 1990); Alice Ogden Bellis and Joel S. Kaminsky, eds., *Jews, Christians, and the Theology of the Hebrew Scriptures* (SBL Symposium Series 8; Atlanta, Ga.: Society of Biblical Literature, 2000).

29. See my essay, "Tanak versus Old Testament: Concerning the Foundation for a Jewish Theology of the Bible," in *Problems in Biblical Theology: Essays in Honor of Rolf Knierim,* ed. H. T. C. Sun and K. L. Eades et al. (Grand Rapids, Mich.: Eerdmans, 1997), 353–372.

30. For discussion of the formation of the Christian Bible, see Roger T. Beckwith, *The Old Testament Canon of the New Testament Church* (Grand Rapids, Mich.: Eerdmans, 1986).

31. James A. Sanders, "First Testament and Second," *Biblical Theology Bulletin* 17 (1987): 47–50.

32. For discussion of the formation of the Jewish Bible, see Sid Leiman, *The Canonization of Hebrew Scripture: The Talmudic and Midrashic Evidence* (Hamden, Conn.: Connecticut Academy of Arts and Sciences/Archon, 1976).

33. Jon D. Levenson, "The Temple and the World," *Journal of Religion* 64 (1984): 275–278; idem, *Sinai and Zion;* idem, "The Jerusalem Temple in Devotional and Visionary Experience," in *Jewish Spirituality: From the Bible through the Middle Ages,* ed. A. Green (New York: Crossroad, 1988), 32–61; Moshe Weinfeld, "Zion and Jerusalem as Religious and Political Capital: Ideology and Utopia," in *The Poet and the Historian: Essays in Literary and Historical Biblical Criticism,* ed. R. E. Friedman (HSM 26; Chico, Calif.: Scholars Press, 1983), 75–115.

34. See "Nomos," in *Theological Dictionary of the New Testament,* ed. R. Kittel (Grand Rapids, Mich.: Eerdmans, 1967), 4:1022–1085.

35. See my essay, "Foundations for a Jewish Theology of the Bible," forthcoming in a volume of essays on Jewish biblical theology edited by Isaac Kalimi, to be published by Eisenbrauns.

36. See Francis Brown, S. R. Driver, and Charles A. Briggs, *A Hebrew and English Lexicon of the Old Testament* (Oxford: Clarendon Press, 1979), 434–436; cf. Lev 10:11; "Torah," *Encyclopaedia Judaica* 15:1235–1246.

37. E.g., Levenson, *Sinai and Zion.*

38. See Levenson, "The Jerusalem Temple"; C. T. R. Hayward, *The Jerusalem Temple: A Non-Biblical Sourcebook* (London and New York: Routledge, 1996); Marvin A. Sweeney, *1 and 2 Kings: A Commentary* (OTL; Louisville, Ky.: Westminster John Knox, 2007), on 1 Kings 6–8.

39. Orlinsky, "The Biblical Concept of the Land of Israel"; cf. Abraham Joshua Heschel, *Israel: An Echo of Eternity* (Woodstock, Vt.: Jewish Lights, 1997).

40. Exod 19:6; cf. Isa 2:2–4; Mic 4:1–5; Ezek 47–48; Zech 14.

41. Deut 9:4–7.

42. See Amihai Mazar, *Archaeology of the Land of the Bible, 10,000–586 B.C.E.* (New York: Doubleday, 1990); Ephraim Stern, *Archaeology of the Land of the Bible, volume II: The Assyrian, Babylonian, and Persian Periods (732–332 B.C.E.)* (New York: Doubleday, 2001).

43. For a translation of the Merneptah Stele, see James B. Pritchard, *Ancient Near Eastern Texts Relating to the Old Testament* (Princeton, N.J.: Princeton University Press, 1969), 376–378.

44. Recent critique of archaeological method now tends to place the major period of ancient Israelite development in the ninth century B.C.E.; see Israel Finkelstein and Neil Asher Silberman, *The Bible Unearthed: Archaeology's New Vision of Ancient Israel and the Origin of Its Sacred Texts* (New York: The Free Press, 2001); cf. William G. Dever, *What Did the Biblical Writers Know and When Did They Know It? What Archaeology Can Tell Us about the Reality of Ancient Israel* (Grand Rapids, Mich. and Cambridge: Eerdmans, 2001).

45. Avraham Biran and Joseph Naveh, "An Aramaic Stele Fragment from Tel Dan," *Israel Exploration Journal* 43 (1993): 81–98; idem, "The Tel Dan Inscription: A New Fragment," *Israel Exploration Journal* 45 (1995): 1–18.

46. 2 Samuel 7; Psalms 2, 89, 110.

47. For studies in ancient Israelite law, see J. J. Finkelstein, *The Ox that Gored* (Transactions of the American Philosophical Society 7 1/2; Philadelphia: The American Philosophical Society, 1981); Moshe Greenberg, "Some Postulates of Biblical Criminal Law," in *Studies in the Bible and Jewish Thought* (Philadelphia and Jerusalem: Jewish Publication Society, 1995), 25–41; Levinson, *Deuteronomy and the Hermeneutics of Legal Innovation.*

48. For modern discussion of the Shoah, see especially Steven T. Katz, *Post-Holocaust Dialogues: Critical Studies in Modern Jewish Thought* (New York and London: New York University Press, 1985); Zev Garber, *Shoah: The Paradigmatic Genocide. Essays in Exegesis and Eisegesis* (Studies in the Shoah 8; Lanham, Md.: University Press of America, 1994); Zachery Braiterman, *(God) after Auschwitz: Tradition and Change in Post-Holocaust Jewish Thought* (Princeton, N.J.: Princeton University Press, 1998).

49. See Emil Fackenheim, *The Jewish Bible after the Holocaust: A Re-Reading* (Bloomington and Indianapolis: Indiana University Press, 1990).

50. Sweeney, *King Josiah of Judah;* idem, *1 and 2 Kings.*

51. James L. Crenshaw, "Theodicy," *Anchor Bible Dictionary* 6:444–447; see also Jon D. Levenson, *Creation and the Persistence of Evil: The Jewish Drama of Divine Omnipotence* (San Francisco: Harper and Row, 1988).

52. Sweeney, *The Prophetic Literature;* Abraham Joshua Heschel, *The Prophets* (New York: Harper and Row, 1962).

53. Newsom, *The Book of Job.*

54. Marvin A. Sweeney, "Absence of G-d and Human Responsibility in the Book of Esther," in *Reading the Hebrew Bible for a New Millennium: Form, Concept, and Theological Perspective. Volume 2: Exegetical and Theological Essays*, ed. W. Kim et al. (Studies in Antiquity and Christianity;Harrisburg, Pa.: Trinity Press International, 2000), 264–275; Jon D. Levenson, *Esther: A Commentary* (OTL; Louisville, Ky.: Westminster John Knox, 1997); Adele Berlin, *Esther* (JPS Bible Commentary; Philadelphia and Jerusalem: JPS, 2001).

55. Marvin A. Sweeney, *The Twelve Prophets* (Berit Olam; Collegeville, Minn.: Liturgical, 2000), 451–490.

56. Exodus 33; Numbers 14.

57. For a cogent attempt to rethink this view without rejecting historical work, see Perdue, *The Collapse of History*.

58. For studies of biblical interpretation and hermeneutics beginning in the Bible itself, see Michael Fishbane, *Biblical Interpretation in Ancient Israel* (Oxford: Clarendon, 1985); idem, *The Garments of Torah: Essays in Biblical Hermeneutics* (Bloomington and Indianapolis: Indiana University Press, 1992); Benjamin D. Sommer, *A Prophet Reads Scripture: Allusion in Isaiah 40–66* (Contraversions; Stanford, Calif.: Stanford University Press, 1998).

59. For an example of how such work might be done, see my essay, "The Democratization of Messianism in Modern Jewish Thought," in *Biblical Interpretation: History, Context, and Reality*, Society of Biblical Literature Symposium Series 26, ed. Christine M. Helmer with T. G. Petrey (Atlanta, Ga.: Society of Biblical Literature, 2005), 87–101.

60. Martin Buber, *I and Thou* (New York: Charles Scribners, 1970).

Let a Hundred Flowers Bloom

Some Reflections on Reading and Studying the Hebrew Bible

Peter Machinist

The Hebrew Bible is a complex book. Its complexity is manifest in a number of ways, three of which in particular emerge from the discussions in this volume. In the first place, the Hebrew Bible is not a single book, but a collection of many: twenty-four, thirty-six, or thirty-nine, depending on the way one counts. These books, moreover, are of different lengths, genres, and content, and in two primary languages, Hebrew and Aramaic, with echoes of a number of others. This plurality is captured in the very label "Bible," derived as it is from the ancient Greek term for the collection, *ta biblia*, which means "the scrolls" and eventually was understood as "the books."

Second, the Hebrew Bible deals with or provokes reflection on a wide range of matters. Those described in the present volume include: the aesthetics of biblical narrative, as exemplified by the story of the encounter between the nascent Israelites and the people of Shechem in Genesis 34; gender, especially the place of women in and through the Hebrew Bible as read in a feminist way; how the Hebrew Bible came to be the Hebrew Bible, namely, the process of canonization and the emergence of sacred authority for a written text; ancient Israelite history and the role of the Hebrew Bible as a, or even the, principal source for that history; the material culture of ancient Israel and how this may be studied through the Bible and archaeological data; a Jewish theological approach to the Hebrew Bible; the nature of biblical law and its setting in the framework of law in the ancient Near Eastern and Mediterranean world; the meaning of sacrifice and the sacrificial system in the Hebrew Bible; and styles of worship in ancient Israel and the Judaism that followed it.

This range of matters, and many others that could be added, point to a third kind of complexity: that on such matters the Hebrew Bible rarely speaks univocally. Not only do the relevant biblical texts more than occasionally disagree, but even within a single passage one can find evidence of tensions or at least a multiplicity of perspectives. One example mentioned in this volume is the slave law in Exodus 21:2–11, which stipulates different treatments for male and female Hebrew slaves, while the law in Deuteronomy 15:12–18, which also treats the Hebrew slaves, expressly requires the same program of manumission for both sexes. Again as noted elsewhere in the volume, the history of Israel found in the books of Samuel and Kings is paralleled by the history presented in the books of Chronicles, but the latter has many differences in detail as well as a decidedly different focus —not on Judah and Israel, but almost exclusively on Judah alone and its center in the Davidic dynasty. The treatment of sacrifices is also not uniform, as these pages have made clear. Deuteronomy 12 allows the non-ritual slaughter of animals that are otherwise fit for ritual sacrifice when they are to be used just for human food, but such non-ritual slaughter is not known in Leviticus (see especially chapter 17). This difference is linked with different perspectives on sanctuaries: in Deuteronomy only one place is mandated for sacrifices to God (see especially chapter 12), whereas Leviticus 17 envisions any number of places. A final example, not explicitly mentioned before in this volume, directs us to the celebrated duel between the youthful David, servant of the Israelite king Saul, and the Philistine strongman Goliath. This duel is recounted in 1 Samuel 17 of the standard Masoretic Hebrew Bible. It reports that after David vanquished Goliath, Saul asked whose son David was, as if he really did not know him, or at least much about him (vv. 55–58). Yet the last verses of the preceding chapter tell us that Saul had, in fact, known all about David and his lineage before the duel with Goliath, for it was at Saul's express demand that David had been taken out of his father Jesse's house to serve at Saul's court (16:17–23).

How to respond to this biblical complexity? Is it possible, for example, to see some interrelatedness, if not coherence, in the range of literary units, topics, and viewpoints represented? The history of the ways the Hebrew Bible has been received and dealt with by various human communities (*Rezeptionsgeschichte*), it may be argued, reveals two perspectives on the problem. The first is historical, and the emphasis on and development of this perspective is due especially to modern biblical study, though, as suggested in earlier chapters, there are many pre-modern anticipations. Here the focus is the Hebrew Bible as a historical artifact: a product of and witness to a particular culture of a particular time and place now passed, namely, ancient Israel. The Hebrew Bible, thus, serves first and foremost as a way of getting at the culture and society that gave it birth and to which it was directed. Accordingly, the differences in literary units, topics, and viewpoints within the biblical corpus are to be explained as differences in worldview, behavior, and historical setting of the authors who composed these texts and of the larger groups in ancient Israel or, more precisely, ancient Israel and Judah, in which they were embedded. These authors may be understood on a horizontal level, that is, as coming from the same time but different places within the communities of Israel and Judah, or vertically, as reflecting different chronological moments and circumstances in Israelite and Judean history.

Chronological change introduces another dimension of the historical, again as the reception history of the Hebrew Bible, especially its modern history, has explored it. Here the Bible itself has come to be viewed historically; that is, the present form of the text in or underlying most current use—the Masoretic text of the late first millennium C.E.—is to be seen as the end product of a long process, which probably started orally before eventually moving into written form alone. That transition was essentially concluded by the latter part of the first century C.E. In this view, the history of the communities of Israel and Judah to which the Hebrew Bible is a witness overlaps, though not completely, the history of the emergence of the Hebrew Bible itself in the various stages of its composition, editing, collection, canonization, and textual refinement. The Bible, if you will, may be imagined as something like a tell—the ruined mound of an ancient village, town, or city that archaeologists excavate—and its successive layers of human occupation. This means that the differences we can observe in the Bible, whether in law, worship, theological outlook, historical perspective, or literary formulation, must be understood as belonging to different strands or stages—different layers—of its history or to different parts of the same layer. These reflect, in turn, the different groups and experiences, scattered over time and, at any one time, over the social spectrum that made up the ancient Israel and Judah from which the Bible emerged. So if Exodus 21 and Deuteronomy 15 differ over the formulation of the Hebrew slave law or if Deuteronomy and Leviticus differ over non-ritual slaughter and the number of legitimate sanctuaries for sacrifice, these differences may be seen as resulting from the different groups and the different periods from which they came within Israel and Judah. The differences thus represent what were historically competing and changing views of the issues at hand. Similarly, if the present, Masoretic form of 1 Samuel 16–17 contains contradictory views about when Saul first learned of David and his lineage, this is the result of different traditions held by different groups within Israel/Judah that have been combined here. These traditions can be recognized and separated by internal analysis of the present text, with the help of the ancient, non-Masoretic versions of the Hebrew Bible, especially the Greek Septuagint, the bulk of whose manuscripts do not have the second recognition by Saul of David in 1 Samuel 17:55–58 and so do not exhibit the contradiction.

How, then, can a historical perspective account for the fact that at the end of its compositional and redactional history the Hebrew Bible has retained different points of view as well as the different topics to which they belong? Would it not have been more logical for these differences to have been eliminated? As a comparison of the Masoretic with the ancient non-Masoretic versions shows (for example, the meetings of Saul and David in 1 Samuel as described above), some differences were indeed eliminated, but still others were retained, so the logical problem is not resolved. A comparative historical perspective, however, suggests that the logic itself is not pertinent: that what the Hebrew Bible represents is not a logical treatise, fully ordered in a rational way, but a traditional literature, of a type known elsewhere in history, including among Israel's Near Eastern neighbors. As traditional literature, the Bible is to be seen as a compendium of the traditions of the society from which it comes, tending to preserve or intertwine competing traditions that were rooted in the underlying societal fabric. In this traditional ambiance, creativity does not strive to proclaim the utterly new, but to rework the inherited. When new views, language, and forms appear, as they certainly do, they are most often expressed as part of an ongoing reality. The differences and similarities among the views, topics, and forms in the Hebrew Bible are, therefore, to be understood in the first instance organically, not as elements of an abstract intellectual structure. They are, indeed, interconnected because they grew out of the interconnected communities of Israel and Judah as these moved through time. The analogy with the archaeological tell again suggests itself, for in the tell later layers continue features of earlier layers, even as they introduce and sometimes substitute new features; moreover, the layers are sometimes separated by destruction and/or abandonment and sometimes not; but all this occurs within the overall continuity of the tell itself over time, as the later layers succeed earlier ones.

We turn now to the second perspective on the complexities in the Hebrew Bible which runs through its reception history. Here the Bible is an object of study and appreciation in its own right, the text itself defining, at least primarily, the world within which it is to be read and interpreted. One formulation of this perspective has been theological: the Hebrew Bible as Scripture, that is, as a canon or sacred collection of texts intended not simply for edification but as the standard of guidance in belief and behavior for those communities that accept its scripturality. The Bible, in other words—and here I describe a traditional religious view of the matter—did not originate with humans, but with God. As such, it is understood not so much as a manifestation of the human society in which it appeared, but as the primary reality, given by God, from which human society derived and still derives, or should derive. Scriptural study, therefore, seeks to clarify the teaching and guidance that the Bible provides to its human communities. In so doing, the study normally centers on a standard, Masoretic text, eschewing the reconstruction of the compositional history of the Bible and the changes in view and form this would have represented, since such reconstruction stands to violate the religious integrity and status of the biblical text. To be sure, the scriptural perspective allows for the recognition of individual differences: among the parts of the standard biblical text (with regard to the kinds of differences in law, historical orientation, sacrifice, and sanctuary mentioned above), among different authors for different parts of the Bible (for example, Moses for the Pentateuch, but David and Hezekiah for the Psalms), and among the interpretations themselves as to what the biblical text may mean. Indeed, traditional biblical commentators were not shy about identifying these differences, in a number of instances relying or expanding on notices in the biblical text itself. Nonetheless, the differences are all to be understood as expressions of a deeper, integrated coherence, if not system. Put another way, the Bible, at its core, embodies enduring, transcendent truths, ones not conditioned by the actual human historical circumstances that gave it birth. It is, then, the purpose of scriptural study ultimately to identify and understand this coherence and these truths, for without them the Bible cannot function as a scriptural standard of guidance.

An alternative formulation of the Bible taken in and of itself is literary. While this was suggested in earlier, even pre-modern centuries, it has become prominent in recent biblical study, particularly over the last three decades. The issue here is what the Bible is as a work of literature. The way into this issue has usually been to focus on a literary unit within the Bible —it could be an individual passage, a set of chapters, a book, a section like the Pentateuch, a category or genre of texts, even the entire Hebrew Bible —which the interpreter seeks to define and appreciate in terms of its structure, themes, language, type (story, poem, law, meditation, list, etc.), in short, to understand what it communicates and how. The assumption is that the unit in question has some kind of literary integrity, even with its internal differences, and the challenge then is to understand what that integrity is and how the differences work within and for it. Such understanding may well involve, and often does, comparison with other texts. In this regard, texts from the ancient Near East in which the Hebrew Bible historically originated as well as those from outside, along with an appeal to general literary theory, are all potentially of equal value for understanding the biblical text at hand as a piece of literature on its own. As with the Bible as Scripture, so with this literary view, the focus has tended to be on the present, usually Masoretic-based text and not on its previous forms and sources. But this time the reason is not one of safeguarding sacral integrity. Indeed, literary critics, as a rule, do not deny the possible existence of these forms and sources. Yet for many critics, it makes little or no sense to give any serious attention to them, because they have largely not survived, but must be reconstructed from exiguous and uncertain evidence. Far better, then, to focus on the present text, which is known and can be read, and which, after all, has an audience of its own already in antiquity.

The literary approach, it may be repeated, does not seek, categorically, to level out differences in the Hebrew Bible in points of view, topics, or literary forms. Differences between literary units of the Bible can be recognized and appreciated as indicative of different authors, different purposes, the result of the conventions of different literary forms, and the like. But within a literary unit, differences need to be considered in the context of the overall parameters of the unit itself.

A return to one of the differences we have discussed will exemplify the interpretive challenge here. The example is the double recognition by Saul of David in 1 Samuel 16 and 17. If a historical interpreter would see the two recognitions as a mark of the source history of the passage, a literary interpreter—and probably a scriptural interpreter also—might well consider them as a reflection by the biblical author on the person of Saul himself and God's judgment on him. The point is that in the narrative of 1 Samuel 15–16, prior to Saul's recognition of David, we are told that Saul had become increasingly agitated, a manifestation of God's decision to take kingship away from him and to bring an evil spirit on him (15:35; 16:14–15). In this light, Saul's second recognition of David, coming after the duel with Goliath (17:55–58), appears not as an inconsistency pointing to underlying sources, but as a mark of Saul's growing mental instability in that he is no longer able to recognize those whom he has already met and even brought into his service.

The two perspectives on biblical complexity that we have been discussing, the historical and the Bible in itself either as Scripture or as literature, are ideal types, to adopt the terminology of the sociologist Max Weber. That is, they are deliberate simplifications, perhaps oversimplifications, of what biblical interpreters have in fact done in order to get at their underlying conceptual orientations. In the practice of biblical study, thus, the line between these types is porous. The two are often mixed, and that is reflected as well in various of the chapters in this book. For example, an examination of gender in the Hebrew Bible may focus on the ways in which this is expressed, or encoded, in literary form, language, imagery, etc., but in the argument that a given literary expression is "a sophisticated political construct that serves the interests of a particular group or class" (p. 82) we move from the strictly literary to the biblical text as witness to a larger historical reality in ancient Israel. Conversely, the analysis of a particular episode in ancient Israelite history may appeal to a biblical source, but not occasionally that source will need to be examined literarily for its type, structure, language, theme(s), and purpose in order to assess its value as historical testimony.

One additional example involves the canon, which, though it is fundamentally a scriptural concern, can nonetheless be approached historically. Historical study of the canonization process, in fact, as considered elsewhere in this book, reveals its conditionality: that there were and are several canons and so several kinds of Hebrew Bible in the course of Jewish and Christian history and that even within a single canon communities sometimes have given more canonical emphasis to one part than to others (so for the Pentateuch, the Torah par excellence, in traditional Jewish practice, over against the books of the Prophets and the Writings). What, then, should a scriptural approach to the Hebrew Bible do with this historical plurality of canons and the different thematic emphases they embody? One can decide that only one canon is legitimate and authoritative, or one can be in some way open and eclectic, giving attention to parts of different canons, perhaps in response to different circumstances and demands, on the assumption that the plurality of canons is a witness to the greater plurality that is God.

The issue of canon raises the more general issue of interpretive authority: on what grounds can we decide what the Bible says or how it is to be approached? How much of a decision do we need to make? how flexible can we be? All the perspectives we have discussed allow some openness on this matter; that is, they recognize that there may be more than one appropriate answer to the interpretation and use of a biblical text and that the answer will be tied to the kind of question asked of the text. But where the limits are and how to draw them is the issue.

A historical perspective on interpretive authority begins with the assumption that the Hebrew Bible is a conditioned phenomenon: only one of many possible sources for the larger history of Israel and Judah from which it comes. Indeed, the Bible itself often raises questions, say, about Israelite/Judaean society and religion, questions it does not provide enough material to answer. Therefore, in approaching the Bible historically, one inevitably has to pay attention to outside sources that put the Bible in historical context and potentially have the capacity to fill in the gaps in the biblical testimony. As the chapters in this volume illustrate, these outside sources tend to be of three kinds: non-written and written archaeological data from the ancient Near East, especially the land of Israel, that mention or otherwise speak directly about ancient Israel and Judah; texts, art, and archaeology from elsewhere in the ancient Near East and the ancient Mediterranean world that serve as points of comparison for understanding cultural, political, social, economic, and physical phenomena noted in the Hebrew Bible; and the artifacts, textual and nontextual, of the Second Temple and rabbinic Judaism and early Christianity that succeed and emerge from ancient Israel/Judah. It is clear that the ancient Israel/Judah a modern historian can reconstruct by using these groups of sources *and* the Hebrew Bible will not always be the same as the Israel described in the Bible alone: as has often been said, ancient Israel is not identical with biblical Israel. How, then, to interpret the Hebrew Bible as historical testimony in this larger mix?

It stands to reason that a plausible interpretation is one that fits the biblical testimony with all the others, but on reflection the matter is not so simple, as evidenced in earlier chapters of this volume. For if by "interpret" we mean evaluating the validity of a biblical statement in regard to a particular historical event or institution, we can find congruence among all the sources, but sometimes we do not: the biblical statement may have no reflexes in the other sources, in which case its validity has to be evaluated on its own, with criteria that are not always clear or universally accepted; or there may be direct contradictions with the other testimonies, which then require an explanation. That explanation may involve a choice as to which testimony is historically valid, say, in terms of what actually happened; but even those judged to be less valid have important historical information to offer about such issues as how events and institutions were perceived and described in ancient Israel. In short, historical interpretation of the Hebrew Bible involves more than deciding on the historical validity of presumed facts, even as it demands an awareness of the partial, conditioned character of our ancient testimonies and of the modern interpreter who is using them.

For the perspective on the Hebrew Bible as Scripture, interpretive authority is often said to reside in the subsequent communities, especially of Judaism and Christianity, in which biblical Scripture is foundational, and these communities try to establish a chain of authoritative interpretive tradition and authoritative interpreters to maintain it. But in each case, there have been and continue to be manifold challenges: as to the validity and legitimacy of particular traditions and interpreters, and involving the demand to do away with a body of official tradition and interpreters altogether and go back simply to the Bible—for Jews, the Hebrew Bible; for Christians, the Hebrew Bible and the New Testament—and interpret it directly out of itself on the basis of certain perceived principles that are assumed to be basic to it. The issue here is not as confused and as unruly as it may appear, because the biblical text does impose some kind of limit on interpretation and because in the histories of Judaism and Christianity certain interpretive options and chains of interpreters have come to dominate or be marginalized, for any number of reasons. Nonetheless, once one reviews the reception history of the Bible as Scripture, there remains a great deal of latitude in interpretation one can observe; and while that latitude, and the pluralist voices in Scripture it allows, have been resisted by some, they have been embraced by others, as we have noted already in discussing the issue of canon.

Finally, what about interpretive authority for those who approach the Hebrew Bible as literature? As several of the earlier chapters attest, recent work in biblical literary study, though not all of it to be sure, has given renewed prominence to the argument that meaning in a text is not only that which the author intended, but that which the reader takes out of it or, even more, entirely what the reader does. On this view, authority is not something given, or entirely given, but conditional, and conditional especially upon the particular reader and the particular moment in which he reads the text. The view here, it should be observed, is not meant for the Hebrew Bible alone; rather, it is for all literature, of which, then, the Hebrew Bible is simply one example. Is the result a free-for-all in interpretation, similar to, but even more intense than for the scripturalists? As with the latter, there is here still the biblical text itself as a phenomenon that has to be reckoned with. But if that text does impose limits on interpretation, it appears that in present biblical scholarship, and again the chapters in this volume are a witness to this, the limits have not been agreed upon. What constitutes a correct interpretation, or membership in the category of correct interpretations, or, perhaps most helpfully, what constitutes an incorrect or improbable interpretation—this is the issue that remains open.

Given this diversity of views and the diversity and complexity of the Hebrew Bible that lie behind it, it is no surprise that the interpretation of the Bible as history, as Scripture, as literature, and in other modes not here considered has been and remains an ongoing process. In that process, as we have seen, the perspectives have often crossed lines. The moral of the story, I am convinced, is that we cannot afford to be dogmatic or narrow about what perspective, what particular approach we choose. The Bible means and carries meaning on a multiplicity of levels, requiring an openness to a multiplicity of perspectives on and approaches to it; and even in dealing with a particular biblical passage or theme, inevitably the understanding will be richer the more avenues we employ in reaching it. All this may appear to be a truism, but the fact is that biblical scholarship has not always been open: all too often we have been told we must make a choice among approaches to a text or issue, and so exclude other approaches that are deemed, on grounds more ideological than substantive, irrelevant or useless. Yet in the end, our inclination must be toward "both . . . and," not "either . . . or," or in the words of the Maoist Chinese slogan, "let a hundred flowers bloom." For unlike what happened to that slogan in China, where its proclamation led to an outburst of critical voices the beleaguered government felt compelled to suppress, in biblical studies the "hundred flowers" and more are the only way to capture the rich texture of what the biblical corpus has to offer.

About the Contributors

Adele Berlin is Robert H. Smith Professor of Bible at the University of Maryland.

Elizabeth Bloch-Smith is a senior staff member of The Renewed Excavation of Tel Dor, Israel and author of *Judahite Burial Practices and Beliefs about the Dead.*

Esther Fuchs is Professor of Jewish Studies and Hebrew Literature at the University of Arizona, Tucson, and author of *Sexual Politics in the Biblical Narrative: Reading the Hebrew Bible as a Woman.*

Frederick E. Greenspahn is Gimelstob Eminent Scholar in Judaic Studies at Florida Atlantic University. He is the editor of *Essential Papers on Israel and the Near East,* author of *When Brothers Dwell Together: The Preeminence of Younger Siblings in the Hebrew Bible,* and author or editor of several other books on biblical studies and interfaith relations.

Leonard Greenspoon is Klutznick Chair in Jewish Civilization at Creighton University and editor or author of fifteen books, most in the Studies in Jewish Civilization series.

Peter Machinist is Hancock Professor of Hebrew and Other Oriental Languages at Harvard University and author, with Steven W. Cole, of *Letters from Priests to the Kings Esarhaddon and Assurbanipal.*

Gary A. Rendsburg holds the Blanche and Irving Laurie Chair in Jewish History at Rutgers University in New Brunswick, New Jersey. He is the author of five books, including a general survey of the biblical world entitled *The Bible and the Ancient Near East,* co-authored with the late Cyrus H. Gordon.

Marvin A. Sweeney is Professor of Hebrew Bible at Claremont School of Theology and Professor of Religion at Claremont Graduate University. He is the author of nine volumes in the field of Biblical Studies, such as *Isaiah 1–39, The Twelve Prophets, Zephaniah, King Josiah of Judah: The Lost Messiah of Israel, The Prophetic Literature, Form and Intertextuality in Prophetic and Apocalyptic Literature,* and *Reading the Bible after the Shoah* (forthcoming).

Raymond Westbrook is Professor of Ancient Law at Johns Hopkins University and editor of *A History of Ancient Near Eastern Law.*

David P. Wright is Professor of Hebrew Bible and Ancient Near East at Brandeis University and author of *Ritual in Narrative* and *The Disposal of Impurity.*

Ziony Zevit is a Distinguished Professor of Biblical Literature at the American Jewish University and author of *The Religions of Ancient Israel: A Synthesis of Parallactic Approaches* and *The Anterior Construction in Classical Hebrew.*

Index

Aaron, 29
Aaron's sons, 126
Abraham, 3, 167
'abrek, 3
Ackerman, Susan, 78, 89
Adam, 80
adultery, 101
Agag, 126
Ahab, 10, 33
Aharoni, Yohanan, 30
Ai, 4, 7, 28, 179
Akiva, 184n3, 185n14
Alalakh, 108
Albright, William Foxwell, 3, 4, 25
Aleppo Codex, 145
allegorical, 45, 106
Alt, Albrecht, 4, 104, 108
Alter, Robert, 48, 52, 82, 88
Amidah, 14, 168, 185n13, 186n21
Amit, Yairah, 62–63
Ammi-Saduqa, 119n15
Ammon, 35, 58
Amos, 177
Amram Gaon, Rav, 169
ancestral custom (*mos maiorum*),
   111
androcentrism, 87
Apocrypha, 66, 196
apodictic law, 104
Aqhat, 89
Arad, 9, 13, 28, 179
Aram, 19
Aramaic, 146
Ashdod, 15
Asherah, 9, 19
Ashkelon, 12
Assyria, 4, 19
Athanasius, 144
Auerbach, Erich, 47

Azazel, 125
Azriyau, 12

Baal, 8, 180
Babylonia, 4, 19
Babylonian exile, 5
Bach, Alice, 77, 80, 88
Bal, Mieke, 78, 83–84, 86, 89
Bar Kosiba, 152, 165, 184n3
Bathsheba, 87–89
beard, 31, 32
Beersheba, 179
Bel and the Dragon, 130
Bell, Catherine, 121, 134
Ben-Tor, Amnon, 33
Bethel, 3, 4
Bethlehem, 179
Bethsaida, 180
"Bible," 209
Biblical Archaeology, 25–26
Biblical Theology movement, 25
bichrome pottery, 33
Binford, Lewis, 25
Biran, Avraham, 25, 26
Bird, Phyllis, 78, 81, 82
blood, 132
Bloom, Harold, 65
Bottéro, Jean, 102
Brenner, Athalya, 78
Bright, John, 4
bull statue, 29, 32
bullae, 8
Bunimovitz, Shlomo, 33
burial, 29
Burkert, Walter, 127

Cain and Abel, 133
Cambyses, 51
Camp, Claudia, 80, 90

Index of Biblical Passages

9	176		132	201
11	176		134:1–2	174
12	176		135:1–2	174
13	176		137	176
16	176		143:5	181
18	176		144:9	178
19	189n47		145–50	176
19:15	181		145:5	181
23	176		145:18	177
27	176		149–50	177
29	176		149:3	178
30	176		149:5	178
32	176		149:6	181
33	176		150:3–6	178
34	176			
44	176		JOB	
46	176		15:4	181
47	176			
48	176		LAMENTATIONS	
50:13	132		2:19	177
55:17–18	175			
58	176		DANIEL	
60	176		2:2	173
63:7	181		6:11	175
69:37	182		9:11	146
74	176			
76	176		EZRA	
77:13	181		3:2–3	166
78:36–37	177		3:6	167
79	176		9:5	175
80	176		9:6–15	177
83	176		10:1	187n29
85	176			
89	207n46		NEHEMIAH	
90	176		8:1	146, 180
93	176		8:3	146
94	176		8:6	188n31
95–99	176		9:2–3	173
102	189n47		9:5	174
103:2–6	184n11			
106:30–31	172		1 CHRONICLES	
106:37–38	137n18		20:5–12	189n39
106:41–47	187n24		21:26	189n38
107	176		29:10–19	189n39
110	207n46			
119:15, 23, 27, 78,			2 CHRONICLES	
97, 99, 148	181		12:1–12	35
119:32	182		18:18	173
123	176		23:18	146
126	176		30:16	146
129	176		32:6	180
			33:6	137n18